DATE DUE		
1408	11/8/06		
1408	11.21.06		
192	3.14.6		
1315	3-24-10		
47	11/8/11		
44	2/8/11		
207	10/25/12		
10/27/16			

No Tomorrows

By

Joanne Connors-Wade

Bloomington, IN Milton Keynes, UK

authorHOUSE™

AuthorHouse™
1663 Liberty Drive, Suite 200
Bloomington, IN 47403
www.authorhouse.com
Phone: 1-800-839-8640

AuthorHouse™ UK Ltd.
500 Avebury Boulevard
Central Milton Keynes, MK9 2BE
www.authorhouse.co.uk
Phone: 08001974150

This book is a work of non-fiction. Unless otherwise noted, the author
and the publisher make no explicit guarantees as to the accuracy
of the information contained in this book and in some cases, names
of people and places have been altered to protect their privacy.

First published by AuthorHouse 8/15/2006

ISBN: 1-4259-4055-2 (sc)

Printed in the United States of America
Bloomington, Indiana

This book is printed on acid-free paper.

DEDICATION

"No Tomorrows" my second published
book is dedicated to my grandchildren

Christina, Tyler, Kaitlyn, Chiara
and
Their Parents

ACKNOWLEDGEMENTS

My appreciation extends to all who contributed to this book. To all law enforcement personnel who have generously given me their time and sharing their personal recollections to each case they were involved in, I say thank you.

To my husband Stephen for his help with the cover design. I couldn't have done it without him.

To the families of the victims, my sincerest appreciation for allowing me into your homes to share the precious memories of your lost loved ones. Your gracious manner is only surpassed by your dignity. It has been my privilege to meet you.

With warmest regards,

Joanne

FORWARD

"*No Tomorrows*" addresses a widespread epidemic that continues to spread.

This non-discriminating epidemic strikes regardless of race, gender, age, or social/economic status and inflicts pain and agony to parents and loved ones left in the wake of tragedy.

The deadly epidemic strikes everyday, throughout the US. There is no cure and it continues to leave heartache, devastation, and suffering in its wake.

The perpetrators/predators are faceless and live among the safe havens as well as the metropolises. No one is immune to the tentacles of a predator. They reach out, snatch and ultimately kill without regret or remorse.

We are all aware of the evil that lurks, but most believe it will strike somewhere else. The families in "*No Tomorrows*" know better.

They will never have 'closure' but seek justice. Some have received justice, some never will, but all live with the pain of losing a loved one.

---

* denotes name and/or description of character has been fictionalized. The
* appears only the first time the name and/or description appears in the story.

CHAPTER 1

It was the fall of 1990. Labor Day, marked the official end of summer and traditionally the start of the school year. By mid October, tour busses `carrying hundreds of tourists, dubbed "leaf peepers" by the local residents, would travel Rt. 2, winding up through the Mohawk Trail. The Berkshires provide the most magnificent display of fall foliage. Once the busses maneuver the hairpin turn they proceed to the summit of Mt. Greylock. Once there, the passengers, with fully loaded cameras draped around their necks, disperse and in a collective 'awe' witness Mother Nature's offering of a panoramic view overlooking four states and treetops painted in arrays of golden, red, and orange.

Berkshire County is located at the Northwest corner of Massachusetts. It shares borders with New York, Connecticut and Vermont.

Pittsfield, the largest city within the county maintains a population of approximately 44,000 residents. For decades, General Electric Co. the city's major industry, provided employment for a large percentage of the blue-collar working class.

By mid October, the children of Pittsfield were back in school. A 12-year-old boy was particularly excited about school that fall. Jimmy Bernardo had attended Crosby Elementary School from kindergarten through sixth grade. Now Jimmy attended Herberg Middle School. Seventh grade was a giant step for him. It was practically Junior High School.

Jimmy was the older of the two Bernardo boys. Robert was 10 attending Crosby Elementary School. Ronald and Mary Bernardo took pride in their boys. Both were excellent students. They lived in a modest home on McKinley Terrace, shaded by picturesque maple trees, and consisted of owner occupied single-family houses. It was the only home Jimmy and Robert had ever known.

The Bernard's were devout Catholics and members of St. Mark's parish. Together the Bernardo family attended Mass regularly. Jimmy served as an altar boy, and Robert looked forward to following his older brother's lead when he reached the appropriate age required to become a servant of the church.

On Monday, October 22, 1990, Jimmy boarded the school bus at the usual time, 8:10 a.m. It was a crisp sunny fall day. The streets and sidewalks were blanketed with the brightly colored leaves that had surrendered from branches of the gigantic maple trees and floated to the ground. The sun was high in a cloudless sky on a picture perfect autumn day.

Orange school busses lined up end to end at the entrance of Herberg Middle School, depositing hundreds of students laden with backpacks and gym bags. The seventh graders were noticeably the most eager, and anxious upon arrival. They, particularly the boys, were also considerably smaller in stature. Jimmy was younger than most of his classmates. He had his

12th birthday on August 13. It would be the year most boys of that age would experience a growth spurt. Puberty and the awkwardness that accompanies that stage of young boys' life would soon be upon them.

October 22nd was going to be a great day for Jimmy Bernardo. The first football practice would get underway immediately following dismissal. Jimmy was a fine athlete. He was active in the City Little League Program, and a natural for most sports. Throughout the summer, he had participated in scrimmages with the neighborhood boys. Most were older than Jimmy, but he was eager to learn. Ronald Bernardo, Jimmy's father, spent many hours practicing passes and various maneuvers with both his sons, while Mary Bernardo watched, pleased with the camaraderie the boys enjoyed with their Dad.

After practice, Jimmy boarded the 'after school' bus that provided transportation for the students participating in extra curricular activities. He arrived home around 4:15 p.m. and called a friend to make plans to meet him at the Cinema Plaza.

Jimmy frequented the plaza almost on a daily basis. He liked to play pool at the Wall-to-Wall Billiards, which included several pinball machines. A 12-year-old could easily spend hours there.

On several occasions, he would go to the theatre that was also located within the plaza. Jimmy and several of his friends had become acquainted with the janitor at the movie theatre and soon they were able to get in to see the movies without paying.

Lew, the janitor had assured them that if he was working they could be let in the back door and get to see the latest movies. Jimmy and his friends took advantage of their adult friend's offer but thought it best not to let it be known. They didn't want Lew to get into trouble on their account.

Mrs. Bernardo placed the meatloaf in the center of the table. Jimmy and Robert took their places around the table and Mr. Bernardo joined his family for dinner. The usual table talk was underway. Nothing out of the ordinary but Jimmy seemed to be in a hurry, glancing at the kitchen clock.

"What's your hurry?" asked Ronald Bernardo.

"I've got to meet Tim* at the Plaza. Can I be excused?" asked Jimmy. He was on his feet, reaching for his plate to be placed on the sink.

"Okay, but be sure to be home no later than 7:00," replied his father.

Jimmy went to the phone, called his friend, confirming he was on his way, and would meet him at the Wall-to-Wall Billiards in a few minutes.

He hung up the phone and ran into his room, tossing his backpack on the bed.

"Where you going?" asked Robert.

"Just up to the plaza. I want to get the new issue of *Sports Illustrated* at the newsstand. I'll be back later."

He donned the denim jacket he had worn to school that day, and scooped up several quarters from his dresser. He pedaled his green Mongoose bicycle as fast as he could; knowing he was to be home by 7:00. The sun was rapidly sinking from the October sky.

It was, perhaps the last sunset Jimmy Bernardo would ever see.

At 7:30, Jimmy failed to return home. Ronald and Mary presumed he had stopped at a friend's house and lost track of time. Mary called Jimmy's friend who lived a few blocks away. His friend stated he had not seen Jimmy. He said he had waited for him because they had agreed to meet at the billiard hall. When Jimmy did not show up, he went home.

After that brief conversation, Mary Bernardo hung up the phone and glanced at the clock. It was nearly 8:00 and it was not like Jimmy to be that late without permission. A look of concern came over Mary's face as she told her husband Jimmy did not show up to meet his friend.

Taking a more casual, optimistic attitude, Mr. Bernardo was confident Jimmy would return with some outlandish excuse for being late.

"Robert, do you know where Jimmy went?" asked Mr. Bernardo.

"No, he said he wanted to get the new *Sports Illustrated* magazine at the newsstand up at the plaza," replied Robert. "He said he'd be right back. He took his quarters, maybe he's playing pinball."

"That was almost three hours ago," exclaimed Mary. "Did he say he was going anywhere else?"

"Nope, just going to get the magazine," answered Robert.

"I'll take the car and look around the plaza. He's probably with some friends up there. He's pulled this sort of thing before. You'd think he'd learn." Mr. Bernardo stated as he picked up his car keys and pulled on a light jacket.

"Okay, and drive over to Clapp Park. He could be at the playground over there. Some older boys hang around there. I've told him I don't want him over there, but you know how he can be."

Mary was becoming visibly shaken. She felt something was not right.

Forty-five minutes passed and Mr. Bernardo pulled into the driveway. Mary looked through the living room window hoping to see Jimmy trailing behind his father. No Jimmy. Her heart jumped. She had called everyone she could think of to locate Jimmy and now Ronald had returned without him.

Mary met Ronald as he entered the house.

"No sign of him around. I stopped into the newsstand to see if he had been in there. George says he'd just started his shift at 5:00 and had not seen him. He doesn't remember if anyone had purchased a *Sports Illustrated* magazine," he reported. I even went to the theatre, but there was nobody there that knows Jimmy."

"Did you check the park?" asked Mary.

"Yes, I drove through the park. There were a couple of kids but they hadn't seen Jimmy."

"I'm calling the police, something is wrong." Mary Bernardo's maternal instincts had kicked in and an ominous feeling was beginning to take over.

"Let's not rush to any conclusions, Mary," Ronald replied. "Let's give it another hour."

"No Ronald, I can't wait another hour. He's been gone for over three hours! He's never done this before. It's just not like him to just take off and not tell anyone. Something is definitely not right here and I'm going to report him missing."

Robert was busy doing his homework and paid little attention to what was going on with his parents in the kitchen. He never imagined his brother would never return home.

The news that would eventually be delivered to the Bernardo family would be devastating and heart wrenching.

"Yes, he's 12 years old. His hair is brown; he's about 5ft. 4in. and riding a green bicycle. He's wearing a jeans jacket, a black tee shirt with fluorescent writing, gray baggy pants and Puma sneakers." Mary was on the telephone with the Pittsfield Police Department.

A Detective from the Pittsfield Police knocked on the Bernardo's door. Mr. Bernardo greeted him and showed him into the living room where Mary was seated. By now, Mary was beginning to feel the pain in her stomach. She called to Robert to join them in the living room.

Sergeant Bernadetto Sciola was seated on an armchair adjacent to Mr. and Mrs. Bernardo. With a small notebook in his hand, he began asking the appropriate questions required to file a preliminary missing child report. The next few hours, at least until morning would unveil what they were dealing with, a runaway or abduction.

Sciola addressed Robert directly, "Now son, if you have any idea where your brother is, now's the time to tell me. Did he tell you about any plans to run away?"

Robert was beginning to feel the tension. The arrival of the police was a silent endorsement of the severity of Jimmy's absence.

7

"No, he didn't tell me anything. Honest, he just said he wanted the new *Sports Illustrated* magazine. That's all he told me. Jimmy wouldn't run away." Robert replied in an almost inaudible tone.

After nearly an hour of questions, the investigator closed his notebook and advised the Bernardo's he would file the report. He also told them the police personnel on the night shift would be alerted of Jimmy's absence.

"I'm sure he'll come walking through that door," he offered. "Boys can be pretty unpredictable at this age. I have a couple of my own. You'll see he'll turn up any minute now."

Sgt. Sciola tried to reassure the worried parents. He looked directly at Robert and said, "Now Robert, if you think of anything else, tell your folks so we can get Jimmy home tonight."

Robert was beginning to feel uncomfortable. Did the police think he knew where Jimmy was? Am I in trouble? Thoughts raced through the 10-year-old boy's head.

"I will, sir, but I don't know where he is."

Ronald escorted the investigator to the door. "Do you think he ran away?" He asked.

"I don't know, Mr. Bernardo. What do you think?"

"No, but what else could it be?" Ronald was searching for some positive reaction from Sgt. Sciola. After all, he must handle this sort of thing all the time. Surely, he would have an idea of what's become of Jimmy.

"I don't know, but I'll keep you posted."

The two men walked to the patrol car occupied by a uniformed officer. Mr. Bernardo refused to entertain the thoughts of abduction. It could not be possible. He didn't even want to say the word. The two men shook hands and the black and white cruiser rolled out of the driveway.

As Ronald Bernardo turned to go into his house, he noticed a neighbor standing on her front porch. She had a sweater wrapped around her shoulders and watched as the cruiser drove away. It was a chilly night, but curiosity has a way of withstanding any temperature.

"Hello Vivian*," Ronald called. "Pretty chilly out here."

"Is anything wrong, Ronald?" Vivian Morriarty* inquired. "I couldn't help but notice the police. Are the boys okay?"

Ronald knew Mrs. Morriarty was genuinely concerned. She was not a 'nosey neighbor' and he felt she deserved an explanation.

"Nothing to worry about Vivian. Jimmy's late coming home. The police are going to keep an eye open for him. When he gets home, he's going to be in a world of trouble!"

Ronald tried to sound casual but deep down he felt an aching.

"Oh, well then, I guess I'll go inside. I just wanted to check if you needed anything. Call me if you need me to stay with Robert."

"Thanks Vivian." With that, Ronald returned to his house.

The porch light stayed on throughout the night. Ronald drove around the neighborhood hourly until dawn with no sign of Jimmy. Mary sat at the kitchen table waiting for the phone to ring. She expected a call from the police or, perhaps the hospital. Mary had called Berkshire Medical Center earlier. There hadn't been any accident victims treated or admitted.

She walked through the living room where Robert was sleeping on the sofa. The stillness yielded to the chime of a domed clock on the mantle. Gently she arranged the quilt that covered her youngest son. It was 4:05 a.m. when Ronald returned from one of his numerous searches with no results. He had stopped by the police station earlier but they had nothing to offer. They suggested he go home and wait. Wait for what? Ronald thought.

"Please try to get some sleep," he advised his wife. "We'll go to the police station first thing. I'm going to take a shower."

"I can't sleep. Ronald, where is Jimmy? What's happened to him?" She blurted out and then crumbled to the floor sobbing uncontrollably. Ronald was exhausted and emotionally drained. He was trying to protect his wife. Mary's thoughts echoed in his mind. She too had already envisioned the worst. The two sat on the floor wrapped in the comfort of each other.

Mary dozed off in the oversized reclining chair and Ronald was busy searching Jimmy's room for anything that might indicate plans Jimmy might have had. He didn't know exactly what he was looking for however he had to do something.

He dumped the contents of Jimmy's backpack onto the bed. In addition to the textbooks, he found candy wrappers, a package of unopened gum, pens, all the usual contents of any school bag. A large white envelope dropped to the floor. Ronald reached for it and recognized the familiar logo. It was the logo of Asterisk Photo. The photographer provided a service each year, taking the school pictures. He opened the envelope and poured the contents onto the bed. There were several pictures of Jimmy. The envelope contained 5 x 7's, 4 x 6's and several wallet sized prints.

Ronald sat on the bed and held the pictures in his trembling hands. After a few minutes, he replaced the photos in the white envelope and set it aside. Sifting through the remaining contents of the backpack, he found the September and October issues of *Sports Illustrated*. The November issue had just hit the stands and typically, Jimmy had to have it.

Robert stood in the doorway, still wearing the clothes he had on from the day before.

"Dad, Jimmy's not back?" Robert's voice was shaky. "What's going on?"

"I don't know son. We're going to the police station in a few minutes. They can probably tell us something. Why don't you take a shower and get dressed? You can stay home from school today. Try not to wake your mother. She's been up all night."

Robert remained silent as he walked to his room. He could not comprehend the situation. If Jimmy had some 'scheme' Robert was sure he would have confided in him.

Mary woke with a start. She reached for the telephone that had jolted her from her sleep. "Hello?"

"Hello, this is Sergeant LaClaire, Pittsfield Police Department. May I speak to Mr. Bernardo?"

"This is Mrs. Bernardo, you can speak to me. Have you found Jimmy? Is he all right? Where is he?"

The questions came end to end. The officer could not break in to answer.

"Mrs. Bernardo, I'm calling to ask if Jimmy has returned or contacted you since you filed last night's report."

"No, no, we haven't heard anything. You haven't found him? Oh God, where's Jimmy?"

By now, Mr. Bernardo could hear his wife shouting. He rushed to take the telephone from her.

"This is Ronald Bernardo. Who am I speaking to?" Mr. Bernardo asked.

The officer identified himself and repeated the purpose of the call.

"What do we do now?"

"The Chief would like you and your wife to come down to the station. We would like you to bring a picture of the boy. We'll need some information from you so we can take the appropriate steps to locate him."

"Thank you sir, we'll be there within the hour," was Ronald's solemn reply to the caller.

Mary stood beside Ronald as he hung up the phone.

"The Chief wants us at the station. He wants us to bring a picture of Jimmy."

Mary was speechless. She walked to the kitchen where colorful magnets held photos of both Robert and Jimmy on the refrigerator door. Most of Jimmy's pictures reflected his participation in various sports. Mary looked them over trying to select the most recent likeness of Jimmy.

She tried to see past the tears welling in her eyes and wondered how does one select an appropriate picture for a missing child poster? She had seen so many of those posters, but never had she given any thought to how they were selected. Now, she was actually faced with the nightmare that so many mothers have had to endure.

Ronald approached Mary and wrapped his arms around her. He was holding the white envelope he had discovered in Jimmy's backpack.

"I have to pick out a picture," she said as she pulled herself from Ronald's embrace.

"I've got the picture." Ronald handed the envelope to Mary. She looked puzzled as she reached for the envelope Ronald was offering.

"Where did these come from? I've never seen them."

"I was looking through his room for something that might help, and I found these in Jimmy's backpack. He must have gotten them at school yesterday."

Mary placed the pictures on the table and gently brushed her hand across the face of her missing boy. The pictures reflected deep brown eyes, and his smooth olive complexion. His smile revealed perfect

13

teeth. He was truly a handsome boy with an uncanny resemblance of his father.

Ronald was of Italian heritage and bore all the 'typical' features one would imagine. His dark, wavy hair framed his European features. He was six feet two inches tall. In high school, he enjoyed the popularity afforded to the captain of the high school football team.*

Mary was a stunning teenager. She was of fair complexion, with contrasting dark brown hair and green eyes. When Mary smiled, her cheeks flashed deep dimples.*

Ronald and Mary were married in 1975 and soon after purchased their house at 3 McKinley Terrace. They planned for their family. Jimmy was born in 1977 then Robert in 1980.*

Until Robert started school, Mary was a stay at home Mom and Ronald continued working at Rising Paper in nearby Great Barrington, MA. He had been there since his discharge from the Army. Once Robert was enrolled in Crosby Elementary School, Mary was hired at the Berkshire Insurance Company.

"Shouldn't we call someone? Should I call Charlotte?*"Asked Mary. Charlotte was Mary's oldest sister.

"No, let's just get to the police station and see what they have to report. We don't want to get anyone else alarmed if we don't have to." Ronald answered in a guarded tone.

"I'll get Robert ready. Do you think he should go to the station or should we drop him off at Charlotte's?" Mary questioned.

"I think the police will want to talk to him too. He may have something to add that will help in the search."

Robert joined his parents in the kitchen. His hair was still wet and matted from the shower.

"Where'd these come from?" he asked picking up one of the photos spread across the table.

"Jimmy must have got them from school yesterday; I found them in his backpack."

Mary picked up a 5x7 and a wallet-sized photo and slid them into her purse. She reached for her sweater, handing Ronald his jacket and the three walked to the car without any further conversation.

It was Tuesday, October 23, 8:00 a.m. and Jimmy had not been seen or heard from since 5:00 Monday afternoon. The clock was ticking and if a search were to get underway, it would have to be soon. Jimmy had been missing for over 15 hours. He could be a long way from Pittsfield by now and Bernardos were beginning to imagine the worst. Robert remained silent during the trip to the police station.

Ronald approached the officer at the counter.

"My name is Ronald Bernardo; this is my wife Mary and son Robert. The Chief is expecting us." Ronald tried to keep his tone steady.

"Yes sir," the desk sergeant replied as he swiveled the logbook around to allow Ronald to sign in. Ronald signed his name as well as Mary's and Robert's glancing at the large Seth Thomas on the wall behind the desk, the time was 8:28 a.m.

In just a few minutes Chief Spadafero appeared and walked directly to the three seated on the wooden bench in the lobby of the station.

Chief Spadafero was a middle-aged man with a warm pleasant smile. A bit overweight, and slightly balding and with his ruddy completion, could easily portray a perfect Santa Claus*. He extended his hand to Ronald as he introduced himself to the anxious parents. Ronald, Mary and Robert stood as the Chief directed them toward the stairway.

"Come on up to my office, let's see what we have."

The Chief sounded optimistic and upbeat. It was a sharp contrast to what the Bernardo's were feeling.

Chief Spadefero sat behind a large oak desk. Papers, reports, file folders cluttered the surface. A picture of an attractive girl encased in a silver frame occupied a corner of the disheveled desk. The Chief noticed Mrs. Bernardo looking at it and broke the silence.

"That's my oldest daughter, Virginia*. She graduated from Vassar last year." He spoke as a proud father.

Mary commented on how attractive she was.

"Now, let's see what we have. Mr. Bernardo, may I call you Ronald?"

"Sure chief, do you have any information about Jimmy? Do you have any idea where he could be? I've been out all night and haven't gotten anywhere. I've checked the hospital and Mary's called all his friends. Robert doesn't know anything except that he went to the plaza to by a magazine."

Mary handed Jimmy's pictures to the Chief.

"Fine looking boy, is this a recent picture?"

"Yes, he just got them from school yesterday," replied Ronald.

"We'll need a list of all his friends. We will talk to them to see what they can tell us about where Jimmy might be. How was he behaving in the last few days? Do you think it's possible he could be a runaway? You know boys at this age can get adventurous."

"If he has runaway, I'll need you to give me some ideas where you suppose he would go. Maybe a relative or a friend? Anyone you can think of?"

The chief detected a look of dismay on the faces of Mary and Ronald.

He was quick to add, "You understand, I'm not saying he has runaway, but we have to consider the possibility."

As he finished addressing the parents, he picked up the phone.

"Is Captain Boyer in the station? Please ask him to come to my office. Thank you."

He turned to the Bernardos.

"Captain Walter Boyer heads up our Detective Division. He will assign a detective to handle this case exclusively. That's how we do things around here."

Ronald and Mary had so many questions to ask, but sat in silence. For all appearances, this seemed to be a routine procedure. Don't they know this is our little boy? Don't they understand how frightened we are? This isn't just another runaway; this is Jimmy!

Ronald cleared his throat and asked,

"Chief, how many of these types of cases come across your desk? Is this 'just another kid' to you?"

17

Ronald was making an effort to maintain control, but he was progressively becoming annoyed at Chief Spadefero's casual manner.

"Mr. Bernardo, eh, Ronald, we get several of these types of cases. Usually, they turn out to be runaways. Until we have evidence of other circumstances, we have to proceed with this assumption."

Mary was not about to tolerate the Chief's patronizing tone. She reached for Robert's hand and started for the door.

"I can't see any purpose of us coming here. You don't seem to understand that Jimmy has been missing since 5:00 yesterday afternoon, and you don't seem to be the least bit concerned. He's not a runaway he's missing!" " We are asking you for help and you're simply 'following standard procedures'. Well, that's not enough." Before anyone could reply, she was at the door when Captain Boyer entered the office.

"Please, Mrs. Bernardo, I apologize if I gave you that impression. Please calm down." The Chief was on his feet and Ronald was at a loss.

"This is Captain Walter Boyer; please have a seat Mrs. Bernardo. My apologies if you misunderstood me."

Mary sat stiffly with Robert standing close by his mother.

Captain Boyer remained standing and addressed the worried parents.

"I've read the report that Sgt. Sciola wrote up last night, and would like to get additional information that will assist us in locating your son."

"Did you bring a picture of the boy?" asked the Captain. "I'll need to get a list of his friends and detective Riello will visit the school to interview them as well as his teachers."

He focused his conversation directly towards Mary. Robert sat quietly, but listened carefully to what was being said. He realized the magnitude of this visit and what it entailed.

"A detective will contact you at your home later today. In the meanwhile if there is anything you can think of, or if you hear from Jimmy, please contact me." Captain Boyer handed his card to Ronald.

"The information we have, description, date of birth, last seen location all that information is being entered into a database, the **NCIC** Missing Persons File. This ensures that any law-enforcement agency in the country will be able to identify Jimmy if he is found in another community."

The Chief stood and thanked the Bernardos for coming and providing the necessary information along with the photo of Jimmy. He tried to offer reassurance that Jimmy would be returned safely. Ronald and Mary were not so optimistic. They feared their worse nightmare was about to become a reality.

As they drove home, they fired questions at their younger son. Robert answered whatever he could, but was unable to offer any additional information.

"I don't know where Jimmy went! I don't know where he is, honest, I'd tell you. I just know he was going to the plaza newsstand and that's all he told me."

By now, the frightened 10-year-old was curled up in the corner of the rear seat, crying.

Ronald pulled into the driveway of 3 McKinley Terrace and Mary rushed to comfort the sobbing boy.

Robert retreated to his room. He could not believe what was happening. Jimmy was missing, and it seemed everyone believed he had something to do with his disappearance. How could his brother just disappear?

He lay on his bed and stared across the room, his eyes fixed on a picture of two boys dressed in cut off jeans and tee shirts holding up their 'catch of the day'. He recalled what a great time they had only a few months before.

Mary and Ronald began making phone calls to relatives and friends. They had to reach the family before the story of a missing boy was broadcasted or appeared in the Berkshire Eagle evening edition.

In an effort to get the calls made in the fastest manner, Ronald went next door to the Moriartys. With a small telephone directory in hand, he rang the bell at 5 McKinley Terrace. A tall, attractive woman answered the ring.

"Hi Ronald, how'd it go with Jimmy? Did he finally get home?"

Ronald looked away and answered.

"No, Vivian. I'm afraid not. Mary and I just came from the police station and we need to make several calls to relatives. May I use your phone? I'm sorry to bother you, but it's the fastest way to contact the family."

"Of course, Ronald come in; let me get you some coffee." Vivian was visibly shaken at the news. She had known the Bernardo's since they moved in nearly 15 years ago.

Mary started making calls. As she related the news to her older sister, she began sobbing uncontrollably. Charlotte told her she would be over right away. She suggested Mary wait before she attempted any more calls. Mary agreed to wait for her sister to arrive.

She went to Robert's room and sat on the bed gathering Robert into her arms. Robert's entire body trembled in his mother's embrace. She kissed his head and tried to comfort the frightened ten-year-old.

Ronald returned home after making several phone calls including one to his parents. They would arrive as soon as possible. The doorbell rang and Ronald peered out the side window of the front door. Detective Riello waited patiently for someone to answer the door.

Detective Sergeant Anthony Riello had been assigned the primary detective on Jimmy's case.

Detective Sergeant Anthony Riello was approximately thirty-six years old. He was promoted to detective in 1984, approximately six years before. His manner was soft-spoken, and very amicable. He was an attractive man, and obviously conscientious of his appearance. The detective sported a Harris Tweed jacket, over a crisp white shirt and paisley tie. His hair was the color of a pristine sandy beach and his piercing eyes reflected the blue of the waters.

"Good morning Mr. Bernardo," he greeted Ronald flashing his charismatic smile.

"Good morning detective, we've been expecting you. I'm surprised you're so early. I'll get Mary, please have a seat. Mary was already entering the living room, blotting her swollen eyes with a tissue.

The detective declined the invitation to sit, but instead walked around the room examining several framed pictures displayed on tables and the mantle.

One picture caught his eye immediately. It was of Jimmy with a familiar broad smile seated proudly on a green bicycle. Anthony Riello was acquainted with Jimmy Bernardo through the many D.A.R.E. classes; a favored project headed up by the detective. He frequently spoke to elementary school children and remembered Jimmy, describing him as a spunky kid. He liked Jimmy and considered him to be a spirited, savvy, streetwise boy.

"Good morning Mrs. Bernardo. I was just admiring this picture of Jimmy." The detective offered the picture to Mrs. Bernardo.

"Was this taken recently?"

"Yes, it was taken this past summer, that's the bike he was riding last night."

"It's a good picture of the boy, and the bicycle which could be helpful. We'll add this picture to the class picture and both will be on the posters." The detective stated.

Mrs. Bernardo agreed and removed the picture from the wooden frame handing it to the detective.

Anthony Riello was a very soft spoken, kind man and the father of an 11-year-old boy of his own. His concern for Jimmy's safe return was genuine and the Bernardos felt confident with this detective.

The sergeant placed the photo under the clip on the board he was balancing on his lap as he sat on the arm of the sofa.

He began to check off the information listed on the 'missing persons' form needed to be entered into the database and begin an investigation.

Ronald and Mary gave the detective their full attention, providing accurate and complete answers to the numerous questions Riello asked.

Charlotte and her husband Gary* arrived and retreated to the kitchen, allowing the detective to conduct his questioning.

"I have the physical description as well as a recent photo." Riello mumbled aloud as he checked his list.

"Does Jimmy have any physical or emotional problems?" he asked.

"No, he's a very healthy, bright, boy," replied Ronald.

"Who was the last person to see him? Did you see him leave the house? Did he say anything about where he was going?"

"No, Robert, his brother, said he was just going up to the Plaza Newsstand to buy the November edition of *Sports Illustrated*. He always wants it as soon as it hits the stands," answered Mary. "That's his favorite magazine. He knows when it hits the stands, and he's right there."

"Has there been any problem that would cause the boy to want to leave home, eh, run away?"

Ronald picked up the conversation.

"He was in a good mood when he left here. He's never even threatened to run away. He's on the ball as far as being home when he's expected. He's usually home by dark unless he's been given permission to stay out later, but he's never been out after 9:00."

"Did you notice anything missing? Personal items, maybe clothes, did he have any money?"

"I didn't notice anything missing detective. If he were going to take anything, especially if he's riding his bike, he would have taken his backpack. As far as money, he didn't have any significant amount of money, I'd say not more than five dollars," replied Ronald.

"I emptied his backpack looking for something that might give me a clue of where he might have gone, but I didn't find anything. You're welcome to look for yourself."

Riello continued to ask the questions and recorded the parent's answers. The questions seemed endless, and in the minds of Ronald and Mary, most were inappropriate. However, they answered them as best they could.

Following the question and answer session, Sergeant Riello was led to Jimmy's bedroom. Mary assured him he had full access to anything in the room as well as within the entire house. She left the detective to search the room in hopes he would find something that would be a clue and lead him to Jimmy.

As the sergeant entered Jimmy's bedroom he looked around the walls. Posters of famed NFL quarterback, Joe Montana occupied every available inch of wall space along with pictures of the 49er's team. It was clear; Joe Montana was Jimmy's hero.

Stacks of sports magazines were neatly piled in one corner indicating the twelve-year-old's propensity for sports.

Meanwhile, the house was beginning to fill with relatives and friends offering support. Vivian Moriarty arrived carrying a platter of various pastries and muffins and rushed into the kitchen. She prepared a pot of coffee and set up the table assuming the role of hostess easing the burden from Mary.

The telephone began ringing. Charlotte screened the calls, taking messages from some and calling Ronald to take the calls requiring information requested by authorities.

Ronald's parents, Alfred and Susan Bernardo arrived. From his bedroom, Robert heard their familiar voices and rushed into the outstretched arms of his grandmother. The elderly woman embraced the small boy; an unspoken offer of comfort.

When his cousin arrived, the two retreated to Robert's room. Heather* was Ronald's niece. Although she was four years older than Robert was, she in addition to all the cousins of the Bernardo family was very close. The entire family enjoyed the close bond, and in the good times as well as times of tragedy, they called upon this bond to get them through. Never had anything come close to the tragedy they were facing now, the unknown fate of Jimmy, and the outcome that would come to pass.

Carol Savery, Mary's mother arrived and as she approached Mary, Carol began to sob. Charlotte was on her feet and assisted her mother into the kitchen.

She prepared a cup of tea and pulled up a chair beside the sobbing woman.

It was nearing 11:00 a.m. and Detective Riello showed himself out assuring the Bernardos he was headed for the station to enter all information into the database. He would visit Jimmy's school as soon as he finished the paperwork at the station. As he handed his card to Ronald, he instructed him to contact him anytime if he thought of anything that might be helpful. He had scribbled his home number on the reverse side of his card.

Just as Sergeant Riello approached his unmarked car, a white van pulled up, blocking the driveway. The van was clearly marked, **WRLP, TV**. The detective took a deep sigh. He had anticipated it would be just a matter of time before the media got the story.

He stepped out of his car and returned to the house. With his shield clearly displayed on his lapel, he positioned himself on the front porch, blocking the entrance.

The camera operators hurried to unload their equipment as an attractive young woman stood under a large maple tree, which served as a natural backdrop. The camera focused on her as she fumbled with a microphone in one hand and notes in the other. She straightened her burgundy suit jacket and passed a comb through her auburn hair.

Anthony Riello recognized Sheryl Pearson* immediately. On several occasions, Sheryl reported Aiello's investigations for the local affiliate of NBC News.

Rob Thomas* noted the badge displayed on the detective's jacket and introduced himself.

"We'd like to interview the Bernardos regarding their missing child."

"I think an interview would be a little premature at this time. The Pittsfield Police Department has gathered all the information required to initiate an investigation." The detective picked his words carefully.

"It's a possible runaway. I don't think the parents are prepared to give you a statement at this time. Please give them some privacy. They are very confused at this time. The family has gathered to lend support."

"Can you make a statement on their behalf? Can you tell us what you know, and the status of Jimmy Bernardo's disappearance?"

The sergeant hesitated for a moment and decided it would be best if he addressed the viewing audience.

Rob Thomas led Anthony Riello to where Sheryl Pearson was positioned in preparation of her evening broadcast. It would be pre-recorded and aired on the 5:00 news.

"Hello Sheryl, you're looking good. I'll speak on behalf of the family of Jimmy Bernardo. At this time, I don't think they are prepared to deal with the media."

"Hi Anthony. It's good to see you. Sure, if you think that's best, let's do it. Before we start the cameras, tell me what you know so far. Is this an abduction, or do you think the boy ran away?"

"There doesn't seem to be any indication of abduction. Right now, we're considering the runaway theory. I haven't anything to go on, only what the family has told me. However, we have to consider all possibilities."

Sheryl knew from experiences in the past with Anthony Riello that he was known to take the most optimistic point of view.

After a brief question and answer session, Sheryl positioned herself in front of the maple tree with Anthony Riello standing to her left.

The cameraman aimed the camera for a 'tight shot' of Sheryl as she began the interview and slowly panned to include Anthony Riello.

"Good evening. I'm standing in front of 3 McKinley Terrace, the home of Ronald and Mary Bernardo. We've learned the sad news of 12-year-old Jimmy Bernardo's disappearance. With me is Detective Sergeant Anthony Riello. Detective, can you tell us about the strange disappearance of Jimmy Bernardo?"

"Well, Sheryl, we don't have much to go on. We haven't ruled out a possible runaway. Jimmy was last seen leaving his home at 5:00 o'clock Monday afternoon. He was riding a green bicycle and according to his brother Robert, was on his way to the Cinema Center Newsstand." Riello replied.

"According to those I've interviewed, nobody has seen him since. We don't know if he ever arrived at the newsstand, and according to his parents, there does not appear to be anything missing that would indicate plans of running away. The Pittsfield Police Department is taking every step to assure his safe return."

"How are the parents holding up? Can you give us some details regarding a description of the boy?"

Anthony Riello's answer came slowly and with caution. He did not want to sound overly optimistic, yet he didn't want to alarm the family and friends of the Bernardo's any more than they were. He was sure they would be watching the broadcast.

"The parents, Ronald and Mary Bernardo, are surrounded by family members and friends who are lending their support. Of course, they are quite upset and worried as would be expected. Posters of Jimmy Bernardo have been printed and are being distributed throughout the city."

The detective continued,

"Jimmy is twelve years old. He's wearing a black tee shirt, grey baggy jeans, Puma sneakers and a jeans jacket. He was riding a bright green, *Mongoose* brand bicycle to the Cinema Center. Anyone who has any information should call the Pittsfield Police Department. (The telephone number flashed across the bottom of the screen) Jimmy was last seen when he left his house around 5:00 o'clock Monday afternoon."

The camera panned the yellow house with the white post and rail fencing that surrounded the manicured front yard; then back to the attractive reporter in the burgundy suit.

"Thank you Sergeant Riello." She turned and looked directly into the camera.

"This is Sheryl Pearson, **WRLP** News, live from McKinley Terrace, Pittsfield. Now, back to you Steve."

Once the camera stopped rolling, Sheryl turned to Anthony.

"Do you think you can introduce me to the family?" She asked.

"No cameras, no 'on the record' statements. I'd just like to meet them."

"Okay, I'll introduce you to them. However, Sheryl, don't forget, this is not an interview for NBC. Agreed?"

"You got it my friend. Thanks, I owe you one." Sheryl replied.

With that, Sheryl excused the crew and proceeded into the house escorted by Anthony Riello. The sergeant introduced her to Mary and Ronald and excused himself. He had plenty of work to do and he had already taken too much time accommodating the media.

Following the 5:00 o'clock news, the Pittsfield Police Department was inundated with phone calls. Each call would be recorded and investigated. Time was critical. Each hour that ticked by would add to the arduous task of finding a missing child.

The search for Jimmy Bernardo would become an all out police effort with Riello taking the lead.

Wednesday, October 24, 1990

PITTSFIELD BOY REPORTED MISSING

The Berkshire Eagle carried Jimmy Bernardo's disappearance as their lead story.

Jimmy had been missing since Monday afternoon. He was last seen riding his green bicycle near the Cinema Center shortly after he left home at 5:00 p.m.

Detective Anthony Riello described the police's efforts of the past two days.

At the request of the detective, Robert Bernardo accompanied by his father disclosed several areas around West Housatonic Street where Jimmy generally rode his bike. It was in close proximity to Clapp Park, both locations were within a half mile from the Bernardo residence. The small group, Robert and Ronald Bernardo, and detective Riello walked the area, hoping to discover something that would lead them to Jimmy. They came up empty, and Riello returned Robert and his father to McKinley Terrace.

The police canvassed the neighborhood and interviewed several acquaintances of Jimmy's.

Neighbors described Jimmy as "a nice, polite boy who was always riding his bike."

One neighbor stated, "I know him to have a lot of friends, but he often plays with two kids on the street. His parents must be very worried."

The McKinley Terrace residents couldn't say enough about Jimmy. They spoke of his participation in Little League and all agreed he was a well-liked boy.

For the remainder of the evening, the search concentrated on the Cinema Center as well as the downtown area. Posters began to appear everywhere in Pittsfield and additionally to the neighboring towns of Lee, Lenox, Great Barrington and several others. Soon they would appear over the Connecticut, Vermont and New York borders. An inter-state search was underway to find Jimmy Bernardo.

Although searchers combed the West Housatonic Street area and parts of the neighboring town of Lenox, no trace of Jimmy was to be found.

The police continued to report they had no evidence to indicate foul play was involved.

Jimmy's age, the poor weather and the fact that he was alone and riding his bike the last time he was seen, was cause for concern according to the detectives.

The Bernardo's described their missing son as a responsible boy and returns home when he is supposed to.

Ronald Bernardo, worked at Rising Paper, and Mary Bernardo, an employee at Berkshire Life Insurance, had taken some time off as the search intensified. Family and friends continued to surround them to lend support to the nearly frantic parents of Jimmy Bernardo. Robert stayed close to his parents and all waited by the phone for some word concerning the whereabouts of Jimmy.

The investigation took on a more aggressive effort. The State Police joined the local police who used a trained Police dog to assist in tracking down Jimmy. It was reported the dog seemed to pick up a scent at Clapp Park, but quickly calmed down turning up nothing.

The wooded areas as well as the railroad tracks were searched. The curves of the Housatonic River, along with the debris on the banks were carefully examined. Because of the rising water level, visibility was poor but volunteers from Berkshire Rescue assisted, hoping to discover some signs that Jimmy had been in the area.

Sergeant Anthony Riello, the spearhead of the Pittsfield Drug Abuse Resistance Education program, visited Herberg Middle School conducting interviews with the students. The only comment from one student, a friend of Jimmy's, was that he had seen Jimmy at Clapp Park around 5:30 the night of his disappearance. He added that Jimmy was carrying a blue duffle bag.

Upon receiving this additional information, Sergeant Riello re-focused on the possibility of a runaway situation. He visited the Bernardo's to get their reaction to the runaway theory that was beginning to develop.

Mary Bernardo went to Jimmy's room and took a cursory check of his clothing.

"Nothing is missing, except for the clothes he was wearing. Jimmy doesn't own a blue duffle bag," she replied when Riello asked, suggesting he may have run away.

Detective Riello asked the Bernardo's to remember everything they could concerning Jimmy's behavior before he left the residence.

Mary and Ronald had been doing exactly that, going over Jimmy's activities that Monday evening.

According to Mary, Jimmy had phoned a friend before he left. He was to meet his friend at the Wall-to-Wall Billiards at the Cinema Center. Robert added that he did say he wanted that magazine and the newsstand was next door to the billiard hall. The parents added that occasionally, Jimmy would go to a movie also located in the Plaza.

Riello scribbled in his notebook. This additional information would give him somewhere to continue his investigation. Surely, someone would recall seeing Jimmy and possibly, who he was with.

The police continued to base their search efforts on the runaway theory.

"I think we may be looking at a runaway situation," stated Officer Daniel Triceri.

Ron and Mary Bernardo were in disagreement; they were sure Jimmy would not runaway. The headlines were disturbing to the family who became concerned the runaway theory would impede the investigation of a missing boy.

State police used a helicopter and four-wheel drive trucks to cover the west side and the wooded areas outlining the city. Aerial visibility of the woods had cleared because of the missing foliage. It appeared that Jimmy had just vanished.

Upon learning of the Barnum & Bailey circus train en route to Akron, Ohio passing through Pittsfield at about 7:30 p.m. Monday evening the runaway theory was bolstered. Did Jimmy jump the train? The Massachusetts State Police alerted the authorities in Akron. Akron police were instructed to search the boxcars of the circus train.

The investigation accelerated and it was believed Jimmy would be found safe and returned home. The inference of abduction was not considered, at least not verbally. On only two accounts to reporters the term 'foul play' was ever spoken. By now, Jimmy Bernardo had not been seen since Monday, October 22. To date he'd been missing for nearly five days.

Detective Reillo visited Jimmy's school again. The leads in the hunt for Jimmy had been exhausted; however, the police stated the investigation would continue contingent upon leads received by the police department.

Riello interviewed one of Jimmy's classmates who had reported seeing Jimmy around 5:30 p.m. off West Housatonic Street and said Jimmy was carrying a blue duffle bag and had mentioned plans to run away.

Detective Riello seemed to be perplexed and frustrated over the circumstances of Jimmy's disappearance. Riello had decided to retrace all the steps he had taken and asked Ron and Mary Bernardo to meet him at the police station. He felt if they repeated what they had already offered to the police, perhaps something would become known that they might have forgotten to mention.

The Bernardo family was barely holding on emotionally. The mere thought of ending the search was simply inconceivable to them. They obliged the detective's request to be re-interviewed although they were convinced it would not shed light on the demise of their son.

Anthony Riello was a very sympathetic man. His usual optimistic attitude was beginning to fade and he was beginning to think 'foul play'.

Riello greeted the Bernardo's and explained, "We're not getting any closer. We've exhausted all our leads, but we will continue the investigation and search." He watched the expressions on the faces of the parents and quite aware his words were not getting through to them.

"We're covering all bases. Whether he ran away or not is irrelevant. What is important is that he is a missing boy. Because of the length of time he has been missing, his age and the weather conditions, we have to treat this seriously."

Now the Bernardo's reacted. Finally, they thought the police were coming to their senses. Ron and Mary had been telling the police that Jimmy was not a runaway. Consequently, days had been wasted by entertaining that concept. Now, they would find him. The Bernardo's felt they had just been given a new ray of hope. Unfortunately, it was 'wishful thinking'. After all, regardless of what theory the police based the search on, the fact remained; searches had been conducted and yielded nothing.

On Saturday morning, hundreds of volunteers from Pittsfield and the surrounding towns gathered at the Cinema Center. The police had copies of gridded maps to hand out to each 'team' of searchers. The maps included Pittsfield as well as all surrounding areas.

There is an abundance of rural area throughout the Berkshires, peppered with small village like towns. Several small lakes and the Housatonic River were included in the search areas. The search was to begin at 8:00 a.m. and continue until dark. The police officers addressed the volunteers offering methods and means of searching. Once the instructions were concluded, the hunt for Jimmy Bernardo was underway.

To Ronald and Mary Bernardo, the hundreds of volunteers were surely an indication they would find Jimmy. Practically every square foot of Berkshire County would be examined. How could he not be found? The volunteers made it clear they would continue searching the following day, if necessary.

Sunday, October 28th, a week after the disappearance of their oldest son, the Bernardo's attended Mass at St. Mark's Roman Catholic Church.

Before the start of the mass, Pastor Roland Durante approached the altar rail and addressed the congregation. He announced the mass would be dedicated to the safe return of Jimmy Bernardo and all would pray that the Bernardo family would find the strength and fortitude it would take to withstand the burden that was placed upon them.

The mass ended and parishioners filed from the colossal church. Strangers approached Ronald and Mary offering them a promise to remember them in their prayers. It was overwhelming to the Bernardos; the outpour from total strangers, sincere wishes and prayers extended to them in the hope that Jimmy would return home unharmed.

It had been a week, and so far, the countless leads received by the police had yielded nothing. It was as if Jimmy had just vanished.

Robert became more withdrawn as the days passed. He was a frightened boy. He returned to school, but refused to ride the bus. Ronald would drive him to school and Mary would pick him up. It was the only way he would agree to attending school. The only time he felt 'safe' was during the school session, and in the confines of his house.

Mary took a leave of absence from Berkshire Insurance Co. After the first week of Jimmy's absence, Ronald returned to Rising Sun; dismissing his boss's offer to accommodate his absence because of the insurmountable circumstances, he was struggling with at home.

For the following three days, the newspapers had nothing to offer regarding the disappearance of Jimmy Bernardo. No mention of any new developments could be reported. Mary and Ron Bernardo were captured in the grips of the unknown. They felt helpless as Detective Riello assured them everything possible was being done. Without any fresh leads and virtually no clues, the investigation was substantially handicapped.

Monday marked the eighth day since Jimmy Bernardo's disappearance.

The New England Missing Persons Bureau offered assistance in the search. They would pool the expertise of people with law enforcement, social services and search operations backgrounds.

A specialist close to the mysterious disappearance of the 12-year-old Pittsfield boy stated he could not confirm reports that the boy had run away or considered a missing person at this point

Sean O'Donoghue offered his speculations after conducting interviews with several of Jimmy's friends. He said it appeared that Jimmy had all intentions of attending school the next day. O'Donoghue concluded this when he was informed that he Jimmy finished his homework and asked his mother for a stamp to mail a letter he had written to a serviceman in Saudi Arabia as part of a class project. The investigator discounted the reports of Jimmy's plans to run away.

The recovery specialist continued to deliver all the information he had gathered from employees of various businesses located at the Plaza. Jimmy and most of the neighborhood boys as well were known around the Plaza. Several employees had seen him there around 6:00 p.m.

O'Donoghue concluded in his opinion, and from his experience in these types of cases, Jimmy could not survive for this long outside. He stated, "If he is out there, someone is providing him with a place to stay and food."

O'Donoghue was a very experienced investigator. He knew how to pose questions to young boys. He asked one key question.

"Do you think Jimmy is safe?" Sean O'Donoghue believed if they were hiding Jimmy, their response would be, "I think so." However, they all replied, "I don't know."

All available resources were utilized. Newspapers carried Jimmy's picture almost daily. TV news broadcasted the circumstances surrounding Jimmy's disappearance.

In addition, the Pittsfield police enlisted the help of the nationally broadcasted television program, *"America's Most Wanted."*

Finally, a new light was shed on the investigation. The producers of *"America's Most Wanted"* agreed to broadcast Jimmy's photograph and a description. It had been ten days since Jimmy was last seen.

The police provided pictures and up to date information regarding the ongoing investigation. The segment would be aired the following day, Friday, November 2.

A renewed feeling of hope was cast over the Bernardo family. Surely, a national broadcast would lead them to Jimmy.

On Friday evening at 8:00, the show aired. It was somewhat of a disappointment because it was such a brief announcement. Most expected they would view a segment but as it turned out, it was simply a bulletin. Jimmy's picture was offered to the viewers; with a narrative reporting the location he was last seen along with a description of what he was wearing.

It was, in all accounts a substantial broadcast considering the producers had prepared it within 24 hours of the police's request. The police anticipated a noticeable increase of incoming phone calls after the broadcast. With the exception of approximately 10 calls from individuals reporting 'sightings' of the boy, it was business as usual at the station. The ten reports were noted and followed up. They did nothing to change the status of the case.

Immediately following the national television broadcast, a new search was coordinated.

The New England Missing Persons Bureau solicited law enforcement officials and private citizens to join them in a major eight-hour hunt to begin at 9:00 a.m. Saturday morning.

The fresh search was professionally organized and would explore previously covered areas, which expanded, to neighboring towns, wooded areas and rivers.

The volunteers were instructed to gather at the Cinema Plaza. They would be divided into groups and dispersed to assigned locations. Eight members of the Milford, MA based non-profit bureau, would supervise the intense search. They had been assisting the Pittsfield Police over the past several days.

The recovery specialists set up an office in the basement of the police station. From that location, they would receive all case related calls. A fax with Jimmy's description along with a request for help in the search was sent to hundreds of police and sheriff departments across the entire state. In addition, the civil defense officials were notified and asked to assist.

Next, the media was contacted and asked to get the word out to citizens who could participate, including divers. Law enforcement officials were urged to provide lighting and other specialized equipment, motorcycles, trucks and even horses if possible.

"We're open to whatever means possible. This will be a well organized, intensive hunt." Sean O'Donoghue, the recovery specialist heading up the search stated.

Within an hour, the switchboard was lighting up. Calls were in coming from citizens volunteering the services and equipment O'Donoghue had requested.

Later in the day, O'Donoghue commented to the media.

"Possible sightings have been reported, but efforts failed to turn up anything. We're wondering if we're following a look-a-like." O'Donoghue added, "We have no evidence he ran away, so we have to look at the disappearance from all angles. In my experience, if he were a runaway, he'd be calling a friend. We don't have that. The Pittsfield police have interviewed his friends and no one has heard from him. We believe they are sincere."

When asked, Mrs. Bernardo said, "The police know more than I do. We don't know where he is. I think the students would have told police if they spoke with him." Mary Bernardo continued. "We're just barely holding up. We're going day by day. The disappearance of Jimmy has put an unbelievable strain on the entire family."

Mary Bernardo could barely speak. She wept openly and turned from the interviewer burying her face into Ron's chest. The reporters respectfully exited the front porch of the McKinley Terrace home. Ron assisted his wife as she retreated to the sanctuary of her home, joining other family members continuing their vigil.

On Sunday, the day after the expansive search, the news was grim. Estimated 150 searchers from the armed forces and police combed the designated areas in vain.

A thorough search of Clapp Park as well as the immediate surrounding areas rendered nothing to indicate where Jimmy could be found.

An additional office was set up in the basement of the police station. A command post was set up at the Salvation Army on West Street, where a radio antenna was installed.

The news was grim, no results, no leads and every possible means had been utilized including

Air Force Civil Air Patrol groups from all parts of Massachusetts and New York. The Missing Persons Bureau contributed countless hours to assist in the search. Two Civil Air Patrol planes were solicited to pass over the entire Berkshire County and overlap into New York, Connecticut and Vermont. The mass searches over the past three days had begun in the morning and continued to dusk. All came up empty. Despite the several sightings reported, the outcome was dismal.

The runaway theory continued to be considered but the authorities expressed concern about the length of time Jimmy had been missing.

Mary and Ronald Bernardo had long since concluded their son had met with foul play. The chances of Jimmy returning home safely was now an impossible wish. It was a difficult concept to accept, but they were certain Jimmy had not run away.

The police extended unprecedented efforts to find Jimmy Bernardo. After two weeks passed since the disappearance, they decided to re-examine all leads.

To date, there had been 60 possible sightings reported. Most were in the Coltsville section of the city. Retracing their steps would be a tedious effort but one the Pittsfield police agreed to, a last ditch effort they believed necessary. They could not determine what future measures they would take.

Detective Sgt. Riello again questioned the parents of Jimmy concerning the statement one of Jimmy's friends had made. The friend was questioned numerous times and each time his story continued to be consistent. On the night of Jimmy's disappearance, he saw Jimmy with a blue duffle bag. The friend said Jimmy mentioned plans to run away.

Again, the Bernardo's were adamant that Jimmy would not run away. Detective Riello never confirmed the boy ran away. He questioned how he would be surviving in the changing weather without shelter, money and a change of clothing. In addition to all those factors, he was sure that runaways generally contact a friend.

The Bernardo's asked the detective about the reports of sightings. "Have you followed up on all those calls?" asked Ronald.

"Yes, we have. I believe the citizens are waiting a little bit before they call in. By the time our units get to the location of the sighting, the boy is gone. We've encouraged people to call in the sightings immediately. We cannot confirm Jimmy was ever spotted. It's likely it's a case of mistaken identity." Riello replied.

"It would be different if we had a definite sighting from a family member or close friend who knows Jimmy," he continued.

"As of yesterday afternoon, we have not received any leads."

It was becoming more and more difficult for Anthony Riello to face the parents of the missing boy. He had nothing to offer that may give them even a glimmer of hope. In his years of experience never had he felt so helpless. Never had he conducted a search of this magnitude only to come up with not even a scintilla of evidence. It was baffling and the longer it went on the odds of finding Jimmy were slim.

Four days passed. The newspapers made no mention of the disappearance of Jimmy. They had moved on to other lead stories. Because of the lack of any progress by the searchers and police, there was simply nothing to report.

A search-related article appeared in the 'local briefs' section of the newspaper. In short, it disclosed the identity of the lead recovery specialist and spokesperson of the Jimmy Bernardo case.

Sean O'Donoghue had been stopped for a minor traffic violation. When he arrived for duty, Captain Boyer ran a computer check on O'Donoghue's automobile registration. The computer revealed a warrant for O'Donoghue's arrest on several charges that included larceny and forgery. The warrants were issued in several towns of Central Mass. The Captain also discovered O'Donoghue's license had been revoked.

In his defense, Sean O'Donoghue believed his lawyer had taken care of everything. He was cooperative with the Pittsfield Police when they placed him under arrest.

Captain Boyer stated, "The incident had nothing to do with the quality of the Missing Persons Bureau. The Bureau has replaced him with Steven Chase."

Boyer expressed his appreciation to O'Donoghue for the efforts he had extended to now in the search for Bernardo.

Three weeks had passed and the mystery of Jimmy's disappearance deepened.

Sgt. Benedetto Sciola of the Pittsfield detective bureau stated, "The boy's absence is puzzling.

We've found nothing. We're baffled. Whatever the circumstances involving his disappearance, the bottom line is Jimmy Bernardo is still missing."

It was becoming evident the searching would be discontinued. The course of action would be decided on a lead-by-lead basis. There was nothing more that could be done. The temporary headquarters at the Salvation Army as well as the one located in the basement of the police station would be disbanded the following Monday unless strong leads were to arise before then.

Jimmy had been missing for three weeks. The family was barely holding up. They wanted to do something to assist in the searches, but there was nothing the authorities and rescue teams hadn't already done.

The Bernardo's were in limbo. What were they to do? What was expected of them? Should they start getting on with their lives without Jimmy? That thought was unbearable, and quickly dismissed. The night of Jimmy's disappearance was replayed over and over in their minds. If only they could remember something, some small detail that would be a clue. Something Jimmy might have said they hadn't thought of; but there was nothing.

The facts remained as they were three weeks ago. Jimmy arranged to meet a friend at the Wall-to-Wall Billiards. He left riding his bike about 5:00 p.m. Monday, October 22. He failed to return and now, three weeks later, they were no closer to finding him.

Ten days passed. No news. It seemed all but the family had given up and life went on. Preparations for the upcoming Thanksgiving holiday were apparent and then the frenzy of Christmas shopping would immediately follow.

Tuesday, November 20, 1990

MISSING BOY'S BIKE
DISCOVERED IN LAKE

A bicycle discovered yesterday in Silver Lake by two youths playing in the area belongs to James Bernardo who disappeared October 22. The boy's father, Ronald Bernard identified the bike as his 12-year-old son's...

The news jolted the community. It put the case of the disappearance of Jimmy Bernardo back into the forefront. The discovery of Jimmy's bicycle confirmed what most refused to admit.

Foul play, Jimmy Bernardo had met with tragedy loomed in the minds of the citizens. The Bernardo's felt the sorrow they could never had anticipated. They were faced with reality. The possibility that Jimmy would never be returned safely was a light of hope that was extinguished. It was a numbing blow.

Upon the discovery of the bicycle, Ronald Bernardo was notified by Detective Peter McGuire who immediately arranged to send the bicycle to the Federal Bureau of Investigation laboratory in Washington, D.C. There, tests would be conducted to determine how long it was submerged in water.

Four state police divers were being brought in from Boston and a specially trained police dog was scheduled to search the 24-acre lake later in the day hoping for more clues.

Detective McGuire knew that Silver Lake had already been searched and nothing was discovered. The lake was located on the opposite section of town from Jimmy's residence and nowhere near the area where he reportedly was last seen.

"We're not sure how long it's been in the lake or how it got there." McGuire stated to Mary Bernardo.

Mary replied, "Jimmy had removed the reflectors from the bike and my husband adjusted the seat so it fit Jimmy by raising it. I don't know what to think anymore."

The two observations Mary had mentioned made Ron's identification of his son's green mud covered Mongoose bicycle positive.

When found, the bicycle was submerged in water about three feet from shore. One of the boys that discovered the bike told his grandfather and it was reported to the police.

"You really had to stand over the water to see it," McGuire added. "We're not sure how long it's been in the lake or how it got in there."

Captain Boyer accompanied by Detective John McGrath and Sgt. Benedetto Sciola spent hours on the lake in a canoe but found no clues.

The following day, City and State Police conducted a more extensive search of the Silver Lake area. The search failed to provide any significant new clues.

The discovery of the bike, served as a considerable development; the first since the investigation began three weeks before.

All sorts of speculation about what the discovery indicated circulated throughout the city. The police declined to offer their theory of what the discovery may indicate concerning what happened to Jimmy.

When Anthony Riello met with Ron and Mary Bernardo to discuss the new developments, they stated they did not believe Jimmy would have discarded his bike. They told the detective that Jimmy paid for the bike from his savings. The cost of the bike was $250.00.

Rewards were offered for Jimmy's safe return. Now, the rewards were offered for information that would lead to the arrest of his abductor. The rewards totaled $1,500.00. They came from Local 1584 of United Paper Workers International Union, Penna's Variety Store of Pittsfield and an additional $500 provided by relatives of the Bernardo family.

The day after Thanksgiving, confirmation of the unspoken conclusion most had dreaded and feared exploded across the front page of the Berkshire Eagle.

Friday, November 23, 1990

PITTSFIELD BOY FOUND STRANGLED
(A picture of the smiling James Bernardo
appeared under the shocking headline)

The body of 12-year-old James Bernardo of Pittsfield was found in woods of a small town outside of Ithaca, N.Y. Authorities determined James Bernardo had been strangled. New York State Police in Ithaca said that the identification was made after an investigation involving the Pittsfield police and an autopsy conducted by the Onondaga County Medical Examiner's Office in Syracuse. Death was due to strangulation.

Ithaca New York is located south of Syracuse and the New York Thruway.

Upon discovery of Jimmy's body, the New York authorities notified Massachusetts State Police. It was imperative steps be taken to assure positive identification. Investigator James Winn performed an examination and comparison of dental records that confirmed the body discovered by the two hunters was James Bernardo. Notification of death to be delivered to the parents was the agonizing task befallen onto Anthony Riello.

With the discovery of Jimmy, representatives of every media gathered at the Bernardo residence hoping the Bernardo's would make a statement, or answer questions for the next newspaper edition and television broadcast.

Ron and Mary were told of the discovery long before it was announced in the newspapers. They remained secluded within their house. Fortunately, because of the Thanksgiving holiday and the day that followed, Robert had not attended school.

Detective Riello anticipated the media frenzy and arrived earlier that morning to shield the Bernardo's from the cameras, microphones and the questions being posed by the reporters.

Alfred Bernardo, Jimmy's paternal grandfather was selected to represent the grieving parents. Included in his brief statement, a plea to respect the privacy of the family was requested and soon the media dispersed. They would seek any further information from the police department.

The police reported they had no suspects at the time. They anticipated the forensic tests would determine when the boy died and other death related aspects. It was necessary to determine exactly when the boy died in order to determine a chain of events leading up to his death.

Captain Walter Boyer stepped forward and announced the Pittsfield police would work in conjunction with the New York police on the investigation. They would re-evaluate all the information gathered during their search, including persons interviewed earlier.

Captain Boyer asked anyone with further information contact authorities.

"The slightest bit of information, however insignificant it may appear, could prove to be a turning point," Boyer said. "Again, we request that people review their memories for anything they may have seen or heard, however minor."

The bicycle that had been found only days before was sent to Washington for analysis. In addition to tests to determine how long it was in the lake, the police were hoping the tests would provide fingerprints of the person who put the bike in the water.

The cause of death was without a doubt, strangulation. In addition to that, the Onondaga County Pathologist determined Jimmy was killed at the scene but the time of death could have been anywhere between when he was reported missing and when he was found. The medical examiner could not say if the killing was sexually related.

Death by strangulation is particularly heinous according to Medical Examiner's accounts. Jimmy's hands were bound which impeded any effort to defend himself. Once the ligature was placed around his neck, he was aware of his dire predicament and undoubtedly experienced insurmountable terror and fear of his impending death.

Manual strangulation renders the victim unconscious within 8 seconds, however, for death to be certain, the ligature must be held tightly for 4 to 5 minutes, ample time for the killer to abandon the killing. There was no doubt, Jimmy's murder was a premeditated plan of a cold, calculating demon, with no purpose.

A full-page newspaper article was dedicated to the sorrowful discovery of Jimmy Bernardo.

Pittsfield police stated, "Jimmy Bernardo was no street kid. He was an average kid who was street smart, but who had never left home before."

Up until the discovery of Jimmy's nude body, the police never classified the disappearance as either abduction or a runaway.

Because of a report that a young friend had told the police that Jimmy had planned to run away, the abduction theory was not official, but was never ruled out either.

The missing person case now evolved into a homicide. Pittsfield Police Detective James McGuire would lead the investigation.The preliminary autopsy reports determined Jimmy had been strangled in the place his body was found. His clothes were scattered nearby and sexual abuse was suspected but not confirmed.

McGuire wasted no time. He spoke to the owner of the Wall-to-Wall Billiards, the pool hall where Jimmy was headed.

Sue Wall told the detective neither she nor any of her staff saw Jimmy that night. In addition, she told the police that Massachusetts law bans children under 18 from pool halls without parental consent. She stated Jimmy's friends were allowed to patronize the pool hall, but Jimmy did not have parental consent.

On Sunday, November 25, 1990, James Bernardo's obituary was published.

James E. Bernardo, 12, of 3 McKinley Terrace, was found dead Wednesday in Newfield, N.Y., after having been missing since Oct. 22. Born in Pittsfield, he was the son of Ronald and Mary Bernardo, and brother of Robert Bernardo. He attended Crosby School and Herberg Middle School, where he was in the seventh grade. He was a communicant of St. Mark's Church and served as an altar boy. He also was active in the city's West Little League. Besides his parents, he leaves his paternal grandparents, Alfred and Susan Bernardo of Pittsfield, and Robert and Rosemary Mazur of Hernando, Fla.; his maternal grandmother, Carol J. Savery of Pittsfield, and his paternal great-grandparents, Fausto and Mildred Bernardo of Largo, Fla., and his maternal great-grandmother, Laura Hitchcock of Lee. The funeral will be Tuesday morning in the church, with burial in Maple Street Cemetery, Hinsdale. Calling hours are Monday evening. Devanny-Condron Funeral Home is in charge.

The investigation of James Bernardo's murder was officially underway. A dozen Pittsfield investigators and four State Police investigators from the Ithaca area were assigned to Pittsfield and began reviewing evidence collected since the boy was reported missing. In addition, twenty investigators worked in the Ithaca area.

A father and two sons had discovered Jimmy's body at about 7:40 a.m. while they were hunting deer near the Edward Kaiser farm in Newfield. The body was discovered in an overgrown, brushy area on the property owned by Mr. Edward Kaiser.

When asked if he had seen or heard anything unusual, Mr. Kaiser said he was in Florida last week. He said he had returned on Saturday afternoon. Jimmy's body was only 200 yards from the farmhouse.

This investigation was becoming one of monumental proportions. The investigators shared all information and frequently brainstormed various theories.

The police theories depended on when the victim died and how and when he traveled to the Ithaca area. One theory being considered was at the time Jimmy was abducted, his bike was left abandoned. Perhaps another person found the bike and kept it for a time before discarding it into Silver Lake.

Regardless of various theories, the key to the murder investigation would hinge on forensic test results, which would include small carpet fibers taken from Jimmy's body and the tape used to bind, gag and blindfold Jimmy.

Police began receiving new tips in the case, including reports that vehicles were seen at times parked near Silver Lake. When the police were able to determine how long the bike had been in the lake perhaps that would be a valuable piece of the puzzle. The reports from Washington D.C. were expected within the week. They were hoping in addition to determining the length of time the bike had been submerged in the lake, it might provide fingerprints.

On the following day, all investigators met and began sifting through all information that had been gathered up to and including the day Jimmy's body was found.

If the boy traveled in a straight line between Pittsfield and Tompkins County, he would have had to be taken through Albany.

They also believed that Jimmy was killed in the woods where the body was found. They were somewhat baffled at that conclusion, as the setting was unusual. It was far from any major highway. If these deductions were accurate, they indicated the abductor/murderer was familiar with the remote area.

According to the medical examiner's office in Syracuse, the body was found lying face down and naked. The hands were bound by duct tape, a rope was around the neck and tape had been placed over the eyes. The clothing Jimmy was last seen wearing were found nearby.

The first step was to compile a list of all business owners and all employees at the Cinema Plaza. It was tedious, and repetitive for the investigators, however it was paramount that all these individuals be questioned. The questions were composed as such that would be appropriate when questioning a potential witness as well as a possible suspect.

Business owners at the Plaza were questioned and provided the police with complete payroll records reflecting all persons, employed.

One individual said he saw Jimmy drinking a soda in front of the plaza's laundromat at 5:30. Another reported he thought he saw Jimmy around 6:00 and he appeared to be heading from the plaza, as if he was on his way home. He reported he still had his green bicycle at that time. Jimmy's friend who was planning to meet him was not able to find him.

Detective McGuire stated days of interviews failed to produce any more than vague accounts from merely a handful of the hundreds interviewed. No suspects were reported.

The following week, a roadblock was set up at West Housatonic Street, near the Cinema Plaza where Jimmy was last seen alive.

Local detectives and New York state troopers stopped over 3,000 cars within the hour from five to 6 p.m. Traffic was backed up for a mile. Police handed drivers a two-page printed bulletin. The bulletin read, *"James Bernardo, age 12, was last seen alive in this area on Monday, October 22nd. If you saw him between 5:00–5:30 p.m. on that day, or if you saw anyone or anything out of the ordinary, however insignificant you may think it is, please call the Pittsfield Police"* (police telephone number followed) The bulletin also included a picture of Jimmy and his bicycle. A similar roadblock was set up in Newfield, N.Y. where Bernardo was found dead.

New York State Police began an additional investigation to determine if there was any link between Jimmy Bernardo's slaying and the unsolved deaths of several N.Y. youths.

One in particular was brought to the N.Y. police's attention. A 15-year old boy from nearby Stephentown, N.Y. had disappeared on June 30, 1990. His body was found July 8, 1990 in a wooded area approximately eight miles from Pittsfield.

A tearful farewell was scheduled for the 12-year-old. Final goodbyes were said and Jimmy would be buried in Hinsdale.

Ronald, Mary and Robert Bernardo followed Jimmy's coffin into St. Mark's Church. The bells tolled and hundreds followed the grieving parents, flanked by an honor guard of Jimmy's classmates and teachers.

Detectives were present watching all who came to mourn the loss of such a vibrant boy. In their experience with homicide cases, it was not uncommon for the killer to attend the services. It seemed to be a part of the scheme in the deranged mind of the monsters.

Reverend Michael Shershanovich began the mass of the dead. His plea to the family for forgiveness to the killer was chilling.

He continued, "If we seek to be forgiven, we ourselves have to forgive, even if it is a person we don't know…a person we may never know." The church was silent as the reverend continued asking that the killer come to his senses.

Immediately following the Mass at St. Mark's Church, the hearse delivered Jimmy's body to the Maple Street Cemetery in nearby Hinsdale. Jimmy's final resting place was beside his great grandmother.

Family members, aunts, uncles, grandparents and cousins encircled Mary, Ronald and Robert and openly sobbed. It was the final chapter in the brief life of 12-year old James Bernardo.

Jimmy's grandfather, the spokesperson for the family, asked reporters to keep the story of his grandson's death alive in order to help catch the slayer.

"I don't want this story to drop. Someone had to have seen something," he added.

"The family has pretty much been kept in the dark about progress in the murder investigation, however we are confident the police will succeed. They are not telling us very much, but maybe knowing less right now is best."

Tears welled in the elderly man's eyes, but he continued.

"Anyone with information about what occurred at the plaza during the time period in which Jimmy is known to have disappeared, please contact the police. Maybe you are afraid to come forward, but you must do so."

"I believe more than one person has to have been involved. Jimmy was a scrapper. He was a strong little kid, and I do believe he fought. There had to be more than one person."

Mr. Bernardo continued and turned to direct his final words toward family members.

"I saw Jimmy two days before he disappeared at my birthday celebration. I'm glad I was able to see him happy that day."

The slaying of Jimmy Bernardo sparked concern bordering on panic to the citizens of Pittsfield. The residents were sympathetic for the family while they feared for the safety of their own children.

The intensive investigation underway in both Pittsfield as well as New York had failed to produce any major developments. Laboratory test results were crucial in determining exactly when the boy died and by what means he traveled into western New York.

Many residents openly questioned how the investigation was proceeding. The atmosphere during the search for the boy and after the revelation of his death was nerve-wracking. Neighbors reported they "are thinking all the time about what went wrong." The children who went to school with Jimmy were particularly upset.

Police were troubled with the fact that Jimmy had somehow traveled more than 200 miles from his home. The citizens were troubled that the killer may still be in the community, since authorities had not ruled that possibility out.

The school planned to make the counseling staff available to students when they returned from the Thanksgiving vacation.

Parents paid closer attention to where their kids were congregating after school — at the mall, at shopping and movie centers. Pittsfield was no longer considered the safe community it once was.

The Onondaga County Medical Examiner in New York announced they would meet with investigators and brief them on results of the studies. In addition, the test results from the FBI were due to determine when the bicycle was thrown into Silver Lake.

Pittsfield police aided by the Massachusetts State Police conducted a second informational roadblock and announced more investigators were being assigned to the case. The parents pleaded for information concerning Jimmy's killer. The medical examiners continued to state they were unable to determine whether Jimmy was sexually assaulted, but they did confirm he died two to three days prior to the discovery of his body.

With this additional information, the question was; where was Jimmy from October 22 through November 20? Three weeks, he was alive, was he with the killer? Nobody had those answers, but it was a haunting question.

Adding to the complex investigation, Captain Walter Boyer reported authorities were investigating an incident which two older teens assaulted an 11-year-old boy on his way to West Side Community School and left him bound and gagged.

The Captain believed the perpetrators might have been "a couple of bullies mimicking the Bernardo situation."

He said the 11-year-old was taking a short cut to school at about 9:00 a.m. and was struck in the back and kicked in the stomach by two youths. The boy's feet were tied with wire, his hands tied behind his back with shoelaces, and a plastic bag was used to gag him.

Boyer said a patron of a nearby variety store heard the boy's muffled cries about 20 minutes later and found the boy. The boy was terrified, but unharmed.

Ronald Bernardo felt he should address the public. After this incident with the 11-year-old, Mr. Bernardo issued a personal message to the citizens of Pittsfield.

"Our son is in our thoughts every moment we are awake. We try to think of the good times we all had together, swimming at Plunkett Lake every Sunday, fishing for bass in the springtime, vacationing in Rhode Island every summer, and playing in the snow in the winter." Ron Bernardo also thanked the police and members of the public for their support.

Ronald Bernardo continued, "We pray to God every day and hope that after hearing me that you will as well. Please pray that the police find our son's killer before he has a chance to kill another child. Our son, Jimmy, is resting now." The tearful father ended his message with, "His pain and suffering are over, yet ours has really only just begun."

The investigation of the murder of Jimmy Bernardo continued throughout the month of December. No clues no leads and no suspects turned up. It was truly a mystery for the detectives and an open wound that would never heal for the family.

The December issue of *Sports Illustrated* hit the stands. The issue was dated exactly one month after Jimmy's body was discovered.

Sports Illustrated announced *"Sportsman of the Year"* and the recipient, no other than San Francisco 49er, Joe Montana was featured on the cover; Jimmy Bernardo's hero.

It would be fifteen years before the *"Sportsman of the Year"* would be named again. The *Sports Illustrated* December 2005 issue would announce the coveted *"Sportsman of the Year"* award. The N.E. Patriots' Tom Brady would be featured on the cover.

A task force was formed to bolster the efforts to find the killer. The task force included Federal, Massachusetts and New York authorities and work out of the Citizens Against Child Abuse interview room in the Pittsfield Police Station.

Captain Boyer stated, "It will be a formalized task-force investigation; a networking. There won't be individual entities. Everyone will work out of the same office, sharing all information."

Alfred Bernardo, Jimmy's grandfather solicited businesses to establish a reward fund to encourage the public to report information leading to the arrest and conviction of his grandson's killer.

In a further effort to spur information, the reward money increased. Ronald Bernardo's employer posted $10,000 reward for information that would solve the strangling death of Jimmy. Thomas Danz, manager of the Rising Paper Co., stated, "We feel we have to do something substantial."

The task force investigating the murder released a photograph of the T-shirt Jimmy was wearing when he disappeared. The photograph was published in the newspaper hoping it would trigger the memory of anyone who may have seen him. It was hoped it would lead to the arrest of his killer.

Repeatedly the task force made public appeals for information regarding "suspicious persons who may have been seen loitering near the plaza on October 22."

By the end of December 1990, the news was grim. The hope of apprehending Jimmy Bernardo's killer was fading with each passing week. The task force continued its investigation but nothing developed; however, the case would remain open.

One year to the day passed since the disappearance of Jimmy Bernardo. October 23, 1991 was the first anniversary of Jimmy's abduction. The investigation of Jimmy's murder remained an open case, but with no suspects or clues, the case was cold.

The news of the arrest of a Catholic priest was widespread. Father Richard Lavigne was arrested in nearby Shelburne Falls and facing two charges of child rape and indecent assault and battery on a child under 14. Lavigne was also the prime suspect in a 1972 death of a 13-year-old altar boy. No charges had been filed in the murder case, but his recent arrest came to the attention of Pittsfield Police Detective Peter Maguire.

Father Richard Lavigne was not considered a suspect in the Bernardo case, but he was added to the list of several people of interest.

"Anytime somebody comes to our attention and is charged with raping a child, we look at him very closely," Maguire said.

The New York State Police investigator contacted the Bernardo family to inform them of the new lead and was quick to emphasize, "He is not a suspect at this time."

Mrs. Bernardo spoke to the press.

"We still have hopes that they're going to get whoever did it. Some days you lose hope then you gain it again, but the New York state police said they will solve it so we have to have faith in them."

McGuire noted the similarities to Jimmy Bernardo. The commonality was Jimmy Bernardo was a 12-year-old altar boy. The priest was facing rape charges and both victims were altar boys.

Jimmy Bernardo served as an altar boy at St. Mark's Church in Pittsfield. Father Lavigne served at St. Joseph's Church, Shelburne Falls only 40 miles from Pittsfield.

The New York authorities declined to comment if the priest would be questioned in connection to Jimmy Bernardo's murder.

Detective McGuire conducted his own investigation into the background of the priest.

He learned Lavigne was 50 years old, and a Chicopee, MA native. He had been ordained in 1966 and celebrated his 25th anniversary as a priest only two months earlier. Further research disclosed the priest was very popular with the parishioners. At the time of a transfer from St. Catherine's Church in Springfield, to St. Mary's also in Springfield it was reported as many as 50 families followed him. He was reassigned to St. Joseph's parish in Shelburne Falls 12 years ago.

Detective McGuire would follow the progress of Lavigne's trial, and perhaps something would develop.

It would be *three years* before Jimmy Bernardo's killer would be brought to justice.

CHAPTER 2

Eighteen months passed since Jimmy Bernardo's death. The investigation was ongoing, but without any new evidence.

On April 15, 1992, Agawam experienced shock as they never had before. They were about to learn of Lisa Ziegert's disappearance.

Agawam Massachusetts is located just southeast of the Berkshires; Hampden County, commonly referred to as the 'foothills of the Berkshires'. Agawam, population approximately 20,000 borders Connecticut.

Traveling along the Massachusetts Turnpike, Rt. 90 Agawam is less than an hour's drive.

Upon graduation, class of 1990, Lisa applied to the Agawam School Department for a teaching position in the elementary school. At the time, there were no positions available and the school was experiencing budget cuts. However, Lisa was persistent.

The school was very impressed with Lisa Ziegert. After all, some of the committee had known her since she attended elementary school. The Ziegert family was well known and respected in the community, and Lisa was offered a position as an assistant teacher for special needs children. Although the pay was somewhat short, Lisa was thrilled, jumped at the opportunity without hesitation, and became a member of the faculty.

In addition to her new position in the public school system, Lisa continued teaching a class at her church. The children were the 7-8 year-olds preparing to make their first communion, an important sacrament in the life of a Catholic child.

Traditionally, First Communion ceremonies are scheduled in May; the classes would begin in September, and continue for eight months of weekly sessions. Lisa volunteered her time. Not only was it an experience in teaching, it was an opportunity to interact with children.

On April 11, only four days before her disappearance, Lisa's classes were complete. The children in her Christian Doctrine class were prepared for their First Communion. They would dedicate the May celebration to their beloved teacher, Lisa Ziegert.

The attractive 24-year-old was a bubbly, outgoing young woman with aspirations that stretched far beyond most. The student councilor, Dick Cowles considered her an exceptional, gifted teacher.

Mr. Cowles was quoted, "Seldom does one come along that stands out. Lisa was that special one."

The entire town of Agawam would be horrified at the story that was about to unfold. Never had Agawam experienced anything so horrific, so unbelievable.

Thursday, April 16, 1992

POPULAR YOUNG SCHOOL
TEACHER ABDUCTED

Sometime after 8:30 p.m. on April 15th Lisa Ziegert, a 24 year-old Agawam schoolteacher was abducted from her part-time job at Brittany's card shop.

The news shocked the residents of this small community. It was inconceivable that an abduction of a 24 year-old woman could take place in a busy, well-lighted strip mall. The store was surrounded by several other businesses and restaurants in the center of Agawam.

Attempting to create a 'time line' the article continued describing the activities of Lisa that led up to the abduction.

Lisa was scheduled to begin her part-time shift at the card and gift shop at 4:00 p.m. The store closed at 9 p.m., but police say Lisa, who was working alone, never closed down Wednesday p.m.

She had completed her day at the elementary school and arrived early at the store. She arrived around 3:45 relieving Sophia Maynard. Sophia was pleased to see Lisa's early arrival. She had several errands to run and those additional few minutes were very welcome.

Sophia prepared the bank deposit and spoke to Lisa about the receipts, which reflected an exceptionally busy Wednesday. Sunday was Easter, so the increase of business was expected for a store that offered a fine selection of gifts and hand designed Easter ornaments.

Sophia placed the bank bag on the counter as she gathered her coat and purse. A few minutes before four, Sophia gave Lisa an affectionate hug and waved goodbye.

"Thanks Lisa, see you tomorrow." With that, she left.

At the start of her shift, Lisa always walked through the store, inspecting the various displays assuring all were in order and attractive.

Shortly after 5:00, Lisa's sister Lynne Ziegert stopped by the store to visit. Lynne and Lisa were close in age; Lynne was older by 15 months. The sisters were also good friends and Lynne frequently dropped by just to visit with Lisa.

There were no customers in the store when Lynne arrived. Lisa was working on sketches, which she shared with Lynne, eagerly explaining the project she planned for her students. They talked about the upcoming Easter Sunday and confirmed that all would gather at their parent's house for dinner.

An hour passed and Lynne left around 6:00. A few customers had come and gone while the two girls chatted but when Lynne left, there were no customers in the store.

Lisa was last seen inside the store at approximately 7:30 p.m.

The following morning, Sophia Maynard, arrived at the store. As she pulled into her usual parking space at the front of the store, she noticed Lisa's car. She glanced into the car; saw a basket of neatly folded clothes in the back seat but no indication of anything wrong.

As she approached the entrance, she noticed the flag indicating, 'OPEN'. That was odd. With her keys in hand, she reached for the handle of the plate glass door and found it was unlocked and the lights were on inside. This was so unlike Lisa to be so forgetful. For a brief moment she considered maybe Lisa had arrived early to work on the assorted hand made gift items they had been preparing.

As Sophia proceeded into the store, she spotted Lisa's sketchpad on the countertop. She walked around the display case, and discovered Lisa's purse, keys and coat were under the counter.

She called out to Lisa. Hearing no response, she called again and approached the storage room located at the back of the store. She swung the door open. There was nobody there.

The following day, the search for Lisa intensified. She had left the lights ablaze, doors unlocked and her purse and keys were left behind.

She had not reported to the Agawam middle school as scheduled. The police began an immediate manhunt with abduction foremost in their mind. They conducted interviews with family and friends. All agreed; Lisa was very responsible.George Ziegert, Lisa's father said, "She would never do anything like this. She would have told us if she was planning on going somewhere."

When asked by investigators, Lisa's boyfriend, Blair Massoia replied, "She's always happy. She doesn't have an enemy in the world. It looks like she's been abducted. I believe she did not leave the store willingly. I think she was abducted."

The Agawam police were assisted by the FBI based in Springfield, as well as the State Police. Lt. Robert Campbell addressed the media stating Lisa's case was being treated as a missing person.

"I'm not going to speculate, anything is possible at this point." Lt. Campbell described the search as that of intense and thorough right at the onset. The Agawam police began combing the fields that surrounded the shopping center. They searched on foot, and the State Police provided the services of a helicopter to conduct an aerial search of Agawam and all the surrounding towns.

Lt. Campbell would not disclose any information that involved the interior of the card shop. Employees as well as patrons of the neighboring stores watched the police activity. Yellow crime scene tape was placed around the card shop to restrain any unauthorized persons from proceeding within 50 feet of the 'crime scene'.

Dianne and George Ziegert arrived at the store soon after they were notified of their daughter's disappearance. Dianne, (affectionately called Dee) assured the police that Lisa was far too responsible to have left the store unattended. She surely would not have been absent from her classes at the Middle School without notification. There was no doubt; Lisa had been taken against her will.

Lisa was single and shared an apartment with a girlfriend. She had been teaching for two years and had worked part-time at the card shop for several years. She was a very stable and dependable young woman. She was close to her family and visited often.

Dee Ziegert recalled the last time she saw Lisa. "She was in her usual bubbly mood. She stopped by my house on Monday to pick up some laundry." She continued, "She put the car seat forward. Put her laundry basket in the back seat, flipped the seat back, big smile, big wave, bye mom. Love you. That's the last time I saw her."

All who knew Lisa were baffled, confused and fearful that Lisa had been harmed. Detectives were inside the store all day. They would not speak to the media who swarmed around the crime scene van backed up to the entrance of the shop. Several items were placed in the van but the identity of these items was not disclosed.

Unsubstantiated rumors were rampant as the investigation got underway, but it was being conducted with little information to be disseminated to the anxious residents. Fourteen officers were assigned to the case. For Agawam, it was a substantial portion of the police department. Lt. Campbell spoke to the press and reported that on the night of Lisa's disappearance a patrol officer did notice the lights on in the store. Generally, the police on the night shift check on local businesses, however as the patrolman noticed the lights he received another call. He responded to the call and was not able to get back to the card shop.

The frequency of calls on the late shift occasionally made door checking very difficult. Incoming calls always took priority.

Campbell added, "It's not like we have a terrific amount of manpower on the late shift." When pressed for more information, the police were sure robbery was not a motive, and Lisa did not leave willingly. The investigation began by interviewing family, friends and acquaintances of the missing woman.

Lisa's sister Lynne was one of the first interviewed by the detectives.

"You don't expect something like this to happen to someone you know, and you damn sure don't expect it to happen to someone you love. She is my best friend as well as my sister."

Lynne Ziegert continued, "Lisa doesn't have an enemy in the world and she wasn't having any problems. She knows we all love her and are just waiting for her to walk through the door."

Lisa shared an apartment with her friend, Deanne Duclos. When the police interviewed Deanne she simply told them, "Lisa is not an irresponsible person. She wouldn't just leave and not take anything with her. She wouldn't just leave the store unlocked and not call anyone." She added, "This (disappearance) is very strange."

George Ziegert, Lisa's father, told police that Lisa had just visited him and Mrs. Ziegert a few days before. She made no mention to them about any plans to go anywhere. Besides, her car was still where she had parked it upon arrival at the card shop Wednesday afternoon.

Police Lt. Robert Campbell was prepared to conduct an aggressive search right from the start. The West Springfield Police, Mass. State Police and Connecticut State Police were already cooperating in the search. A search of the area by police and a tracking dog, along with a helicopter and boat search of the nearby Westfield River, failed to provide leads.

"Right now, we're sifting through volumes and volumes of information." Campbell said. "We only get one shot here, so we're trying to cover all the bases. If we miss something, it's hard to go back six months from now."

Police began collecting items from the gift shop that included a display case and two rear doors in an effort to find clues to Lisa's disappearance.

Joseph O'Neill, the owner of Brittany's Card and Gift Shoppe was at the store overseeing the efforts of the Agawam Police who had been joined by the FBI.

"Lisa was very trusting and whoever it was, had to be someone she was intimidated by." Mr. O'Neill was very emotional as he commented about Lisa's disappearance. He had known Lisa since 1989 when she started working for him at the shop.

"Lisa is a very sensible young woman, I don't think she would have allowed herself to let in a suspicious character...it may have been someone she knew." Joe O'Neill's statement was chilling.

O'Neill continued, "The action by police indicates she was lured to the back of the store before she vanished."

Rumors were rampant. The police would neither confirm nor deny that blood was found in the rear of the store.

Lt. Campbell confirmed that the items taken from the store would undergo testing. Robbery was not considered, as the cash register had not been disturbed.

"We've received several leads, and we've run them all down, however at this time, we do not have a suspect."

James Dent owned Carpets and More, a carpet store next door to the card shop. When interviewed, it was determined Dent was the last known person to see the missing woman.

According to Mr. Dent, he was closing his store at 7:30 and he said Lisa had waved to him. He entered the card shop and talked with Lisa for about 15 minutes.

He recalled with a chill what they talked about.

"It must have been somebody she wasn't intimidated by, or someone she knew because she had a panic button right by the counter and she never used it." The visibly shaken storeowner continued,

"Lisa mentioned occasional problems with a customer. I told her just to let things like that go. When I realize I was the last person to see her, it sends a chill right through me."

Family and friends had gathered at Lisa's parents' home and waited for news. Prayers were offered for Lisa during the Saturday Easter services at Sacred Heart Church. As the community prayed, the police continued their search.

"As of Friday morning, we have classified this as a kidnapping," said Lt. Campbell. "We have ruled out a number of possibilities, and we feel Lisa did not leave on her own."

The investigation was intense, but provided very little to the whereabouts of Lisa Ziegert.

Lisa's picture and details of her mysterious disappearance were broadcasted on all major TV networks. The newspaper carried her picture and information surrounding the circumstances of her disappearance in every edition.

Her picture reflected a beautiful young woman with a charismatic smile and the following description; brown hair and blue eyes. She was wearing a white blouse, light blue peasant skirt and brown suede boots. The telephone number of the Agawam Police followed every broadcast and every news article.

Through information provided by the store receipts, the detectives were able to determine she was abducted some time after 8:21, when she last waited on a customer. About 9:05 another customer reported she had come into the store but nobody was there so she left without notifying authorities.

The investigation was particularly baffling because of the location of the store.

The suburban shopping center had been buzzing with activity. The restaurants and bars in the small strip mall were open. Dozens of bowlers were in and out of the Agawam Bowl, right next door. Yet, during the peak bowling rush between 8:15 and 9:15 an unknown assailant was able to take Lisa from the shop.

The Agawam Bowl co-owner was questioned. Bob Tetreault said, "This is one of the things I have the most difficulty understanding." Tetreault referred to the fact that over 100 people went in and out of the bowling alley that night. The noticeably shaken business owner continued, "I really wonder if someone was watching the whole situation and because of a lot of movement going on, people might not notice another car."

The circumstances of the disappearance continued to grip residents, prompting endless speculation and rumors throughout the community.

Most agreed Lisa must have known her abductor and many were heard to say, "When they catch whoever did this, we're going to know him."

The police did conclude it was likely that Lisa had been taken out a side door in the rear of the card shop, which leads to a service road between the shop and the bowling alley.

They had removed two doors and a display rack that appeared to have bloodstains to be examined as well as possible fingerprints.

It had been four days and Lisa's family waited and worried secluded in their home. It was tough on everyone, particularly George Ziegert.

AGAWAM WOMAN FOUND DEAD

The desperate four-day search for Lisa Ziegert ended on Easter Sunday. It was a tragic ending when police found her body in a wooded area less than two miles from where she had been abducted.

The Ziegert family was informed of the discovery of Lisa's body. When Dee Ziegert came to the door, she knew the detective was not there to deliver good news. His expression that of pain as he said, "Dee, we found her…"

Dee Ziegert spoke before the detective could finish,

"She's dead," was the two words Dee uttered as she felt her knees about to buckle.

In the days following the murder, the family remained secluded, watching television and reading news accounts of the killing.

Later, Dee Ziegert would say, "We kept thinking, this is not happening. It's not denial, it's disbelief. Your head knows, but your body, mercifully..., gives you a very numb feeling."

Friends gathered on the front lawn of the family home after learning that police had found the body.

Only hours before, a special Easter mass was said for the safe return of Lisa Ziegert. Twelve churches in Agawam were handing out white ribbons as a sign of support for the Ziegert family.

Although authorities had not positively identified the body, Lt. Campbell believed it to be Lisa.

The Agawam Police were notified by a passerby who had discovered Lisa's body. The police rushed to the reported location and immediately roped off the area.

Late into the day police worked in the roped-off area where Lisa had been found. Spectators gathered and quietly watched as the detectives and forensic technicians continued sifting through the debris hoping to find something that would lead them to whoever had deposited her body.

The search continued for over eleven hours. Floodlights were brought to the site, but the police would not explain why the work was taking so long.

gawam Police refused to discuss any details of the Ziegert murder. They reported that they had received a call from a man who had been walking in the woods with his two young sons and believed he had found Lisa's body. The police responded to the scene that was less than two miles from the gift shop and even closer to Lisa's residence.

The officer who arrived at the scene disclosed that she was "pretty well beaten up." They would not share any potential clues or if they had any suspects. The police refused to speculate on any motive for Lisa's murder.

The area was swampy and drenched from days of steady rain. It was difficult for the police to reach the body.

Lt. Campbell confirmed that more than 20 witnesses had been interviewed, but none was named as a suspect.

"I think whoever left her here had to know the area," the Lieutenant stated. "You need a four-wheel drive to get through the mud and there are a lot of different entrances to this place."

As the Lieutenant spoke, he shouted over the noise of a helicopter hovering overhead that had been called in to photograph the area.

Lisa's body remained at the site for over twelve hours after the discovery. It was necessary to leave Lisa's body untouched until all evidence had been gathered.

The Medical Examiner arrived around 2:30 a.m. and released the body to be transported to Springfield Municipal Hospital where an autopsy would be performed. The results would be delivered to the Agawam Police Department as soon as they were available.

Lt. Campbell scheduled a news conference and discussed progress of the investigation.

One of the 20+ witnesses questioned was an employee of Healthy Habits, an all women's fitness club across from the card shop.

Lisa worked out at the club everyday around 3:00 p.m. The witness described a "man who would show up every day when Lisa was there. The man would buy frozen yogurt at the club's juice bar."

"We thought he was weird." She said he never approached Lisa and was not intimidating, but she hadn't seen him since April 14. Lisa disappeared on April 15.

Another witness told police that around 9:15 p.m. the night Lisa disappeared, he saw a full sized utility vehicle such as a Ford Bronco enter the woods where Lisa's body was found.

Detectives searched for the person who killed the 24-year-old teacher. They concentrated on the man regularly seen leering at her as she exercised in the local health club.

The investigation turned to the witnesses' accounts that had been received immediately following the discovery of Lisa's body.

One witness, a member of the health club was questioned extensively. The woman provided the description of a man about 5-feet, 10 inches tall, in his mid-30s. She noted a 'beer belly' and wavy, dirty, light brown hair. His clothes were always soiled and she expressed how surprised she was to see him drive away in a fancy red sports car. She was shown mug shots of men who resembled the man she described, but did not recognize any of them.

Another member of the club stepped forward and added she along with employees of the club complained about the man that continually leered at the all-female members because he was spending too much time at a club meant for women only.

When the club manager (male) was questioned, he stated, "That's the first I've heard of it, which is sad."

District Attorney William Bennett held a press conference. With the exception of the questioning of a few witnesses, Bennett advised the police were purposely keeping quiet and at this point it would be better that the public not really know all the facts. He concluded that too much information provided to the press could "screw up the investigation."

Lt. Robert Campbell, the lead detective on the Ziegert homicide shared the results of the autopsy. The report confirmed the cause of death was a single knife wound to the throat.

He addressed the statements from a handful of witnesses who claimed the body was found naked. "That is an unsubstantiated rumor," the Lieutenant stated adamantly. He advised that a sexual assault could not be determined at this time.

Lt. Campbell was very professional; however, he felt the pain personally. He knew the Ziegert's and Campbell's son attended school with Lisa's younger sister Sharon.

Others on the force were equally affected from the discovery of Lisa's body.

Sgt. Wayne Macey's daughter also attended school with Sharon. Gerry O'Keefe, another officer of the community's police department had known Lisa since she attended high school with his daughter. Following high school, the two girls attended Westfield State College together.

The loss of Lisa Ziegert was particularly personal in the small community. Lisa touched many lives; she would not be forgotten.

It was a continuing effort of law enforcement to dispel rumors running rampant. One high ranking State Police Officer responded to the rumor circulating that the body was badly mutilated.

"That is entirely false," he contended.

From the onset, there were no less than 15 detectives on the case. Campbell assured the anxious residents in the small community that all evidence was being carefully analyzed and all leads were being followed up. With the assistance of the Massachusetts State Police, the theory evolved that Lisa's assailant could be a local resident who would have knowledge of the obscure dirt road that led to the wooded area where the body had been discovered.

The theory offered by the police was chilling and transmitted a wave of fear that stunned the entire community. It was conceivable the killer could be having lunch at the next table or seated beside you at church. Everyone walked beneath the umbrella of suspicion.

The steps of the Agawam Police Department was the chosen site where news conferences would be held to deliver updates to the media. Agawam residents outnumbered the reporters, photographers, and TV cameramen vying for the best position to hear the latest information and progress of the investigation.

The business owners from the shopping center gathered and expressed their shock of the only homicide they could recall in their community.

"We're all family here," said Ed Borgatti, the owner of EB's Specialty Chicken located only a few doors down from the card shop.

"My wife walks out there every night and we've never had any fears of abduction."

All agreed that with a guitar shop, bowling alley, barbershop, pet store and several bars and restaurants, the small but bustling section of Agawam attracted a number of young as well as adult shoppers.

The owner of the barbershop commented, "It's one of the most popular places in town. No one here has ever been afraid."

A lifetime resident expressed his personal concerns, "This is a very big happening and it's a bad one. It will have a lasting effect."All agreed that the memory of Lisa Ziegert's murder would color the town for years to come.On Wednesday, April 22, 1992, the wake for Lisa Ziegert was scheduled at the Colonial Funeral Home and Sacred Heart Church. The funeral would be the following day, a capsulation of Lisa's 24 years appeared in the paper.

Lisa Ziegert was a teacher's aide in the special education department at Agawam Middle School and a clerk at the Brittany Card and Gift Shop in Agawam. She also worked at the Perry Lane Camp for four summers.

Lisa was a communicant of Sacred Heart Church and taught Confraternity of Christian Doctrine classes there.

While in high school, she played tenor saxophone and flute in the concert band. She had also been a drum majorette for the school's marching band for two years. She worked for the school newspaper and literary magazine, Unicorn.

She was a member of the National Honor Society and the American Field Service.

She leaves her parents, George and Diane "Dee" (Goodreau) Ziegert of Agawam; a brother, David G. of Los Angeles; two sisters, Lynne A. and Sharon L. Ziegert of Agawam; her grandparents, Edwin O. and Bertha (Beaulieu) Ziegert of West Springfield and Charles A. Goodreau of West Springfield.

The Colonial Funeral Home crisis team will be available for counseling and support programs Wednesday at the funeral home. A special program will be held for children under the age of 16 in the morning. An adult program will be offered in the evening.

Calling hours will be Wednesday afternoon and evening.

Memorial contributions may be made to the Lisa M. Ziegert Memorial Fund, in care of Jack Patterson at Heritage Bank, 1325 Springfield St., Feeding Hills.

The police continued the intense investigation. Nothing was taken for granted everyone associated with Lisa would be questioned.

The son of a former Agawam police officer was questioned.

Edward Borgatti worked at his father's restaurant only 30 yards from the shop where Lisa worked. Rumors were widespread and Borgatti faced accusing citizens and became the topic of conversation in the wake of the questioning.

The police insisted the questioning was a routine matter because of his friendship with Lisa and because he was in the area when she was abducted. When asked where he was between 8:00 and 9:30 on the night Lisa disappeared, Borgatti said he was working at the restaurant.

Borgatti also shared an apartment with Blair Massoia, Lisa's boyfriend. Blair Massoia had been questioned earlier in the investigation.

The Borgatti family was well known in the community. His father, Edward Sr. was a former police officer. The senior Borgatti was infuriated as the rumors spread throughout the area.

"They have not charged him with anything," he said, claiming his son was never told his rights at the time he was questioned.

Mr. Borgatti contacted District Attorney William Bennett and the Agawam Police Chief pleading with them to dispel the rumors.

Agawam Mayor Chris Johnson took to the airways and made a statement on behalf of the Borgatti family.

"It's unfortunate, but you are not going to stop the rumor mills. The Borgatti family are very good members of our community and don't deserve this."

When District Attorney William Bennett was asked specifically if Ed Borgatti was considered a suspect the D.A. replied, "I'm not going to make any comment on that."

He added that the rumors were 'unfair' and 'unsubstantiated.'

The Mayor of Agawam offered a $5,000 reward for information leading to the capture of Lisa's killer. In addition to the reward, he authorized $20,000 in funding for the costs accrued by the investigation.

Hundreds of people lined up to attend Lisa's wake at the Colonial Funeral Home. Children accompanied by their parents attended to give their beloved teacher a final goodbye. Some wept, some simply stood beside their parents not able to comprehend the finality of this gathering for Lisa Ziegert.

Close friends of the family sat by George, Dee, Lisa's 2 sisters and brother. They listened as many related the feelings they held for Lisa.

The music director for the school system remembered, "She was always willing to give her best, a real sweet kid."

Others stated that upon learning of Lisa's disappearance they felt complete emptiness and absolute disbelief.

One of Lisa's co-workers described Lisa as, "An all-around person. She was someone anyone would be happy to have as a daughter, a sister, or a friend. She was someone you would be proud to know."

The following morning, mourners began filing into the church around 9 a.m. even though the Mass was not scheduled to begin until 10 a.m. Many wore the white ribbons that had been passed out at the Easter Sunday service; Lisa's body was discovered only hours after the Mass. Tremendous bouquets of flowers blanketed the procession of limousines that carried family members.

The limousines slowly pulled to the curb directly in front of the church. Funeral directors assisted Dee and George Ziegert, Lisa's sisters Lynne and Sharon and Lisa's brother David. Another limousine followed and Lisa's grandparents, assisted by the somber funeral home assistants joined the family to file into the church.

When all were seated, the music began and the choir sang a special tribute, "On Eagle's Wings" as the pallbearers slowly walked beside Lisa's flower laden coffin. The trembling gloved hands of six young men clutched the rails. Thomas Petrillo, Robert Sibley, Paul Joseph, Jay Mercandante, Todd Connery and Edward Borgatti were Lisa's final escorts.

As they entered the church, the solemn procession was flanked by an honor guard. John Calabrese, Mike Marmo, Chris Sanchez, Mike Desmond and Eric London and bowed their heads as their friend passed before them.The mourners stood as Lisa passed, row by row. When the six bearers reached the altar and the awaiting priest, they genuflected and took their designated seats, joining the over 800 attendees.

Standing before the altar, decorated with white Easter lilies and mums, Father Joyce faced the congregation to deliver his eulogy. The priest, donned in deep purple vestments began by expressing that he could not explain why the prayers on Easter Sunday offered for the safe return of Lisa went unanswered. He suggested mourners take their hint from the gospel:

"Come to me all who find life burdensome…I will fill that void you feel."

"Today the church calls on us to change our focus. Lisa sought to have her faith nourished by the church and in turn helped nourish it in others. Jesus calls us to open our hearts to Him; nothing can separate us from our love of God, not even death itself."

He turned and slowly walked up the carpeted steps of the altar and began the Requiem Mass of the Dead.

At the portion of the mass that customary accommodates a sermon, Reverend James Martone addressed the throng.

He said he was there to celebrate Lisa and all the happy memories she had left him and hoped others would do the same.

In a wavering voice, he told the mourners that Lisa and his own daughter made the stole he was wearing. The stole was emblazoned with a red cross and he expressed how much love went into the stole. As he spoke, he removed the stole, clutched it in his trembling hands and laid it on Lisa's casket.

The Reverend continued, "Lisa is happy, it is we who are sorrowful because we will miss her. She brought love to everyone."

When the service ended, members walked out under blue skies, their faces reflecting a silent sorrow to deep to be consoled by words or endless tears.

The 800 mourners included grief stricken friends, students, local business owners, faculty members and police officials. D.A. William Bennett, Chris Johnson, Mayor of Agawam, State Senator, Linda Melconian, State Representative, Michael Walsh, Members of the Town Council and School Committee members.

The procession walked to the Springfield Street Cemetery. Father Joyce offered final prayers as the sobbing grew heavy.

The Most Reverend John Marshall, bishop of the Diocese of Springfield prayed over the casket. He was assisted by several clergymen who were friends of the Ziegert family.

As part of the investigation, law enforcement officials attended the funeral and videotaped the crowd that gathered at the burial. They would review it carefully hoping to find the person who just didn't fit.

William Bennett said local and state police as well as the FBI continue to work around the clock on the case, but declined to offer anything further.

Rumors continued to spread throughout the small community. One rumor was particularly disturbing and unsubstantiated. District Attorney William Bennett attempted to squelch rumors of an arrest in Lisa's murder.

One of the pallbearers at Lisa's funeral continued to be plagued with rumors contending he was responsible for Lisa's murder. It was becoming more than he could bear. The community continued to target Ed Borgatti despite the Mayor's earlier efforts to dispel the rumors.

The Ziegerts' were equally disturbed and continued to offer moral support to withstand the rumor mill. Ed Borgatti expressed how painful the rumors were to his family and his concern that they were not likely to vanish soon.

All Lisa's friends and family members had been questioned in the investigation. The questioning in no way was to suggest that any of them had done anything wrong.

Borgatti concluded that the rumors were started because police had examined the tires on his Jeep to see if they matched the tracks left at the site where Lisa was found. Although the police had examined others, which included family members, Borgatti continued to be the target of the unsavory rumors.

In addition to the rumors, prank calls were received at his residence and business, the EB Specialty Chicken, located only 30 yards from Brittany's Card and Gift Shop.

When a resident approached him outside his business, the annoyed Borgatti replied,

"Would the Ziegerts' have asked me to be a pallbearer if they thought I'd killed their daughter?"

Finally after several calls to the District Attorney, William Bennett issued a written statement. In part, the District Attorney stated,

"A widespread story that the son of a well-known Agawam resident has been arrested or implicated in the crime has no basis in fact, and should be ignored."

"People should be calm and understand that police who are investigating are trained people. The release of information about the murder has been sparse, but necessary. A full effort is being made and the public should have confidence and be mindful before making any assumptions."

He was careful not to name the person referred to in his statement.

As the investigation continued, the Agawam Police Department were working with police in nearby West Springfield.

Lt. Campbell met with Sgt. Paul Finnie of the West Springfield Police to look into a possible tie between Lisa's abduction and an attempted kidnapping of a 21-year-old woman on April 9, only one week before Lisa was murdered.

An unknown man was reported to have followed a young woman as she was driving along Rt. 20, West Springfield. She stopped at a gas station and the man passed her, but began following her again as she left the station.

When she stopped at a restaurant further down the street, she got out of her car and the man grabbed her around her waist, putting his hand over her mouth. He threatened that if she yelled, he would kill her. The woman stated she had not seen a weapon.

Fortunately, people inside the restaurant heard her screams and ran to assist the woman. The man simply walked to his car and drove away.

The suspect's description was similar to that of the man who had been reportedly seen leering at Lisa at the health club she frequented, but not to impede the investigation, the police would not comment any further.

Leads were being received hourly at the Agawam Police Station. The owner of the local car wash contacted the police when he discovered articles found in the trash barrel of one of the bays. They were hopeful they would discover another piece of the puzzle.

The owner of a local car wash had discovered a man's insulated shirt and a large piece of black and red carpeting stuffed in a trash barrel inside one of the bays. The carpeting was described as the type that could be used in a van or truck. The bay was caked with mud, which is commonly left from four-wheel-drive vehicles.

After close examination, the shirt had pinkish stains on it that could have been blood, or, caused by the red in the carpet. Forensic testing would determine the origin of the stains.

The results of the investigation were being disseminated to the media on a daily basis. The residents were uneasy and needed to be assured the case was being classified as top priority and an aggressive search was being conducted to find the killer.

Seeking a sense of security, more than 400 people signed up for weapons permits. One by one they stepped up to the counter at police headquarters.

The applicants, primarily women, came from every walk of life. A waitress working the night shift, the aerobics instructor who lived alone, a man who swore he would never allow a gun in his house were just a few seeking a means of security that had vanished from their lives.

They wrestled with a mixture of grief and fear of the possibility that the killer was a local man. A pall blanked the community.

Business owners in the area where Lisa had been abducted reported a noticeable decline in business.

The manager of the video store placed a hammer and tire iron behind the counter. At J.W. Wimpey's Restaurant/Bar, the crowd thinned out after dark leaving the once popular nightspot much quieter than previous Friday nights. One woman quit her job rather than work the night shift.

While the community's concerns seemed natural to some residents, others considered it borderline hysteria. Officials worried about the number of people arming themselves and believed the torrent over the crime had reached irrational proportions; but people wanted answers, how, why, and mostly, who did it?

The lack of information created a fertile ground for fear and anxiety and caused rumors to spread like wildfire.

The authorities were reluctant to release information that would jeopardize their investigation. Reporters were besieged with calls from angry residents wanting to know why certain aspects of the case were not in the papers. The callers referred to the rumors and considered them facts; the reporters felt a moral obligation to present the rumor to authorities to determine; rumor or fact.

Dealing with a tight-lipped police force the reporters were compelled to decide whether they should mention rumors in their stories despite the reluctance of authorities. Occasionally their decisions would be unfavorable and backfire. It was a no win situation for the news media.

It was no secret that rumors and innuendo dominated both the newspapers and television. Decisions were considerably perplexing as to what means should be taken. The reporters were advised to consider each bit of information received and deliver a careful presentation of the facts to the readers.

Two weeks had passed since Lisa's disappearance. The investigation was aggressive and intense, but the abductor was yet to be apprehended.

The man who had who had visited the juice bar of the Healthy Habits Club where Lisa Ziegert exercised was located, and brought in for questioning.

Lt. Campbell said the man had been interviewed and his alibi checked out to the satisfaction of the police. The disclosure dispelled the rumors and the man, which police would not identify, was eliminated from the list of suspects.

The man was not aware he was being sought and it was unclear why he frequented the all-women's health club, but he said he was unaware that he was staring at the women or that he was intimidating in any way.

"He is definitely on the back burner."

The Lieutenant also addressed the results of the undershirt and piece of carpeting that had been discovered at the car wash.

After reading of the discovery, the man who had discarded the shirt and carpet contacted the police. The police interviewed the owner of the discarded items and determined he was not a suspect.

With the exception of the two men being eliminated as suspects, there were no new developments that could be reported to the public.

Nearly a month passed and funding the extensive investigation was of concern.

Christopher Johnson in addition to being the Mayor was the acting Police Commissioner.

The town council had authorized $35,000 for police overtime and $20,000 was slated for the Ziegert case. Two weeks passed and most of those funds had been spent.

The Agawam Police had been working 16-hour-shifts in efforts to track down Lisa's killer.

Johnson approved additional funding and ordered the investigators to ease the 16-hour shifts and continue working eight to ten hour stretches. However, he was quick to assure the public that the investigation was no less aggressive and was far from over.

The extra patrols that had been assigned two weeks earlier were dropped and the appropriated money would be used to pay investigators extra hours. Most of the detectives had been working the Ziegert murder case seven days a week and many over eight hours a day

Lt. Campbell devised two separate shifts covering the hours between 8 a.m. until midnight. He made it clear that the case remained No. 1 priority but expressed concern that his men would soon 'burn out' if the schedules were not reduced to more realistic hours.

Finally, after a month into the investigation, a witness surfaced. He had been hesitant and debated whether or not to get involved in the on going investigation..

The witness told police he saw the vehicle enter the wooded area at about 9:15 on the night of April 15. He provided a description of the vehicle stating it was a late model, full-size utility vehicle.

"Similar to a Ford Bronco or a Chevrolet K5 Blazer," the unidentified witness added.

His description was remarkable in detail. He added the vehicle he saw was dark in color. He wasn't sure but thought it was dark blue.

It had an externally mounted spare tire with a light cover. The tires were described as oversized and the vehicle was equipped with mud flaps. The extensive description included a silver band across the back and on the top was either a roof rack, or possibly an air deflector.

Lt. Campbell believed the new information was credible and that the time frames fit, indicating Lisa was taken from the store to the woods within an hour.

This witness's account bolstered the police's original theory that a four-wheel drive would be able to enter the swampy area more readily than a passenger car.

Upon receiving the information, the authorities issued a lookout for a late-model utility vehicle resembling a Ford Bronco or a Chevrolet Blazer. They noted the vehicle could be garaged, or for some reason not being operated on the road. Investigators asked that if anyone was aware of a vehicle that had 'suddenly dropped out of sight' to notify the Agawam Police Department.

"I'd be very interested to know of a vehicle that all of a sudden fell off the face of the earth," Lt. Campbell commented.

Detectives from Agawam and the State Police had a list of several vehicles in the area they planned on checking into.

As the description of the vehicle became known, the police received nearly 200 tips with 24 hours.

A renewed hope was reflected when Lt. Campbell addressed the media.

"This is what we want. We will sort it out, we've got to keep banging on doors," he said. "This case remains top priority, we haven't given up."

Weeks passed with little progress of the investigation. News articles reporting information of the Lisa Ziegert murder began to dwindle.

The community began their recovery. The shopping area once again bustled with young boys zooming by on bikes, senior citizens shopped and young women visited the tanning salon just doors away from Brittany's Card and Gift Shop. Slowly, the community began to recover.

The thoughts of what happened to Lisa Ziegert died down, but it would never be forgotten.

On May 30, six weeks after Lisa's murder, Joseph O'Neill locked the doors of Brittany's Card and Gift Shop for the last time. He had anguished over Lisa's murder and felt a deep sorrow for the Ziegert family.

His decision to close the store permanently came after careful consideration. His effort to hire help that would be willing to work the evening hours was futile, and business had dropped substantially. He flipped the sign that read 'Closed' and drove away.

Two months later, the police were still keeping quiet about the case and the community was still at a loss to understand how it could have happened.

Lt. Robert Campbell faced the demanding reporters. Because the pace of the investigation had slowed, detectives had returned to their regular working hours and some were assigned to other cases. He confirmed the pace had become slower, but maintained leads were still out there. State Police that had been assigned to the case were relieved.

Lt. Campbell stated, "Certainly, the leads are not as plentiful, but we continue to receive forensic information. We never close a case until the crime has been solved."Robert Campbell continued to work on the case full time. It was the biggest case the 20-year-veteran had worked on and by far the most grueling.

The Ziegert family was forced to cope with the loss of their daughter. Friends and strangers alike offered their support to Lisa's family. Dee and George Ziegert believed that by talking about Lisa's death, they might prompt someone who may have information to talk to police. Police continued to investigate, but the leads had substantially dwindled.

Since Lisa's death, Dee and George Ziegert tried to get on with their lives.

They returned to work a week after the funeral. Dee Ziegert spoke about the need to focus, and that without focus you become trapped in the remembrances of the horror.

"You realize she's gone, but to accept that, I still can't," she said. For a time, "I didn't want time to move ahead. I was afraid things would change and we'd forget."For years to come the Ziegerts' would be comforted by displays and special events assuring them Lisa would never be forgotten.

When asked how he was coping, George Ziegert replied, "You have your good days and your not so good days. There's no predetermined amount of days of grieving."

Lisa's mother added often times she felt she would like to wrap her children in cotton batting and keep them in their rooms, but then added, "You can't do that to a child, it's not fair." She thanked everyone who had contributed their time and efforts for the special tributes and ceremonies for Lisa.

At least one family member would attend all the events despite the difficulty; they needed to show their appreciation for all that was being done. It was an effort to maintain composure during the events, because, "We're so proud of her. We're so proud to be her parents and we want her to be proud of us. Lisa wouldn't want us to forget there are other people still with us." Lisa's parents thanked all those who had supported them and continued to support them through countless benefits. Mr. and Mrs. Ziegert were overwhelmed by the cards, letters and notes they had received from total strangers. Some postmarked from as far away as Hong Kong.

Mr. Ziegert said, "It is so overpowering to us. We know Lisa was good; she was our kid." George Ziegert said he never expected so many others to have seen in Lisa what the family saw. The Ziegert family continued to plead to the public trying to address perhaps a reluctant witness to come forward. The police had many pieces of the homicide puzzle, but more were needed and they could only be found by someone coming forward.

If or when the killer was caught, the Ziegert family would have to relive the murder over and over, but there was no easy way.

"No one should have to go through this. No one has a right to take someone else's life." Dee continued, "We're not even looking for answers why, because there won't be any. It doesn't make sense."Mr. Ziegert expressed his feelings for his daughter.

"Lisa was a beautiful person. She was a nice girl...she liked people and people liked her. I can't imagine who would want to kill my daughter."The Ziegert's both agreed that the Agawam police had been genuinely concerned and compassionate. They frequently stopped by the Ziegert's home to assure them they were continuing to work on the case.

"I have nothing but the highest praise for them; they care, it's personal," said Mrs. Ziegert.Another month slipped by. Police Chief Stanley Chmielewski addressed the City Council in a confident tone. He was sure the Ziegert case would be solved.

His appearance at the City Council meeting was meant to assure the Councilmen who had inquired about the status and, if any, progress of Lisa's murder investigation.

The Chief responded, "I firmly believe we're going to get the guy." He advised that the leads were still strong but declined to discuss the specifics.Chief Chmielewski sounded optimistic despite the fact that nearly three months had passed since Lisa's murder. He told the Council that ample physical evidence was available and indicated the police were getting closer every day.

He acknowledged that the police had a tight lid on the investigation, keeping nearly all the information to themselves, but added that the police were exhibiting excellent police procedure in a matter of such magnitude.

Representing the community, the City Council voiced the concerns of most of their constituents.When the Chief was asked directly about the reduction in investigators, which led to speculation that the case was a lost cause, the Chief replied,"This investigation has never come to a lull." He expressed his strong faith in Lt. Campbell's handling of the case and described the lieutenant as "book smart and street smart."

The Chief would not comment on whether or not an arrest was imminent, or whether there were any suspects. The Chief thought for a few seconds then declined any further comments. He would not confirm or deny the matter of suspects and simply described the case to be a day-to-day type of thing, and it would be inappropriate for him to risk jeopardizing the investigation with his comments.

Mayor Christopher Johnson stated that no additional overtime would be spent unless a strong lead was to break. The small community simply could not allocate any additional funds. The overtime money had already been transferred from the reserve account.

As weeks turned into months, the investigation continued, but the pace was substantially diminished.

Benefits were held annually and the funds collected served to continue the Lisa M. Ziegert Memorial Fund.

Throughout Agawam, the memory of a vibrant 24-year-old schoolteacher who gave so much to so many remained in the hearts of all who knew her.

Lisa was a loving daughter to George and Dee, a caring sister to Lynne, Sharon and David, a devoted teacher, and a cherished friend.

One can only imagine the fear and terror Lisa was forced to endure the last minutes of her life at the hands of her killer.

Lisa Ziegert's murder remains an open case; to date (2006) it remains unsolved.

CHAPTER 3

On Sunday morning, November 6, 1992 forty-year-old James Lusher raced from his house shouting,

"Jamie is not with his grandmother; she hasn't seen or heard from him. I thought he was going to stay with her for the weekend. She hasn't seen or heard from him."

The father of Jamie Lusher gasped as he called to his fiancée, Christine.

On November 6, 1992 only six months after Lisa's murder, Westfield, just over the line from Agawam, faced the bizarre disappearance of Jamie Lusher.

With a population of approximately 42,000, Westfield residents felt secure and safe in a city that boasted minimum crime.

Jamie, a 16-year-old special needs student was enrolled at the Westfield Alternative School. The 16-year-old was described as having the intellectual capabilities of a 12-year-old.

At the start of the school year, the school advisers recommended Jamie be transferred from the Alternative School for children with special needs, and 'mainstreamed' into Westfield High School.

Jamie's father, James Lusher was not in total agreement with the decision. He was not convinced his son was prepared emotionally or academically to cope with the change.

The alternative school by no means was the best environment for Jamie. The majority of the students were a step away from being placed in a supervised correctional center for youths; once referred to as a reformatory.

Jamie's exposure to the sorts of classmates at the Alternative School began molding Jamie's personality. He became arrogant and somewhat of a scrapper. He developed an abrasive manner. Jamie was well known throughout Westfield and had several acquaintances, but rarely developed any meaningful friendships.

Jamie was a difficult child. He was difficult to love. His father had an arduous job as his guardian, but he loved his son. Because of his problems, Mr. Lusher was prepared to care for Jamie for the rest of his life. It was a commitment he made from the time he took custody of Jamie and his 17-year-old sister Jennifer in 1986.

On Friday morning, November 6, Jamie asked his father if he would bring him to stay with his maternal grandmother for the weekend. His father advised his son he would contact Jamie's grandmother and see if Jamie's plans would be suitable to her.

Jamie was excited about staying in Blandford with his grandmother this particular weekend because of the dirt bike meet scheduled to take place beginning Friday evening.

On Friday morning, the senior James Lusher said goodbye to both Jamie and Jennifer. He assured Jamie that if his grandmother agreed, he would bring Jamie to Blandford later that day, once he'd returned home from work.

Mr. Lusher failed to contact his former mother-in-law. Knowing how difficult Jamie could be, he preferred not to place Jamie in her care for an entire weekend; possibly disrupting any previous plans, she may have made.

When he returned from work around 5:30 Friday, November 6 Jamie was not home. His bicycle was not in its usual place by the garage and Mr. Lusher, knowing how determined Jamie could be, assumed he had contacted his grandmother and rode his bike to Blandford. The trip to Blandford by bicycle was a lengthy one but not for Jamie. If he wanted something bad enough, he would find a way to get it.

For James Lusher, Saturday was much the same as any other. Jamie's sister, Jennifer made plans to go out with friends and sleep over at her girlfriend's house. Her father made it very clear to Jennifer she was to be home early Sunday morning. He planned to clean out the gutters on the house that had become clogged with the autumn leaves. Both front and back yards were covered with the variegated autumn leaves and needed to be raked. Jennifer assured her father she would be home Sunday morning.

Mr. Lusher and Christine planned to attend an Elvis impersonator concert that evening in nearby Chicopee. He hadn't felt a need for concern for Jamie's whereabouts. He believed Jamie had arrived at his grandmother's, attended the dirt bike meet and stayed over in order to return for the continuation of the meet on Saturday.

Sunday morning, November 8 was exceptionally sunny and mild. James Lusher woke early, made coffee and read the Sunday paper. An hour passed and Christine shuffled into the kitchen.

"Morning Jim," she said as she poured herself a cup of coffee.

"That was a great concert last night. I had a good time."

"Me too, those guys were really something. They actually had talent."

"I'm going to try to get the yard cleaned up today. I've put off raking those leaves long enough. Before you know it, it'll be snowing. I could use some help," Mr. Lusher replied.

"I'll give you a hand. Between you, me, Jen and Jamie, we'll have it done in no time."

"I told Jennifer to be sure to be here early. Jamie should be calling for someone to pick him up at his grandmothers," Mr. Lusher replied.

With that, he went outside to face the leaves that blanketed both the front and back yards.

He was a little annoyed that Jamie had not been responsible enough to get home by now. He hadn't counted on much help from Jennifer, but he did expect Jamie to be available.

After about an hour, Mr. Lusher became more and more agitated and decided to phone his mother-in-law and speak to Jamie. Jennifer had not returned home as she had promised which left Mr. Lusher and Christine to clean the yard.

He reached Jamie's grandmother by phone and after speaking to her, Mr. Lusher's anger transformed from anger to panic. Jamie had not arrived at her house, she had not heard from Jamie.

Mr. Lusher had not seen his son since Friday morning when he left for work. Now, it was Sunday and he could not account for Jamie's whereabouts.

He wasn't sure what to think. One thing he was sure of was that Jamie would never stay away this long without telling somebody. He just wouldn't stay away this long period!

After Saturday night, the dirt bike weekend rally was over. Because Jamie had very few friends he would likely attend the event by himself. It was possible he could have met someone there, but he would have gone to his grandmother's to sleep. Every conceivable scenario passed through Mr. Lusher's mind. None of them fit Jamie's pattern of behavior.

He instructed Christine to stay by the phone while he headed for the police department.

As he reached his car in the driveway, Jennifer was pulling in.

"I'm going to the police. Jamie is missing. Call your mother and see if he's been there," he shouted to Jennifer.

"I thought he was at Grandma's," Jennifer replied.

"He's not there, she hasn't seen him. Just do what I said, call your mother and anyone else you can think of that might know where he is and stay put until I get back."

Upon his arrival at the Westfield Police Department, he asked to speak to the chief. The desk sergeant informed James the Chief wasn't in and offered to assist Mr. Lusher.

"My name is James Lusher. My son, 'Jamie' is missing and I need to file a missing child report right away."

In an abbreviated version, James Lusher related the concern he had for the whereabouts of Jamie.

"Now, tell me Mr. Lusher, how old is the boy and when was the last time you saw him?" asked the sergeant.

"Jamie is 16 years old sir and the last time I saw him was on Friday morning. I left for work, he went to school and when I got home, he wasn't there."

"Did he give you any indication of his plans to go anywhere?" asked the officer.

"Well, one thing, he's not an ordinary 16-year-old. He's a pretty puny kid, and intellectually challenged. He pretty much measures up to a typical 12-year-old. Even his physical appearance would be considered closer to that of a 12-year-old. He's…"

The Sergeant interrupted James Lusher.

"Does he have a car? You know 16-year-old boys sometimes have a mind of there own. It's a tough age for a boy."

Mr. Lusher again attempted to explain Jamie's intellectual handicap but his words were ignored. The officer hadn't even taken down any notes. It seemed all he was basing his evaluation of the situation on was that Jamie was a 16-year-old male. Some believe gender plays a part in these situations. Had this been a missing 16-year-old female it would likely have been taken more seriously.

Mr. Lusher explained the reason he was remiss in reporting Jamie's absence. He explained it was a miscommunication, or for lack of a better word, lack of communication. He admitted he should have confirmed Jamie was in the care of his grandmother.

That very thought haunted him from the time he learned Jamie was nowhere to be found. He regretted he had not called Jamie's grandmother, a burden he would continue to carry for years to come.

Just as the anxious father was concluding his account of the past days, the phone lit up, indicating an incoming call. Without hesitation, the sergeant accepted the call and raised his hand to Mr. Lusher indicating, 'hold on, I'll be with you in a minute'.

Mr. Lusher was enraged at the sergeant's casual demeanor. Frustrated, he stood quietly at the counter, feeling like an eavesdropper as the telephone conversation continued for what seemed like much more time than it should have.

When the call was finally ended Mr. Lusher was advised it would be best to "give it until Monday morning. If he doesn't show up for school, give us a call." It was clear to James Lusher the discussion had ended.

Mr. Lusher left the station. He was at a loss for words. Surely, this was not standard procedure in a missing person's case, particularly a missing child. He'd heard time after time, how important the first 48 hours were to an investigation of this type. Jamie had not been seen or heard from for nearly three days!

Christine met James at the door. She listened as he told her of the disturbing encounter at the station.

He was confused and felt an ache that began in his chest, up through his throat and made normal breathing difficult. He was sweating profusely and feared he was experiencing a heart attack. He rushed to the sink, splashing cold water over his face. He had suffered a severe panic attack. Never in his 40 years had he ever been so frightened and felt so helpless.

"My God, you're as white as a sheet! Jim, are you all right?"

Once he was able to gain his composure, he assured Christine he was okay and sat at the table to begin to tell Christine all he knew at the time.

"Where's Jen?" He asked.

"She's in her room. I think she went back to bed. She said she'd been up late last night and wanted to get a little more sleep. She called her mother, but there was no answer."

"I'm going to drive around and see if I can find him. I don't know where he could be, but I can't just sit here until tomorrow morning. The police said to wait until tomorrow and if he doesn't show up for school, to give them a call."

The distraught father left without any further explanation.

Sunday evening, November 8 was the longest one James Lusher had ever experienced. He'd been out most of the daylight hours searching for Jamie, driving the route Jamie would have taken if he had headed to his grandmother's house in Blandford.

Rt. 20 twists through rural mill towns. James Lusher made frequent stops along the way, searching through wooded areas in hopes of finding anything indicating Jamie had been there. He pictured Jamie pedaling up the winding hills toward Blandford. Had he been offered a ride, there was no doubt, he would have accepted. Mr. Lusher couldn't dismiss that possibility.

It was dark when Mr. Lusher returned home. Jennifer was on her way to Blandford to stay with her recently widowed grandmother.

Jim called his daughter and assured her he would call as soon as he heard anything.

Christine placed a cup of coffee and a sandwich on the coffee table. James had drifted into a restless sleep.

Christine returned to the kitchen and began cleaning up the dishes from earlier that day, feeling sadness for James.

James was always such a strong man tolerating no nonsense from his children, particularly Jamie. He would have like to be a friend and father to Jamie, but that was not possible. Instead, James cared for Jamie with a 'tough love' attitude. It was the only way to keep Jamie from harm.

She knew James was blaming himself for Jamie's disappearance; that's how he was. Christine wanted to offer comfort but James could not accept any display of caring from her until he had the opportunity to resolve things in his own mind.

Christine and James had dated since 1990 and often discussed marriage. James was deeply in love with Christine and Christine could not imagine her life without James.

Christine was well aware of James' plan for Jamie's future. She understood that Jamie would be a permanent member of his household.

B y 7:00 o'clock Monday morning, James Lusher was showered, shaved and prepared to file the official missing person report at the police department.

Christine anticipated the early morning plans and prepared to accompany James. With the photos gathered the night before, James and Christine drove the short distance to the Westfield Police Station.

Upon their arrival, James asked to speak to a detective, hoping he would receive more cooperation than he had experienced with the desk sergeant the day before.

Detective John Camerota ushered the couple down a short corridor leading to the detective division.

Almost immediately, James Lusher felt at ease with Lt. Camerota. The detective showed the couple to a small round table and offered Christine and James a cup of coffee. He joined the exhausted father and his friend in the cordial atmosphere he had created.

The interview with Jamie's father included the usual information required for any missing person's report. After all the information was obtained Detective Camerota's demeanor changed. He conveyed a sincere interest in what Mr. Lusher had to say about his missing son.

Camerota listened while James Lusher related the special circumstances concerning Jamie. When he handed Jamie's photo to the detective, it was obvious; Jamie did not appear to be a 16-year-old. His small frame and general appearance would be more like that of a 12 or 13 year old.

The detective explained all information would be entered into a database that served to inform all law enforcement agencies throughout Massachusetts, as well as national coverage. Posters would be printed and distributed throughout Westfield and all surrounding towns.

As the detective concluded his explanation, Mr. Lusher breathed an audible sigh of relief. He felt assured the police would initiate a search for Jamie. He felt he had done everything and had confidence in Lt. John Camerota.

"We'll get started on this right away, Mr. Lusher. I'll be in touch with you. Michael McCabe will also be working closely with me, so feel free to speak to him as well. Here's my card, call Mike or me anytime. Either Mike or I will visit you at home and take a look around Jamie's room if you don't mind."

"I appreciate your help. Stop by anytime if you think that will help," replied Mr. Lusher.

"Do you investigate a lot of this type of thing? Tell me, detective, do you think you'll find him?"

Mr. Lusher knew it was a question impossible to answer, but he was hoping for a positive response.

"We do get missing person's reports all the time. Usually, that's what they turn out to be, either a runaway, or simply a person who decided to take a little trip without telling anyone."

"Rarely are they subjects of foul play. I can't tell you how this will turn out. Surely you know that, but

I can assure you Jamie's case will be a priority and we will use every resource we have to bring him home."

James Lusher left the station and drove directly home. He felt a little sense of relief, and also realized how exhausted he was.

Christine was at a loss for words as she watched Jim begin to fall apart. It was so out of character for him. He was always able to maintain control. She felt her silence would be most appropriate at a time like this; besides, what could she possibly offer that would ease the burden James was bearing?

The phone rang. Jennifer assured her father that she had reached her mother.

Jennifer's mother was married to William Levakis. They lived in Westfield. The divorce had not been an amicable one, and rarely did James and his ex-wife communicate. James knew that under these circumstances he would have to put his feelings for Joanne Levakis aside and cooperate with her.

Joanne Levakis would not be so willing to reciprocate her ex-husband's consideration.

James anticipated Joanne's call, but it never came. Instead, Joanne contacted the police and demanded that any information concerning Jamie was to be directed to her. She had no intentions of receiving second hand information from her ex-husband, James.

Detective Michael McCabe spoke to Mrs. Levakis. He explained the procedure the police would follow. After a lengthy conversation, the detective sensed the hostility that existed between Jamie's mother and father. This would be an obstacle the detectives would have to deal with.

Tuesday, November 10, 1992

16-YEAR-OLD REPORTED MISSING

After four days passed, Jamie Lusher's disappearance became newsworthy.

Although the newspaper account of the circumstances of Jamie's disappearance was inaccurate, stating he was last seen riding his bicycle to Blandford, the newspaper served to get Jamie's picture into every home in Westfield. His disappearance was finally becoming the focus of a police investigation.

Admittedly, the trip to the rural town of Blandford was a 12-mile trek; Jamie was a tenacious and determined kid.

Only two weeks earlier, October 15ᵗʰ, Jamie celebrated his 16th birthday. He was qualified, by age, to get his driver's license; however, Mr. Lusher was adamantly opposed to Jamie getting behind the wheel of a car at 16, or any other age. To compensate Jamie and realizing his need to have means to get around, Mr. Lusher presented Jamie with a new bicycle on his birthday.

Detective Michael McCabe arrived at the Lusher's residence around 10:00 o'clock Tuesday morning. He was instructed to examine Jamie's room for any clues that might be significant to fortify the runaway scenario. Similar to John Camerota, James McCabe

119

exhibited sensitivity and concern toward James Lusher.

Jamie's bedroom was in total disarray. Clothes covered the floor, his bed was unmade, and a small wastebasket overflowed with discarded soda cans. On the nightstand was a partially eaten slice of pizza.

Before the detective had a chance to comment on what he was seeing, James offered his disapproval of Jamie's living conditions. The detective laughed and seemed to understand the habits of some teenage boys. He was observant and noticed with the exception of Jamie's room, the house was very well kept.

After a cursory look around the disheveled room, it was pretty certain nothing helpful to the case was to be discovered there.

Detective McCabe had a brief conversation with Mr. Lusher, and assured him everything possible was being done to find Jamie.

The detective stated a state police helicopter and all the efforts of the Westfield police failed to turn up any trace so far. He added, in addition to the air search, police on foot searched bike trails in Westfield and the surrounding hill towns.

The state police from nearby Russell barracks joined in the aerial search. They were confident the search had been thorough, however unsuccessful.

Mr. Lusher was assured once again that everything possible was being done to find Jamie. Posters were printed and distributed throughout the city and extended to the surrounding hill towns.

James Lusher, although he kept it deep within, knew he would never see his son again. He knew all the searching would not bring Jamie home. He was gone, and in Mr. Lusher's mind, there was no doubt.

Jamie's mother, Joanne Levakis addressed the media whenever the opportunity presented itself.

"We just want him back," she stated. "He's very naïve and has a trusting nature. I believe someone could have talked him into accepting a ride, and abducted him."

Mrs. Levakis continued, "Jamie is a whimsical teen-ager who liked to take off on his bike. He left his father's home once to stay overnight at a nearby friend's house without telling his father."

She continued, explaining that Jamie had been punished for giving the family such a scare and she doubted he would try to do something like that again.

Police investigators questioned residents of Blandford, including the organizers of the dirt bike meet that had taken place. Although several stated they knew Jamie, no one had seen him at the meet.

The police continued to search for Jamie but their searches proved fruitless. They were unable to find Jamie, or any clues that might lead to the missing boy.

The police assured James Lusher they would keep him abreast of any progress. They had not contacted him since he had filed the report. It had only been a couple of days, but he thought he deserved information before he read it in the newspaper. The only information he had was the same as the newspaper subscribers.

The article described Jamie, and the clothing he was wearing the last time he was seen.

The police department received numerous telephone calls from people in the community asking questions about Jamie. Some reported they had seen him. None of the sightings turned up any additional information to assist in the investigation.

In addition to every resource imaginable, a local woman contacted the police claiming to be a psychic. Despite a degree of skepticism, the police followed instructions the psychic offered.

The woman claimed she had a vision where she thought Jamie would be found. As instructed, the police traveled to Woronoco, a small mill town Jamie would have passed had he been headed for Blandford. There was no trace of the boy.

The police department was baffled. They were treating the case seriously, although they had received a call from an individual claiming to have seen Jamie riding his bike in downtown Westfield on Sunday evening.

At this point, it really didn't matter to Jamie's father. He was acquiescent to his belief Jamie was gone forever. He was already preparing a 'comfort zone' that would provide him the emotional strength necessary to support loved ones when the official news came.

The following day, the news confirmed Mr. Lusher's preclusion.

On Thursday, November 12, 1992, the police reported Jamie's bike had been found. A hunter made the discovery in a field on the north side of the city.

James Lusher answered the door and faced Sergeant Brian Boldini. The sergeant informed Mr.

Lusher the discovery of what they believed to be Jamie's bike.

"We'd like you to come with us to identify the bicycle, Mr. Lusher."

James Lusher traveled to the remote area at the north side of the city. There, in the middle of an open field, beside a small pond was the mud covered grey *Huffy* with the distinctive bright green forks. He confirmed the bicycle belonged to Jamie.

It was becoming too dark for a thorough search the scene. The police would return at daylight to look for clues. The location was not disclosed for fear others would gather and disturb any possible evidence that might be discovered.

Regardless of the newfound evidence, (the bike) Sergeant Boldini continued to state his belief that Jamie was a runaway.

Another individual, a waitress at the Friendly's restaurant where Jamie was known to frequent told police she served dinner to Jamie around 7:00 p.m. Sunday.

Jamie's mother, Mrs. Levakis when hearing the statement from the waitress felt it was a reliable source. The waitress was a high school student who knew Jamie personally.

She added, "Jamie was also spotted Friday during school hours by employees of Burger King. I think my son got scared. The Burger King employee threatened to call the school and report his truancy. I think he was afraid he'd get in trouble for skipping school."

Mr. Lusher offered his speculation.

"If he's dodging now, it is because he's fearful of what will happen if he comes home. His fears have always been out of proportion."

He shook his head in frustration.

"Who knows what's going through his mind? I just wish he would know that I want him back, and of course his mother does too."

Until the parents of Jamie learned of the sightings, they feared he had been abducted or had suffered from the extreme cold nights. They did not believe he would know how to care for himself or find shelter on his own. Mrs. Levakis was certain someone was helping her son and he was not alone.

Mr. Lusher silently disagreed.

Lt. Camerota said, "In light of the information we've received, at this point we believe the boy is alive and well and just doesn't want anybody to locate him."

James Lusher became increasingly frustrated with the Westfield Police Department. How much more did they need to be convinced Jamie's disappearance was the result of foul play? Didn't the discovery of Jamie's abandoned bike provide basis for law enforcement to revisit the case and continue the investigation on the premise Jamie was abducted?

The area the bike was discovered, a remote area, certainly contradicted the theory that Jamie was "last seen headed to his grandmother's house in Blandford."

The north side of Westfield is completely opposite of the route he would have been on had he been traveling to Blandford.

When Mr. Lusher asked for updated information after the calls had been followed up, he received little cooperation. With the exception of the lead detective, John Camerota, communication with the father of the missing boy was minimal. Most news was delivered to Mr. Lusher through the newspaper.

The location the bike was found was disclosed. It was a remote area where area teens were known to 'party'. On the property was a man made pond surrounded by open fields of grass nearly 6 feet high.

The intensive search of the 100 acres of land off Bennett Road failed to turn up any new information. Firefighters scoured the area using two Fire Department boats to drag the pond at the site where the bicycle was discovered. It became late afternoon and the search was halted. They would resume the next day and also planned to use the aid of a search dog from the state police in nearby Northampton.

Lt. Camerota was on the scene of the search and advised the media, "We'll regroup and figure out which direction to go in tomorrow. We cannot continue into the night. It's too dangerous."

It did appear every effort and every available resource was being put into action but still Jamie was nowhere to be found. With the exception of his bike, there were no additional clues to determine what had become of him. Foot searches were conducted looking for evidence Jamie may have camped out in the woods close by the area where his bike was discovered.

No sign of a campfire, food wrappers, items of clothing, anything to confirm the police's runaway scenario; yet they refused to give it up.

Mr. Lusher was growing increasingly agitated. He went to the police station and asked to speak to the chief.

His visit with Chief Benjamin Surprise was brief. When asked why the runaway theory continued to be the focus of the investigation, the chief replied, "Mr. Lusher, take it easy. He's probably in Florida having the time of his life."

Mr. Lusher's reply was nothing short of anger and rage. He expected more from the Chief of Police and did not hesitate to convey his feelings. Is that the attitude he was passing down to the detectives? How could he be so flippant? Any respect James Lusher might have had for the chief of the police department was now diminished to disgust, lack of sensitivity and professional incompetence.

Sightings of Jamie were abundant but the police believed many reported may be mistaken identities.

Although each reported sighting was investigated, none panned out. The mistaken leads, in fact, led to a grilling of Jamie's sister, Jennifer.

Jennifer drew interest from the Westfield Police when she drove to a sighting after someone called her house. At the time, the police had no knowledge of the call. Lt. Camerota became suspicious when he was notified Jennifer had been seen letting a youth into her car.

Two detectives and one female patrol officer arrived at the local K-Mart where Jennifer was working her regular shift. They approached Jennifer and escorted her to the break room of the store. Jennifer was frightened and confused.

After undergoing a lengthy questioning by the lieutenant, police excused her. They were satisfied with Jennifer's explanations of her actions; she was chasing leads on her own. They made it very clear that they needed to be told about any other leads that she might receive.

Jennifer thought she had located Jamie, but it turned out that it was another teen that looked very much like her brother. She opened the car door to admit the boy into her car. Just as he was about to get in, Jennifer began crying.

"The boy looked identical to Jamie," Jennifer told the police.

In an effort to dismiss any doubt of Jennifer's statements, a lie detector test was scheduled for the following day. Jennifer, James Lusher, Joanne Levakis, and Jamie's elderly grandmother were subjected to lie detector examination.

After the questioning of Jennifer, John Camerota was convinced the citizens kept mistaking Jamie's picture with another teen whose physical appearances were very similar to those of Jamie.

"Everybody says they keep seeing Jamie, but it's not him," Camerota stated.

After this statement, came a report from a 9-year-old girl who lived near the Lusher's home. She told the police she saw Jamie on Saturday. The young girl knew Jamie and told the police she spoke to him. She asked him why he was hiding.

He replied, "I'm afraid I'm in trouble." He did not tell her where he was staying or how he is managing on his own.

The firefighters began the task of draining the pond. James Lusher was at the sight and watched as a steady stream of water shot out from a hose and the pond drained slowly.

"I'm certainly hoping they'll drain this thing and there won't be anything in it that anybody cares about," Mr. Lusher commented to an onlooker.

During the week, Mr. Lusher had independently spoken to four psychics who told him his son was hiding. All four were in agreement. What Mr. Lusher was not aware of was his ex-wife Joanne had also consulted with a psychic. She contended the physic she conferred with was in total agreement with the other four. All assured the parents of the teen that he was indeed alive, but afraid to come home because he felt he was going to be in a lot of trouble.

"We've gone over it and over it and over it. I think because of all the time and effort that's been spent, he's afraid he'll be reprimanded for it," Camerota contended.

"It's the farthest thing from the truth," Mr. Lusher remarked. "We just want him to come home."

One of the psychics led James to Robinson State Park in Agawam. The psychic said Jamie was hiding in a shack. When Mr. Lusher went to the location, he found a tree fort, but no sign of Jamie.

Only to be disappointed again, Mr. Lusher stated in a tired defeated tone,

"Only God and Jamie know where he is. At this point, I have no idea."

After two weeks, Westfield Police Captain Michael Avonti stated the field searches for Jamie would be halted. He added however, that the investigation into the disappearance of the 16-year-old boy would continue.

The police had come to an impasse. They felt a comprehensive search, from checking out bicycle trails on foot as well as from the air, to draining the pond near where the bicycle had been found was sufficient.

The spokesperson for the Westfield Police Department stated it would be a waste of time to go into the woods without any direction. They continued to speculate that Jamie was purposely staying away from home and could be hiding out with friends.

Captain Michael Avonti addressed the media.

"There's really no place to go. We have nothing concrete and really no leads. It's totally frustrating."

The calls that had once numbered 30 to 40 a day had stopped. The police were beginning to believe Jamie had left the area.

Weeks past, and December brought the first snowfall. No further news of the teenager was reported.

Although in his heart, he held no hope of Jamie being returned safely, Mr. Lusher continued to search and urged others to do the same.

Joanne Levakis, Jamie's mother also refused to give up hope.

Delving into the details and circumstances of the parent's divorce would serve no purpose. Whatever reasons the parents of Jamie and Jennifer led to the Lusher's acrimonious divorce was particularly sad. Both parents suffered the grief and anguish over the mysterious disappearance of their son but would not lend comfort to each other.

Joanne Lavakis was able to find comfort from her husband, William, however, there was no way Mr. Lavakis could imagine the pain she was suffering. James Lusher had a compassionate friend in Christine who offered solace; however, only the parent of the missing child could feel the enormity of the loss.

As the New Year approached, police delivered updated information to Jamie's parents. Occasionally, they would visit with the parents to assure them that Jamie's case remained active.

Because of the time that elapsed and the fact Jamie failed to come home for Christmas, the police were concentrating on other reasons behind his disappearance.

"He would be easy to pick out, and I just can't believe that a law enforcement person somewhere in this state hasn't run across him. I thought he would be spotted before this," Lt. Camerota said at one of his visits to Mr. Lusher.

He disclosed the results of the lie detector testing. All had passed satisfactorily, although Jennifer's could not be determined one way or the other. This happens occasionally and he assured Mr. Lusher his daughter was not in any way considered under suspicion.

The detective also told Mr. Lusher he had written to a psychic in New Jersey who had worked with law enforcement officials in the past, but he had yet to receive a response.

Both of Jamie's parents had consulted psychics during the original search, but failed to come up with additional clues.

Mr. Lusher made every effort to celebrate Christmas for Jennifer. He went through the motions as best he could, but his efforts were not genuine. Jennifer felt Christmas without her brother just couldn't be the same.

Regardless of the constant sibling bickering between Jennifer and Jamie, Jennifer expressed her feelings for her brother. Additional responsibilities were placed with Jennifer regarding the care of Jamie. Mr. Lusher came to depend on Jennifer.

Jennifer made sure Jamie was up and dressed for school every morning. She prepared his breakfast and dispensed his medication. When Jamie needed clothes, Mr. Lusher would give Jennifer a credit card and Jennifer would take Jamie shopping. She brought him to his doctor and dentist appointments. When his hair started looking shabby, Jennifer brought him for a haircut.

There was no doubt there were times Jennifer resented the burden Jamie could be. After all, she was a teenager and like most teenagers, she had friends she liked to hang out with.

Jennifer was not the perfect daughter and liked to party with her friends. Never the less, she was always aware of how much her father had come to depend on her. She loved her brother. Because she was only 15 months old when he was born, Jennifer never knew life without Jamie. She genuinely felt emptiness and a loss.

There was no Christmas tree at 148 Riverview Terrace in 1992.

The Pittsfield Police Department continued to struggle with the unsolved murder of Jimmy Bernardo, two years earlier. The Pittsfield Police initially believed Jimmy to be a runaway. They looked into the similarities of the Bernardo and Lusher cases and found substantial reason to contact the Westfield Police Department.

After two years, the investigation into Jimmy Bernardo's murder remained active but unsolved.

Investigator Bruce Eaton of the Pittsfield detective bureau was unaware of Jamie Lusher's case. It was brought to his attention, and after a brief description, the Lusher case got his attention.

In early January 1993, Bruce Eaton contacted Lt. John Camerota at the Westfield Police Department to compare notes of the two cases. .

Lt. Detective Camerota was aware of the Bernardo case but hesitated to consider them to be linked before reviewing the file. A meeting would be scheduled with Pittsfield police after Westfield had the opportunity to evaluate both cases.

Although Jamie Lusher's case remained open, very little if any progress was being recorded. The disappearance of the teen simply went cold. With nothing to go on, the police had no choice but to wait for a break.

Mrs. Levakis was not so quick to simply wait. She contacted the National TV show "America's Most Wanted" and requested Jamie's story be televised. She faxed copies of recent newspaper stories to the show. She hoped John Walsh would take an interest because his son Adam Walsh had been abducted and murdered.

In addition to that, Joanne Levakis contacted the producers of *"Unsolved Mysteries"* which also airs segments about missing people.

When asked, Mrs. Levakis replied,

"I believe the Westfield Police are doing a great job in their efforts, but they don't have any further leads. This can't hurt."

Chief Surprise commented the police had no problem with more national exposure.

He added, "Any help that we get is always positive."

A week after Mrs. Levakis contacted the TV producers she received the disappointing reply.

"In a case such as this, if the law enforcement agency does not feel it is a stranger abduction, we can't get involved," was the response from the representative for *"America's Most Wanted."*

They further explained that after contacting Chief Benjamin Surprise they were unable to get the abduction confirmed. The spokesperson for the TV show explained that right from the beginning, the main criteria is it has to be a stranger abduction, and the police have to classify it as such.

Mrs. Levakis was angry and confused. She contacted the Chief to find out exactly the status of Jamie's case. When she was finally able to reach Chief Surprise, she demanded an explanation.

"Although we'd like to cooperate with the producers of *"America's Most Wanted,"* replied Police Chief Benjamin Surprise.

"Without solid evidence we cannot support an abduction classification."

He continued, "There is absolutely nothing to indicate Jamie was abducted or anything violent occurred to him. There was no damage to the bike, no pieces of clothing, no blood, nothing to point in that direction."

Mrs. Levakis was flabbergasted. She could not believe what the Chief was saying.

The news of Jamie's disappearance would not be aired came as a crushing blow. The producers informed her of the response from the police department and the idea of airing the story had to be scrapped.

Joanne Levakis expressed her feelings to the Chief as well as Captain Avonti and Lt. John Camerota.

"You've ruined my only chances. You said you would welcome any help I could get. You have totally sabotaged everything. I'm so furious. You've bungled this case so much."

She was visibly shaken, but she added, "I don't know what I'm going to do. That was my last hope!"

Detective Lt. John Camerota offered his sympathy to the distraught mother and pointed out that police have followed up on all possible leads.

"I wish I could find the kid, I really do," he added.

The Chief responded, "Every avenue possible to this point has been checked. We will continue to use whatever options are available without putting out a major capital investment, which we cannot afford."

Three weeks passed, and Mrs. Levakis received the unexpected notification that Jamie's segment would be televised.

On January 29, 1993, nearly three months after Jamie's disappearance, the popular Fox television network show featured the segment they had previously prepared. Viewers were shown a picture of Jamie and given an 800 toll free number to call if they had any information to offer.

It was apparent the Westfield Police Department had reconsidered their earlier comments. The show could not be aired without confirmation of a stranger abduction. Confirmation had to come from the Chief of Police.

Both Joanne Levakis and James Lusher were pleased with the show. It served to rekindle a spark of hope the show would be seen by someone who could offer information that would lead to the safe return of Jamie. They expected immediate response; however, response would be slow coming.

Three days passed. The show had not generated any leads. Again, the parents of Jamie began the downward spiral into a hopeless abyss.

What they didn't know, was the responses were submitted to the television show. The show acted as a clearinghouse, forwarding the tips on to the Westfield Police Department.

On February 3, about four days after the broadcast, John Camerota began receiving the responses. They came in the form of fliers sent by the staff of *"America's*

Most Wanted." Each flier described a telephone tip the show received in response to the Lusher broadcast.

Seventy-two fliers had been received. The tips were from all over the country and one from Canada. The tips described possible sightings of Jamie. Some were out in left field and didn't make any sense. A few looked promising.

One of the promising responses came from a Long Island girl claiming she saw Jamie in the company of a few other teens. The detectives were instructed to contact the police in the cities and towns from which the more promising leads originated.

Now a new light was cast on the investigation. The search was now crossing over state lines. Westfield police planned to seek the help of the Federal Bureau of Investigations. Jamie's disappearance was about to be assisted by the FBI.

Another week passed. Daily phone calls to the police department offered no encouragement to Mr. Lusher.

Finally, after almost two weeks, Captain Avonti announced that although a great number of tips were received, none turned up anything. The Long Island tip turned out to be a look-alike.

The FBI commented it did not look good because Jamie had been gone for so long. His age was a major factor, they said, kidnappers tend to keep younger children longer. The case would remain open and be activated on a lead-by-lead basis.

The Lushers agonized over the mysterious disappearance of Jamie. They came to the reality Jamie had been abducted and killed, but the agony of not knowing was cruel and inhumane. No funeral, no memorial could be arranged.

Jamie Lusher has a birth certificate but no death certificate.

Families suffering pain the loss of a child forces them to endure never find closure. The families can only hope they be allowed to provide a final resting place for their beloved child.

They look for justice. Some find both, others, have neither. The book of Jamie Lusher's life can never be closed.

To date, Jamie Lusher has never been found. The case remains unsolved.

CHAPTER 4

Rick Piirainen faced his two young sons.
"Where's Holly?" he demanded.
Five-year-old Zackary replied,
"I don't know she wasn't at the puppies' house."

Rick looked to eight-year-old Andy for answers. Andy handed a single white sneaker to his father and replied,
"We found this in the road."

With both boys in tow, Rick headed up the road, retracing the steps his three children had taken only minutes before...

Sturbridge Massachusetts is often referred to as the 'Heart of New England' and boasts of the charm that lies within its past and present - in rolling hills and hiking trails, in summer concerts and covered bridges, in historic taverns and cozy country inns.

August is the busiest time of year for the residents and merchants of Sturbridge Village. The village is 200 acres of historic shops recreated to reflect the 1800's. Throughout the spring and summer, it is the destination of well over 500,000 tourists. It is surrounded by several villages and towns none exceeding population 5,000.

Unfortunately, Sturbridge, similar to other villages and towns spackled throughout Western Massachusetts, is not immune to tragedy.

The Piirainen family enjoyed the amenities the scenic area had to offer. Since childhood, Rick, Carla and Karen Piirainen frequently spent warm sunny days at the family's cottage on South Pond.

Mr. and Mrs. Lemieux, the mother and stepfather of the Piirainen children, enjoyed their family and the comfortable serenity of their summer get away. Sturbridge was a short trip from their home in Grafton making even a day trip easily accessible.

As the three Piirainen children became adults and married, their children were endowed with the enjoyment of visiting their grandparents' cottage just as their parents had the generation before them.

Richard Piirainen married Tina Harrington and soon began a family. First born, January 19, 1983 was Holly. Two years later, Andrew and three years after Andrew, Zachery was born.

Rick's two sisters, Carla and Karen also married and before long, Mrs. Lemieux enjoyed seven grandchildren.

Holly was an exceptional little girl. She was precocious and sensitive. A few years after Zachery was born, she took it upon herself to watch over her brothers. She was a responsible little girl and simply quite amazing.

In 1991, Holly was 8 years old. In the wake of the Trade Center bombing she expressed a genuine concern about what was going to happen because of the tragic event; something few eight-year-olds would even be aware of.

In addition, in 1991, Holly's mother and father separated and divorced. They were concerned about the effect the divorce would have on the children. The welfare and well-being of Holly, Andy and Zack was foremost in their minds so Rick and Tina agreed on flexible visitation resulting in joint custody. The children fared very well with that arrangement and the support of their extended family.

The Piirainen children had both paternal and maternal grandparents, aunts, uncles and cousins. They lived in close proximity to each other enabling them to develop a strong family bond.

Rick Piirainen accrued vacation time and thought it would be well spent with his three children at the family cottage. The children looked forward to the frequent visits and the secure surroundings the rural neighborhood afforded.

On August 5, 1993, 10-year-old Holly Piirainen and her brother Andy spent most of the morning swimming in South Pond, directly behind the cottage. Rick sat leisurely watching as Zack played at the edge of the water.

At about 11:30 a.m., after the three had changed from wet bathing suits, Holly asked her father if she could go to a nearby cottage to see a new litter of puppies.

Rick advised, "Okay, but take one of your brothers with you. I don't want you going anywhere alone. Be sure to make it quick, we're going to McDonald's for lunch."

Holly took 5-year-old Zack by the hand and headed up the dirt road that led to the cottage at the corner of South Shore Road. Rick watched and smiled at Holly's long golden ponytail bobbing in rhythm with her hop-skipping pace. She held Zack's hand swinging his arm in exaggerated loops, causing Zack to laugh aloud. Rick watched until they turned the bend in the road.

About twenty minutes passed and Zack returned to the cottage alone.

"Where's Holly?" asked Rick.

"The puppies weren't out on the porch. Holly wanted to wait to see if they would come out," was Zack's reply.

Rick instructed 8-year-old Andy to take his brother and go back to get Holly.

Rick reached the house at the corner where South Pond Road intercepts with Allen Road. The puppies were not on the porch as they had been the previous day and Rick was sure Holly would not have ventured beyond that house. The children were not allowed past the end of the dirt road onto Allen Road, a more heavily traveled paved road

There was no sign of Holly. He picked up Zachery and began running back to his mother's cottage with Andy trailing close behind.

The police were called and within minutes cruisers headed down South Shore Road toward the cottage.

Rick stood in front of the cottage with both boys close by his side as an officer emerged from the cruiser. Rick was visibly shaken as the officer approached him.

He handed the small white sneaker to the officer, and related what had transpired only minutes before.

As Rick addressed the officer, Mr. Lemieux, Rick's stepfather arrived. Ed and Maureen Lemieux were planning a weekend vacation and had arranged for Rick to care for their dog. Mr. Lemieux arrived with the dog as planned. The presence of two cruisers, with lights flashing caused concern as he stepped out of the car and approached Rick.

Andy and Zack rushed to their grandfather and began spouting that Holly was missing and, "Dad called the police."

One of the police officers approached the older man and asked for identification and the purpose of his arrival. Mr. Lemieux explained his relationship to the family and that he was simply there to drop off his dog, pointing in the direction of his car where the muzzle of a Golden Retriever squeezed through the partially opened rear window.

Satisfied with Mr. Lemieux's identity, the officer granted the grandfather access to the house. Ed Lemieux went to the phone and called Rick's mother, Maureen. She was at work and upon receiving the call, left and headed to Sturbridge. Once there, she contacted Holly's mother, Tina.

Before long, the entire family had arrived at the Sturbridge location. Neighbors walked down the dirt road and stood in shock as the news of Holly's disappearance began to spread.

Soon additional law enforcement arrived. Detectives and investigators from the Sturbridge police department began an immediate canvassing of the neighbors on South Shore Road, asking for any information that might lead to the safe return of Holly.

The appropriate steps were taken to get all information into the databases and distributed throughout the state as well as the national network for missing children.

Friday, August 6, 1993

GIRL 10, MISSING IN STURBRIDGE

The next day, the disappearance of Holly Piirainen covered the front page.

Eighty police officers and firefighters, using dogs and helicopters began a search for the 10-year-old.

Dick Butterworth was the director of the local civil defense and spokesperson to the press. Holly was still missing at 9:00 p.m.

Butterworth stated, "At this point, we're treating it strictly as a missing person."

The family of Holly was sure it was more than a 'missing person' case. They were stricken with grief that would become reality in the months to come.

Holly was described by her grandmother as a typical preteen. On January 19, 1993, she had a slumber party. It was on her 10th birthday. She thought "The Simpsons" were cool and she loved puppies.

Rick Piirainen spoke to the media. He was already haggard but expressed his belief that Holly was abducted by a stranger.

He added, "That's what I thought right from the beginning. The discovery of that one sneaker is what scared me right away. The children have been told time after time not to talk to strangers."

Rick described Holly as "savvy about strangers" and not a naïve girl.

Mrs. Lemieux, Holly's grandmother thought the serene, wooded setting of her summer cottage in Sturbridge was surely safe enough to let her granddaughter walk to a neighbor's place to look at the pups. She was wrong. Most in the area shared a misconception. Not even the beauty of the backwoods of Sturbridge could protect a lovely child like little Holly Piirainen.

The following day, close to 80 State and Sturbridge police officers joined by firefighters searched for over nine hours without success.

State Police with infrared equipment searched through the night covering a 3-mile area of Holly's disappearance. The search continued until nearly 1:00 a.m. and the family was assured the search would continue early the following morning.

Sturbridge Police Chief Kevin Fitzgibbons said he was not ruling out the possibility that Holly was kidnapped. Fitzgibbons added that a full ground search would begin at 7:00 a.m. and advised any volunteers to meet at the Burgess Elementary School.

An anguished search continued with high-tech tools. Authorities tapped into satellite television, color fax machines and other high-tech devices to spread word of the missing girl's case around the country.

More than 350 volunteers poured over more than five square miles in the South Pond area looking for Holly. The search included the aid of Massachusetts State Police K-9 unit as well as helicopters with heat sensors that would detect a person's body temperature in the dark. The search continued until after 9:00 p.m. Chief Fitzgibbons and State Police Lt. Timothy Hackett commander of the Sturbridge barracks took charge of the search efforts.

The media were on the scene and continued to interview family members.

Rick Piirainen commented, "All we can do now is let the authorities do their job and pray Holly is okay."

The Chief assured the family Holly's disappearance was being treated as urgent because, "it fit a pattern known as stereotypical kidnapping," in which a child between ages 5 and 12 is seized by a stranger along an isolated highway.

The police shifted their search efforts to a criminal investigation. They questioned a Sturbridge man and after searching his vehicle determined he was not a suspect. Earlier in the day, Chief Fitzgibbons interviewed an individual who had some pertinent information on the case, although he was not considered a suspect.

By now, the family was besieged with media to the point of exhaustion. The repeated questions were frustrating to the family who had no new information to offer. Rick and Tina, Holly's mother and father expressed their appreciation to the media for covering

Holly's disappearance, but requested state police bar reporters from the premises.

Rick Piirainen walked up the road to the house where the puppies were and spoke to his neighbor expressing his willingness to consult a psychic to help.

"I believe she is still alive," he said. "I have to keep believing until they come up with a body. Until then, I will keep looking."

As the police wound down a massive but unsuccessful three-day search, authorities began focusing on the possibility Holly had been abducted.

The State Police as well as the Civil Defense joined in the search efforts. The family gathered at the cottage to lend support as the focus of the probe shifted to a criminal investigation.

Ed Lemieux, Holly's paternal grandfather, made numerous calls to missing children's hot lines and television programs that feature missing children.

Rick spoke proudly about Holly's Girl Scout accomplishments. Recently she had earned her babysitting badge. His voice wavered with emotion as he looked directly into the camera,

"All I want is to get Holly back. We're open to anything. I received a call from a psychic suggesting where to look."

Within 24 hours, the producers put together three TV spots and fed them by satellite to several New England TV stations in addition to Fox television stations around the country.

The police advised the parents to refrain from participating in the search. In addition to every available means, the State Police had bloodhounds roaming the five-mile area and the scent from the parents could confuse the dogs.

Lt. Timothy Hackett of the State Police reported they had not ruled out she was out there somewhere, but cautioned the family the chances of finding her in the area were beginning to dwindle.

Hackett described the search thus far as meticulous in a 5-mile radius. He confirmed reports of suspicious people and vehicles had been checked. In addition to the investigation, a local man was questioned. After a thorough interview, the police were satisfied and stated they felt they had no further interest in him.

Holly's aunt, Carla attended an ecumenical service. Her seven-year-old daughter, Julie wept in her mother's arms. The children could not comprehend the magnitude of Holly's absence.

Fliers were circulated throughout the area and handed out by police working the roadblocks stopping motorists traveling nearby roadways.

The fliers reflected a wholesome, exceptionally beautiful child with long blonde hair framing an angelic face. Holly had a smile that would melt the heart of even the coldest of heart. Her abductor had to be a heartless monster.

Hackett faced the cameras and appealed to the public. "Some people see things that they may think are nothing, but it may help us find this little girl. Please contact the authorities with any information you may have."

As the search continued, it expanded to include parts of the neighboring town of Brimfield. All known convicted deviant sex criminals that had been released were contacted, questioned, and subsequently released. No arrests were made.

As the unsuccessful efforts of numerous searches and hundreds of volunteers continued, parents began offering grim reminders about dangers.

Shocked neighbors turned a watchful eye on their own children. They warned their children about the dangers in their seemingly 'safe haven' advising them to have a friend with them – never to go any place alone.

All the warnings that had been given to the children on countless occasions were reiterated repeatedly in the wake of Holly's disappearance.

Several residents were watching their children far more carefully and had even restricted some playtime activities.

One resident moved to his Allen Road home five years ago from New York City. He thought he had escaped the fear of city living, but the shock of what had happened to Holly awakened his fears that nowhere is safe.

Rick Piirainen added, "I grew up here and I considered it safe, but no place is safe. It could have been anyone's kid."

State Police Lt. Timothy Hackett suspected Holly and her abductor might have stayed in the area.

"Because of the remoteness of the area, I believe he's probably from the area."

This was a haunting concept. How could that be? How could it be a local resident, possibly a neighbor?

Hackett's hopes of finding Holly safe were beginning to dim. The detectives continued to knock on doors and track down more than 100 leads, sightings of vehicles in the area.

The police searched for a woman that was seen bicycling with two children. They felt she might have noticed something more than passing vehicles.

The family members continued to face cameras and plead for the return of Holly.

A haggard Rick Piirainen, wearing a Homer Simpson T-Shirt that read "All American Dad" and a Harley Davidson cap, made a heart-wrenching plea,

"Please return Holly. Just drop her off at a mall, or convenience store. We are not interested in revenge." In addition, the family considered the tips from psychics. Maureen Lemieux accompanied by her two daughters, Karen and Carla, visited the nearby Catholic Church.

"There are supposed to be miracles if you pray to St. Ann," she said.

A week after Holly disappeared, *"America's Most Wanted"* aired Holly's story. Approximately 15 to 20 million viewers nationwide were expected.

The segment presented interviews with Rick Piirainen and Tina Harrington, Holly's parents. Holly's grandparents, Maureen and Ed Lemieux and Holly's maternal grandmother, Mary Harrington-Cooper were also included in the segment.

Holly's picture and vital information that surrounded her mysterious disappearance was broadcasted into the homes of millions of viewers across the country.

Maureen looked directly into the camera and repeated her plea,

"Please drop Holly off in a safe place. We are not interested in revenge. We just want her back. Holly, we love you and pray you will be home soon."

Tina Harrington, Holly's mom addressed her daughter directly,

"Holly, keep trying and keep praying; we are all still looking for you and love you very much." She then sent a message to Holly's abductor,

"Whoever has Holly and has been keeping her against her will please let her go or contact us as soon as possible."

The moderator asked Tina how Zachary and Andy were reacting to Holly's disappearance.

"I don't think Holly's absence has sunk in yet on her two brothers. They still think she is coming back." Tina choked back tears and added,

"No one has given up hope. There are so many people praying for her. People are still searching. Please, don't give up hope."

Rick faced the bright lights and looked directly into the camera. His statement addressed the possibility of a kidnapping for ransom.

"If money is what you want, we can get it. Just contact us. We can get the money."

"I think Holly is still alive and in the area and haven't found anything to make me think different," her father said.

Next to speak was Holly's maternal grandmother, Mary Harrington-Cooper. She held up a favorite stuffed animal of Holly's and expressed her feelings,

"The worst thing is not knowing. Many times, it ends with an anonymous tip. That is what we are hoping for here."

The searches continued after the TV show.

Searches focused on previously untouched areas of the woods near South Pond.

Following a previous search that discounted a grim tip that a body had been sunk in the swamp nearby, authorities began their seventh day of searching with as little evidence as they had at the start.

Residents were interviewed throughout the quiet neighborhood on South Shore Road and Allen Street.

The search continued for Holly and with each passing day, the hope that she would be found safe and returned unharmed was a flicker in the hearts of all.

By now, the rescuer's search evolved into a hunt to recover Holly's remains and move on to find the person who had harmed her. It was the harsh reality seasoned detectives and police officers had come to accept days before.

Scores of state troopers now joined by FBI agents and personnel from towns throughout Central Massachusetts and northeast Connecticut joined in the search.

Again, Rick Piirainen faced the television cameras to plead for his daughter's return.

"We're begging anyone with any information; please let us know where she is. Holly, if you can hear me, call 911 or do something to help yourself."

Holly's mother, Tina Harrington was noticeably absent from any of the searches. She remained secluded in her Grafton home and declined any opportunity to comment.

The Sturbridge Police Chief, Kevin Fitzgibbons offered further information concerning some initial impressions about Holly's disappearance.

He disclosed that 5-year-old Zackary had made a statement to the police the day of Holly's disappearance. Initially, Zackary told the police he and Holly ran apart after being scared off by a large dog. Fitzgibbons stated that account was no longer believed.

Ernest Jolin, husband of Rick's sister Karen, gently questioned the small boy. Zachary was more at ease speaking to his uncle and stated he just turned around and walked away, toward home. The 5-year-old could not have been a reliable source and either version did not change the investigation one way or the other.

As he was being tucked into bed, Zackary asked, "Where is Holly going to sleep tonight?" His mother did not answer.

The search was endless. School busses from surrounding towns were filled with volunteers, transported from a central location in various surrounding towns, and dropped off to participate in the search. After a full day of walking through wooded areas, which included rugged forest terrain, the searchers boarded the bus and returned to their places of origin.

Several local businesses, including the local McDonald provided food and drink for the hundreds of searchers. Holly was not to be found.

All means imaginable were put into action including donated Motorola Radios communication equipment. A local real estate management company allowed employees to participate in the search and rounded up its consulting foresters to help.

The grandparents of Holly's best friend stepped forward. Mr. and Mrs. Adams offered the first pledge toward a reward for any information to Holly's safe return. As he contributed $1,000 toward the fund, Mr. Adams said, "I'd love to raise $50,000." He offered the bank name and address that all pledges were to be sent.

"I hope somebody, somewhere who knows about this terrible incidence will come forward, and Holly will be returned safely to her family." Rick's sisters, Carla and Karen, his mother Maureen Lemieux and stepfather Ed Lemieux stayed at the cottage throughout the search. They remained there day and night hoping for Holly's return.

Early Thursday morning, August 12, a young man appeared on the doorstep of the Lemieux's cottage.

He was in his early thirty's, barefoot and barechested. His hair was disheveled and he looked in need of a shower and shave. His appearance was assumed that of one of the tireless searchers. Maureen came to the door.

Robert Armes introduced himself to Holly's grandmother and presented her with a selfless offer. His intention, he explained was to conduct a vigil to raise money to help find Holly.

He explained how when he had heard about the massive search for Holly, he was stricken with sorrow because he was the father of three daughters and a son ranging from 3 to 12. He wanted to spearhead the activity with help from friends and neighbors because,

"If I put myself in your shoes, I can't imagine the pain and torture you are going through."

He continued by explaining the account would be the "Find Holly Piirainen Fund" and was to be set up at the Country Bank for Savings in West Brookfield. It would be separate from the fund that was seeking pledges for a reward for information leading to finding Holly, and suggested the family use it to print fliers and fund a continued investigation if needed.

Maureen was astonished at the stranger's proposal. She invited him in to discuss his intentions further with the family members who were present.

After a lengthy discussion, the family gave their approval for the account to be opened and thanked Mr. Armes for his concern and efforts it would take to organize such an event.

The vigil was scheduled to take place on Saturday, August 14, and continue through Sunday until 9:00 p.m.

Saturday, August 14th arrived and the vigil was scheduled to begin at 7 a.m. at Brookfield Elementary.

Armes anticipated close to $10,000 from the expected hundreds of people, including Holly's family. Several local businesses contributed food and drinks for those who attended and all would be given pink ribbons, balloons and stickers.

Holly's maternal grandmother, Mary Harrington-Cooper attended, however Holly's mother was not present. Mrs. Cooper spoke to the gathering crowd.

"This has got to stop. We have to say we are fed up with it and that abductions are not going to keep happening to our children." She spoke with a firm, angry tone.

"This has already happened to parents a thousand times before. This time it is our names in the blank. This is not just Holly that is gone. It is everybody's child."

Mr. Cooper, added, "People are reacting like it's their little girl. I'm gratified by the response."

The distraught grandmother continued to address the crowd that had gathered, saying the family is feeling strained. They are tired and depressed, but still hopeful that Holly is alive.

Throughout the day, strangers approached several members of the family asking how they were holding up and if they had received any favorable news. The family members were gracious and appreciative of the concern displayed by those who had gathered for the vigil. Unfortunately, they had nothing to offer regarding any developments in the search for Holly. They did discuss the dozens of psychics that had contacted them. Most of the information offered by the psychics was too vague to be useful right now, but all claimed Holly was still alive.

The news of the vigil caught the attention of a Dairy Co. as far away as New Britain, Ct. The Vice President of Guida-Seilbert Dairy Co. decided to resurrect a practice it had started back in 1985, but ended it a few years later.

Guida said milk customers could expect to see Holly's missing-child poster imprinted on a side panel of the half-gallon milk cartons starting within two days. The photo would appear on 250,000 cartons per day, and distributed throughout Connecticut, Massachusetts and Rhode Island.

Mr. Guida followed Holly's case on the news and decided to use the missing-child panels again because it was a local case they felt they could respond to. He added there were no plans to do this for other missing children.

In response to that statement, Mr. Guida replied,

"Doing this again may offend some people, but we feel the benefits far outweigh the negatives."

In spite of the drizzle and fog in the morning, the vigil continued throughout the steamy afternoon.

The raindrops were referred to as 'Tears for Holly'.

State Trooper Bruce Hopper of the Sturbridge barracks stated the police were getting hundreds of leads at the rate of one or two calls per minute. The dispatcher agreed adding that the phones stayed lit 24 hours a day. The family was assured each lead would be investigated but because of the volume, it may take days before all were contacted.

Detective Sgt. Roger Smith attended the vigil and recalled a case that continued to disturb him. He spoke of 4-year-old Andrew Amato who was last seen at 10:30 a.m. on September 30, 1978. He was playing with his sister and cousin in the woods behind a trailer park in Sturbridge.

He ended the story saying,

"It's going to be 15 years at the end of next month. We're still carrying it as an open case. That's why this terrible situation in Sturbridge bothers me. I know exactly what the family is going through, how frustrated they must feel."

Smith turned to the family of Holly and expressed hope that Holly would be found alive and well.

"I know exactly what you're going through. It jerks your heart around."

He added, "Police Chief Szamocki retired with this unsolved mystery weighing heavily on his mind. He carried the pain of the Amato boy's disappearance to his grave."

Another memory was aroused in the midst of the vigil. The similarities were striking. An off duty police officer recounted the story of 10-year-old Sarah

Pryor's disappearance from Wayland, MA while walking near her rural home.

Sara was abducted on the afternoon of October 9, 1985. The Pryor family moved to Wayland from Pittsburg only weeks before believing the sleepy, quiet rural town was a welcome change and a surety of a safer environment.

Despite the intensive search by law enforcement and every resource available at the time, Sarah Pryor was never found. The case remains unsolved.

As the day ended, a friend stopped by to see how the effort was going. Armes estimated over 300 people had been there. It had been a slow, steady stream of people. He was pleased at the response on Saturday and hoped the vigil/fund raiser would be equally attended through Sunday, reaching its anticipated monetary goal.

During the overnight stretch, a gas-powered lantern lit the hand-lettered sign - **FIND HOLLY PIIRAINEN.** The crude sign was visible from nearby Route 9. At 1:30 a.m., two women arrived with coffee and doughnuts for those on the vigil. They stayed until 5:00 a.m. Several heartwarming gestures were exhibited by total strangers, some just passing and noticing the sign stopping by to contribute. Many expressed how heartsick they felt as they thought of their own children and their safety.

Sunday, August 15, 1993

FAMILY'S SORROW REKINDLED

The family of Jamie Lusher who disappeared from Westfield over nine months ago, offer words to the Piirainen family…

Jamie had been missing for more than nine months.

Joanne Levakis's life was thrown into turmoil, but the mother gradually found ways to cope with the disappearance of her 16-year-old. By returning to her job at Berkshire Industries, she began to keep her emotions under control.

When Joanne Levakis heard the news of Holly's disappearance, she realized the flood of memories and thoughts about Jamie had never been tucked away. The news triggered the emotional struggle anew. She found herself empathizing with the Piirainen family. She was prepared to shut out the world.

"I saw the news and I just went into one of those black moods. You just don't care about anything you can't concentrate on anything. I suffer depression now. I want to lock myself in my room and shut out the rest of the world," replied Joanne Levakis when asked how she felt about the news of Holly Piirainen's disappearance.

Jamie's father, James found his own way of dealing with the loss of his son.

"I'm sure that by this time most people wouldn't agree with me, but I've never given up hope that my son is somewhere else," he said. "I've gone through hell, but I can't focus a lot on it because I have a daughter to consider."

The Westfield Police department expressed their intention to return to the pond where Jamie's bike was found. The pond had been drained in the fall, when the bike had been discovered. Now, police would use dogs to see if they could pick up any scent.

"As time goes by, hopes fade," John Camerota commented. He was not optimistic.

James Lusher understood the detective's comment all too well.

"I would say that you cannot give up hope until the evidence is found," Mr. Lusher said.

"It's like an emotional roller coaster. At first, you're in shock. Then you're hopeful, you can't sleep, you can't eat. You want to run all over the world and look under every nook and cranny."

When Mrs. Levakis replied, she had mixed feelings.

"I would rather have seen him dead than having someone abusing him and hurting him, with him not being able to get help. In a way, the idea of death is comforting."

Mrs. Levakis continued to consult psychics stating that she didn't believe in them 100%, but it was the only hope she had left.

In nearby Sturbridge, all hearts went out for Holly. The vigil held over the weekend was considered successful. The six donation cans on the table at the Brookfield Elementary School were filled and emptied hundreds of time. A thousand pink ribbons were tied onto vehicles and 800 pink balloons were sent home with local children. The organizer of the event was more than pleased. Robert Armes spoke to the media,

"This has been a thousand times better than I ever thought. The outpouring of support and media coverage has been overwhelming."

Television crews and newspaper reporters besieged the supporters and were welcome. All were thankful for the exposure they had created. The goal was to keep the pressure on and to get the word out. It was a tremendous effort and exceeded all expectations.

The one tragic fact remained; Holly was still missing. The search continued but hopes diminished as each day passed.

Since the first week of Holly's disappearance, cards and letters of encouragement and sentiments were received. Hundreds were received, but one had a poignant significance. Written in the penmanship of a ten-year-old was the following letter...

My name is Molly Bish. I am 10-years-old. Some day I would like to come see you. I   am very sorry. I wish I could make it up to you. Holly is a very pretty girl. She is almost as tall as me. I wish I knew Holly. I hope they found her.

*Author's Note - Molly Bish, Warren, MA 10 miles away, was abducted seven years later, on June 27, 2000. It would be three years (2003) before Molly Bish's remains were discovered. Molly's murder remains unsolved. When Molly went missing, Maureen Lemieux reached out to the Bish family and shared the letter. The two families have lent each other support over the years, attending Masses and Vigils for both girls. Maureen and her two daughters, Carla and Karen, have become active volunteers for the Molly Bish Foundation.

The Armes family tallied up the donations from the vigil. Although they had anticipated a larger sum, Robert Armes stated he was still satisfied with the results. Maureen Lemieux was contacted by a local radio station and agreed to do an interview with the host, Upton Bell.

With her hands wringing in her lap, Maureen stared straight ahead, as she answered Bell's questions. She publicly thanked the Armes for the vigil and announced the money raised over the weekend would go to hire a private investigator.

"I have no idea how much a private investigator costs, I suppose it can vary depending on how long the investigation takes." She continued to answer questions from callers, and expressed her purpose for being on the show.

"I want to keep Holly's disappearance in the public eye. I hope this might touch someone's heart and hope they'll have a change of heart and bring her back."

Maureen addressed the unsavory telephone calls she and members of her family had received. She described the callers as hurtful and insensitive. "I'd rather not quote the caller's accusations; however, my response is simply, 'Don't judge anybody until you've walked in their shoes.' The majority of calls are encouraging, and the family truly appreciates the concern of so many."

CHAPTER 5

On August 18th , in the midst of the intensive search for Holly, another girl was reported missing. Bulletins were sent out, and posters were being circulated just as they had for all the cases being investigated in Massachusetts.

Twelve-year-old Sara Anne Wood, from a small town in upstate New York, not far from the location Jimmy Bernardo's body had been found 2 ½ years before, was now showing up on the national database.

It just didn't seem to stop. One case dovetailed the other and without resolution. To date Western Massachusetts was involved in the investigation of Jimmy Bernardo, *(Pittsfield, October, 1990)* Lisa Ziegert, *(Agawam, April 1992)* Jamie Lusher, *(Westfield, November, 1992)* and Holly Piirainen *(Sturbridge, August, 1993)* In addition to these cases approximately 70 others were also being investigated.

Local police from their respective stations together with State Police and the FBI were working in unison to find a link, or clue, a suspect or a lead that might solve these disappearances. So far, they were led to dead ends.

Jimmy Bernardo and Lisa Ziegert's bodies had been discovered. Their killers had not.

Jamie Lusher's body had not been found. He was assumed dead, but neither the body, nor a suspect had been found.

Now, in the midst of the intensive investigation into Holly Piirainen's disappearance one more girl had gone missing.

Sara Anne Wood, the 12-year-old daughter of Robert and Frances Wood had disappeared. She was last seen riding her bicycle to her family's residence on Hacadam Road in Frankfort, New York on August 18, 1993. Sara was returning from Norwich Corners Church on Roberts Road in Frankfort, where she attended summer Bible school. The area she was last seen in was in close proximity to where Jimmy Bernardo's body had been discovered.

Sara's father, Robert Wood was a pastor at the small church in the community. He appeared on local news as well as the national networks pleading for the safe return of his daughter. A description of Sara Anne Wood was published and posters were circulated throughout the New York, Vermont and Massachusetts area.

The posters reflected a smiling 12-year-old in a red and white cheerleading outfit as well as a cropped shot of her face. She had brown hair; blue eyes and weighed approximately 96 lbs., 5' tall.

Her poster displayed the same information the others had. The National Center for Missing and Exploited Children (NCMEC) toll free 800 number as well as the NY State Police telephone number was included in bold type on the poster.

Another child missing and another family's dreams and hopes diminished. The Woods also believed what was now becoming an apparent misconception. These small rural hometowns were not the safe haven where children were free to grow up. There was no haven that protected them from the crimes and brutality occurring in inner cities and broadcasted on the nightly news. He concluded there was no safe place, not even your own backyard.

Working closely with the Pittsfield Police and the Massachusetts State Police, New York law enforcement agencies shared leads and information.

After over two years, Massachusetts failed to have any suspects in the Bernardo murder. The police were baffled and frustrated.

The New York police discovered Sara Anne Wood's bicycle, and coloring book and crayons hidden in some brush. She was wearing a pink t-shirt with the phrase "Guess Who," turquoise shorts and brown sandals.

With the exception of gender, the Sara Anne Wood and James Bernardo cases seemed to have similarities. Both had very dark hair, both were riding bicycles that had been abandoned and both were twelve years old.

Sara's bicycle was discovered very near the location Jimmy Bernardo's body had been found.

The authorities continued to compare the circumstances of Jamie Lusher's disappearance and included Jamie in the equation.

Jamie although 16, had the physical appearance of a twelve year old. His mental capabilities were considered that of a twelve year old. Jamie also had very dark brown hair and Jamie's bicycle, like Bernardo and Wood's, was also abandoned.

Investigators had no leads to indicate where to expect the abductor to be. New York had a missing girl, believed to be murdered; Massachusetts had a Pittsfield boy, murdered and found in New York. The medical examiner confirmed Jimmy Bernardo had been killed at the New York location, but remained baffled when faced with the question of how Jimmy had traveled 200 miles from Pittsfield. Was the predator a Pittsfield resident, or had he traveled from New York to Massachusetts and return to New York with Jimmy? It was a puzzle with too many missing pieces.

Sara's father spoke to the press on a daily basis.

"My faith has been shaken in the past and it will be in the future," said Robert Wood. "My relationship with the Lord doesn't depend on me, it depends on His ability to hang on to me, and that's what He's doing."

Robert Wood tried to keep his family in control. He was certain Sara had been abducted and the small community continued searching with every means they had at their disposal.

The women of the church created ribbons tied in bows of aqua and pink; symbolizing the colors Sara was last seen wearing.

A State Police command center was housed under a temporary Red Cross tent set up on the church grounds.

As the search extended to over five days, the state Department of Environmental Conservation rangers relied on up to 200 trained searchers per day so they could say with certainty, "no stone had been left unturned." They had combed the surrounding marshes, woods and cornfields.

A spokesperson from the forest rangers felt the search was very extensive and that they had a 95% guarantee that,

"If the girl was in the area, some sign of her would have been found." They believed they were doing everything they could to find Sara.

Sara's posters were seen in the windows of every business in town. The local market placed the posters in every customer's grocery bag. Neighbors offered food to the volunteers as well as the family of Sara Anne. Every car and truck that passed through the small hamlet displayed a poster in the rear window.

The residents displayed worry and grief for Robert and Frances Wood. One neighbor of the Wood family expressed her concern, "It's so close to home. Nothing like this has ever happened around here."

Robert and the entire Wood family took solace in their faith.

The search was about to go national. People that had planned vacations stopped by the command posts to pick up piles of fliers to be distributed to tollbooths, stores, restaurants and rest areas as they traveled.

The search continued on a lead-to-lead basis. The New York State law enforcement personnel took on the primary investigation and search for Sara Anne Wood. Information was shared with Massachusetts if it appeared to be linked to the Bernardo homicide.

Sara's story was highlighted along with other missing children, including Holly Piirainen on the television program, *"48 Hours"*

The senior producer for the show followed the investigation and interviewed the families. He and his television crew were convinced Sara's story was worth telling.

"We were touched by the families and friends up there. We have created a short documentary that reveals the disappearance and the investigations that followed ending with the present."

All hoped a nationally broadcasted CBS program would provide more clues to Sara's whereabouts.

During the televised interview, Robert Wood addressed the attention paid to Sara's case.

"Thanks to neighbors and supporters of my family a $150,000 reward has been amassed for Sara's return. People are amazed at the effort and some have asked why so much attention is being paid to Sara? Our hope is that if anything else, her case sets a standard for how child abduction cases should be handled because it's a national problem."

Chapter 6

The Sturbridge search for 10-year-old Holly Piirainen was ongoing. Warm summer months had now surrendered to the crisp autumn temperatures.

The Piirainen family heard of Sara Anne Wood's disappearance but New York investigators did not believe there was a connection.

It was September and Holly's brothers Andy, 8 and Zachary, 5 were scheduled to start the school year. Maureen Lemieux, Holly's grandmother would return to her job also. Since Holly's disappearance, Maureen had taken time off from her dental hygienist job.

Waiting day after day, then week after week resulted in a helpless feeling. Staying home just didn't seem to make sense anymore and became very difficult for the anxious family members.

Holly's family continued to bear up under the strain of knowing nearly one full month had passed with no news about their little girl.

Holly's mother, Christine Harrington spoke briefly to the media.

"I just deal with it day by day. I have to keep going for her. I just wake up and try to be hopeful that I'll hear about her soon; otherwise I wouldn't want to wake up."

She also described how her 8-year-old son was coping.

"Andy found his own way of coping with the disappearance of his sister. He pretends she's still at 4-H camp."

The New York police were notified of Holly's disappearance by tourists who traveled from Sturbridge to upper New York via the interstate highway. As travelers learned of Sara Anne Wood's disappearance, they called police to alert them of Holly's case.

With the information they gathered from the travelers, they began comparing the two cases noting the cases had similarities. Both girls were last seen in remote areas and were close in age. From there, New York investigators contacted Massachusetts police.

Geographically, the small town in New York and the equally small town of Sturbridge were connected by Interstate 90 the Massachusetts Turnpike and the New York State Thruway. Could there be a Route 90 link?

Police in three states were sharing data in their searches for Holly, Sara, Jimmy and Jamie's killer. They were delving closely into the possibility there was a link in the case through the interstate road system.

A month passed since Holly Piirainen was last seen walking up the dirt road in Sturbridge, MA.

The police had given up an active search for Holly but assured the family they intended to follow any leads they might receive.

A call from a couple of anglers prompted the police to search a nearby lake. The fishermen said they caught what appeared to be human hair on their lines while fishing. They reported the blondish hair came up twice.

Police divers responded. They recovered a shoe, but it did not match the one found where Holly was last seen.

State Police Lt. Timothy Hackett said that no analysis could be done on the hair because the anglers threw it away.

"We don't have anything to say that's a solid lead or anything of that nature."

Chief Fitzgibbons announced Detective Christopher Donais was assigned full time to the case. In addition, a room had been set up at the police barracks for investigators.

"We still continue to get information on almost a daily basis," the Chief said.

"The police continue to check a lot of individuals because callers are giving different names including those with past sexual offenses or pedophile profiles."

The family of Holly continued every conceivable effort to keep the search for Holly in the forefront.

Over the weekend, Rick Piirainen and his mother Maureen Lemieux distributed over 20,000 pink ribbons at a local fair that took place over the Labor Day weekend. They took the opportunity to speak to as many fair goers as possible.

"We're asking people to keep their eyes open. If they see anything strange, don't think they're being foolish if they call police with a tip. Please pray for

Holly," were the words of the missing little girl's grandmother.

October marked another month without Holly and with no progress in the investigation.

The Piirainen family hired a private detective to work the case. Carl Westerman passed information on to Rick Piirainen that seemed to be encouraging and bolstered the family.

"You follow up leads and hope it ends up where it's best. I have a good feeling that it's going to turn out good, and I have three solid leads," Westerman disclosed. The investigator was quick to discount rumors flying about. He commented the facts suggested Holly was a victim of a random abduction.

"That makes it more difficult to track, because it is an unpredictable move." Carl Westerman stated to the press.

"I don't want to say anything that will hurt Mr. Westerman's investigation, but there are things that lead us to believe Holly is still alive," stated Holly's father when asked by reporters.

Rick continued, "We don't get hundreds of calls per day like we did before, but we still get a few calls from people who think they've seen Holly."

Lt. Timothy Hackett countered with his statements,

"With four full-time investigators on the case, we haven't backed off at all." The Lieutenant admitted the leads were getting slimmer but the few they had received of late seemed to be more concrete.

Lt. Hackett, commander of the Massachusetts State Police dismissed the detective's reports of strong leads in the investigation. He referred to them as a figment of imagination. Hackett did not approve of Westerman's optimistic attitude and feared he was delivering false hope to the Piirainen family.

"If somebody wants to come in and tell us something they know, we'd be more than happy to check it out if it has any substance to it." However, the leads continued to dwindle.

Maureen Lemieux continued to wait for confirmation from Westerman regarding the breaks in the investigation. She became distressed because of the lack of communication between the family and the investigator. Maureen also worried the funds donated to pay for the investigator would soon run out. Regardless, the Piirainen family had vowed they would not give up their search for Holly.

Holly's grandfather, Ed Lemieux, was an active participant in the search efforts and contacted the Interstate Association of Stolen Children.

Jeff Malone a certified clinical therapist from Dallas headed the investigation.

Once he learned the aspects of Holly's disappearance, he went to work developing a profile of possible suspects in the case. When the profile was completed, he met with the family and the press.

In his first interview with the press, Malone stated,

"I've got a real good feeling about this one. As far as I'm concerned, Holly is alive and well. We just need to find her."

He refused to elaborate on his reasons for believing Holly had not been harmed, and would not divulge the profile of a possible abductor

Although the Interstate Association of Stolen Children was a non-profit organization, Malone's expenses were expected to be paid.

Maureen realized the family did not have enough to cover Malone's airfare, rental car and hotel. Once again, as she had on numerous occasions, Maureen was determined to find a way to overcome this financial obstacle.

Without hesitation, she contacted several people who had made offers to help and her aggressive approach proved to be successful.

A local business owner donated $1,000 to cover the airfare. Another independent offer covered the car rental as well as the hotel expense. The generosity of strangers was quite overwhelming to the Piirainen family.

One had to wonder why all 'outside sources' were convinced Holly was alive. The psychics, a private investigator, and now this non-profit organization were all in agreement. On the other hand, not all law enforcement agencies were so optimistic.

Hunting season was just around the corner. There was the hope hunters would aid in the search. Perhaps they would go into remote areas that hadn't been previously searched. At best, the hunters may turn up something that would give the dwindling investigation some new direction.

Saturday morning, October 23, 1993, Rick Piirainen was home with Zachery and Andy when he answered the knock at the door. Lt. Timothy Hackett stood in the doorway. Rick felt the ache in his stomach almost immediately.

"Rick, may I come in?" The trooper's tone was solemn.

"Sure, Lieutenant, sure, come on in," Rick replied.

"I think we've found Holly's remains." The officer was obviously finding this the most difficult message he'd ever had to deliver.

Rick took a few steps back and dropped into a chair. He was speechless. He had been anticipating the news for nearly three months, and thought he would be prepared to receive the horrible news, but now he realized he was not even close to being prepared.

He called to the two young boys playing in the next room.

"Andy, Zack, get your jackets on, I've got to go somewhere with Lt. Hackett. Gail * will watch you until grandma gets home."

He hurriedly delivered his two sons to the neighbor who had watched them on numerous occasions. He avoided telling her what he had just learned of the discovery. Gail Magnant sensed something was wrong when she spotted Lt. Hackett seated in the cruiser parked in front of her neighbor's house.

Rick began a barrage of questions wanting to know the details of how and where Holly was found.

Lt. Hackett answered as best he could but when Rick insisted he be taken to the location of Holly's remains, the officer was firm and adamantly advised Rick he was delivering him to the Sturbridge Police Department.

In spite of the distraught father's protests, he was driven to the Sturbridge Police Station.

A short time later, Maureen and Ed Lemieux returned from shopping. As they entered the house, Maureen called out,

"Hello everyone, I'm home." There was no answer. She was accustomed to Zachery racing to her with a jubilant greeting. It became obvious, nobody was home, and yet the door was left unlocked.

Maureen began putting the grocery's away and Ed sorted through the mail.

The phone rang and Maureen answered, "Hello?"

"Mrs. Lemieux? Is this Holly's grandmother?"

"Yes, who is this?" Maureen asked.

"I'm a reporter from the Springfield Union, do you have any comments now that Holly's been found?"

Maureen gasped.

"What are you talking about? I don't know what you mean?"

There was a brief silence followed by a sincere apology from the caller.

"No, no, don't hang up. Tell me what you know!" Maureen shouted into the phone.

The reporter shared the little information he had and repeated his apology for his call.

Maureen raced from the house filling in her husband as she headed for her car. Ed and Maureen drove directly to the Sturbridge Police Department.

As they entered the station, they looked around hoping to see Rick. They were advised by the desk sergeant that Rick was with Chief Fitzgibbons.

"I'm Rick's mother; I need to see him right away." Maureen was close to hysteria. Ed wrapped his arm around her shoulders in an effort to support his wife.

The sergeant escorted the couple to the Chief's office. Upon seeing Rick, Maureen wrapped her arms around her son and sobbed. Regardless of every effort to maintain control, Rick broke down when he witnessed his mother near collapse. Until now, Maureen had been the strength of the family throughout this horrible ordeal.

Ed assisted the grieving grandmother to a seat and drew another chair close beside her.

Chief Fitzgibbons conveyed his sincere sorrow for the three family members seated before him. Once they were able to regain their composure, he filled them in on the details of Holly's discovery. He was careful to advise them positive identification had not been determined and would not be confirmed until a medical examiner completed his examination.

Maureen asked to use the phone. She had to notify the family before they began receiving phone calls similar to the one she had received.

She called her daughter, Carla and asked her to make the necessary calls to notify Holly's mother, Tina and other family members. The only information Carla was able to obtain from Maureen was that

Holly's remains had been discovered by two hunters in the neighboring town of Brimfield.

Rick insisted the police bring him to the location where his daughter had been found. Despite his insistence, the Chief remained steadfast and refused to allow Rick to subject himself to view the skeletal remains of his little girl.

Tina Harrington, Holly's mother, was not home when Carla tried to reach her; however, the news was delivered to Tina as she drove her car through downtown Grafton.

Hearing the newscaster on her car radio forced her to veer off to the shoulder of the road. Once she collected her thoughts, she made a U-turn and headed directly to the Sturbridge Police. She could not believe; would not believe what she just heard. It had to be a mistake. Surely, the media would not air this information before the family was notified. She was angry, and her intention as she drove toward the police station was to express how she felt about the broadcast she had just heard. At no time did she believe it to be accurate.

When Tina Harrington pulled into the parking lot of the Sturbridge Police Department, she spotted Maureen's car. It was at that moment she knew Holly was never coming home.

Rick tried to remain optimistic as he spoke to his mother,

"I'm hoping there's some kind of mistake, but if it is her, at least the body has been found."

Rick returned to his house and his concern quickly turned to his two sons.

He would have to deliver the news of their sister's death to an eight-year-old and a five-year-old. It was a gut wrenching task but it had to be done soon. Maureen went to the neighbor and picked up her two grandsons.

Maureen and Ed retreated to the bedroom while Rick faced the two boys. Two innocent faces stared at the man slumped before them. Rick tried to convey the bitter news as gently as he could, but found there was no gentle way to tell two little boys that their sister was dead.

Rick mustered every ounce of strength he had and told the two boys as much as he thought they needed to know about how Holly had been found.

"Dad did the girl they found have dark brown hair?" asked eight-year-old Andy.

"No Andy, why would you ask that?"

"They aren't sure it's Holly. If she has dark brown hair, then maybe it's Sara Wood," Andy replied. "Sara has dark brown hair and she's missing. Do you think it could be her?"

Rick reached for his oldest son and held him tightly.

"Andy, I'm so sorry. They're pretty sure it's Holly."

Upon hearing these words from his father, Andy began to cry. Zachery began to cry and yes, Rick sobbed uncontrollably.

Maureen Lemieux appeared in the doorway of the kitchen.

The grandmother of the abducted little girl was emotionally spent. She had drawn on every fiber of her being to provide support to her family during the three months of uncertainty, spearheading fundraisers and administering the finances resulting from each event. Maureen was the emotional rock that all depended on throughout the three month search for Holly.

Only hours earlier, she listened as the police delivered the dreaded news of Holly's demise, but now, the sight of her son and two grandsons huddled on the floor sobbing, was more than she could bear.

Within a short time, family members began arriving at the George Hill Road residence. Aunts, uncles, cousins, and grandparents arrived and soon the old farmhouse was filled with those who loved Holly; each bearing their own burden of grief and sorrow over the loss of Holly Kristin Piirainen.

Sunday, October 24, 1993

CHILD'S BODY IS FOUND IN WOODS

On Sunday morning, October 24, the newspaper announced the tragic news.

The nearly three-month search for Holly Piirainen had come to a tragic end. The skeletal remains were discovered on Saturday, October 23 the first day of pheasant hunting season.

At 8:45 a.m., two hunters notified the local police of the gruesome discovery of what appeared to be the skeletal remains of a small child.

State Police Col. Charles Henderson described the body of Holly as badly decomposed. The location were she was found was only five miles from where she had been taken. It was a heavily wooded area in a neighboring town of Brimfield.

Col. Henderson commented there was no forensic evidence to make a positive identification but the authorities believed there was strong indication it was in fact Holly Piirainen.

The initial examination of the remains of Holly indicated that there were no signs of trauma to the body, no gunshot or knife wounds but the medical examiner could not determine the cause of death, the means of death was undoubtedly homicide.

An autopsy would be performed at the University of Amherst, Worcester, MA

The discovery of Holly's remains immediately triggered a joint investigation to be conducted by the Massachusetts State Police and the district attorneys from both Hampden and Worcester counties.

District Attorney William Bennett presided over Hampden County, where Holly's remains were discovered.

District Attorney John Conte presided over Worcester County, where Holly was abducted. Both D.A.'s were called into the investigation.

The media began releasing information as it was received from the authorities.

Holly's decomposed body remained in the wooded area overnight to allow authorities to complete their investigation of the site. State Police guarded the entrance to the crime scene throughout the night.

The owner of the property where Holly's remains were discovered had spoken to the hunters who made the gruesome discovery. Wilfred Bertrand offered the information he learned from the hunters.

Bertrand did not get the names of the hunters but they told him they 'stumbled upon a skull and a sneaker'. As he disclosed the information he learned from the hunters, Mr. Bertrand appeared to be shaken.

The authorities failed to include the area during the intensive 3-month search. Five Bridge Road, the location of Holly's remains, led to a dirt road that provided access to the woods for hunters and anglers. The abandoned railroad right-of-way was referred to by area residents as 'the dead road'.

The local residents agreed whoever was responsible for Holly's death must have known the road. A stranger would not even know it was there, particularly in the summer with all the trees in full bloom. It was dense, and hardly allowed access.

One resident lived only 100 yards from where Holly was found.

"The guy who did this had to know the area because you have to know the road is here. It makes me sick to think that she was so close and probably needed help and I had no idea."

"It makes me feel sick. She might have been crying for help and we were so close," she said.

Rick Piirainen reflected on the efforts that had been made over the previous three months to find his daughter.

He was convinced the killer was still in the area because a stranger would have been lost in the dense location. He also believed the killer would hunt down another child.

Rick remembered being near the area during the search acting on a psychic's tip. Dozens of psychics had provided tips during the search, but this one stood out in Rick's mind. He resolved to seek out this psychic in hopes to obtain additional information. The police assured the family they had no suspects.

Rick tried to avoid the media. He had nothing to offer but his sorrow and anguish. On one of the few interviews he participated in he said,

"Holly's disappearance has been a nightmare I've lived with every day since August 5th. I've cried every day."

The interviewer pressed Rick asking how he felt about Holly's discovery.

"At least the search and the terrible feeling of not knowing where Holly was, is over." When asked how Holly's mother was holding up, Rick answered,

"She feels about as bad as can be expected and does not want to talk about it."

Maureen Lemieux was present at the interview. Maureen added, "At least we know now what happened. We aren't going to be wondering for seven years like the Pryor family has had to."

Mrs. Lemieux referred to 9-year-old Sarah Pryor of Wayland who disappeared in 1985. The case remains unsolved, and Sarah's body has never been found.

After the family gathered at the Grafton house, Holly's brothers ran through the house filled with weeping adults. Since the divorce, Holly's mother, Tina rarely came to the house but she arrived with other members of her family. Her three children lived in this house on weekends when they visited their father.

When Tina arrived, Zachary and Andy tried to snuggle close to their mother, but Tina's tears would not stop. The two boys ran outside.

The distraught family exchanged theories and thoughts of what was to be tended to next.

Rick addressed the family,

"We now know where she is and we don't have to go to any more benefits and relive the story a million times."

As the family consoled each other and expressed the weight of their sorrow, the authorities were busy at the scene.

After investigators had thoroughly scoured the wooded area, the remains they believed to be that of Holly were removed to be delivered to the State Medical Examiner's office in preparation for an autopsy.

The investigators dug and sifted through mounds of dark soil, leaves and other forest debris about 50 feet from the riverbank in search of evidence and possibly more remains.

A skull and a sneaker that matched the sneaker left at the scene of Holly's abduction were placed in the Medical Examiner's van. State police cordoned off an acre of woods then covered a 20-foot wide primary search area. The investigators worked literally on hands and knees, sifting and digging with their fingers and small hand tools to assure no evidence was overlooked.

A two-tier wire mesh was provided to sift through the dead leaves, small stones, dirt and pieces of tree limbs gathered and shoveled into large plastic trash bags. Once sifted, the debris was deposited into brown paper bags to be transported to the crime lab for further examination.

The State Dental Examiner's Office announced identification from forensic dental evidence would not be available for another week.

The investigators recalled following up a tip from an out of state psychic. They responded with the aid of a scent-sniffing dog and came within a mile of where the remains were found. The letter said, 'check a leaf pile' but it was very vague.

The letter also referenced gates and stone walls. The letter did not reveal names, or the name of the town, but its descriptions led searchers to Brimfield.

It was believed that if the searchers had entered the dense wood from a different point, they would have found the remains sooner, they just did not go far enough. However, it was believed while the remains would have been discovered sooner, the outcome would not have been any different.

Carl Westerman, the private investigator hired by the family had stated just the day before the gruesome discovery,

"I've got a good feeling about this. I believe she's still alive and I have three solid leads to investigate."

When asked his thoughts about the physic Westerman replied,

"I've been through an awful lot of psychics and if any were good, we would've had Holly a long time ago."

The paid private detective, who produced zero evidence and contributed nothing to the investigation and search, dismissed the letter as a 'wild guess'.

Residents of the small town of Brimfield reflected anger and fear. Generally, they feared Holly's killer was still at large and in the area.

A professor, who studied serial killers for over ten years, offered his evaluation and conclusions to the type of person that would be likely to have abducted and murdered Holly.

Professor Jack Levine, a professor of criminology and sociology believed it unlikely the killer was a stranger who decided to abduct Holly Piirainen at random. He added the killer is more likely to be someone who knew the girl and her family

Because of the lack of physical evidence and no crime scene, it would be a very difficult case to solve.

Professor Levine's extensive research of cases similar to this indicated few kidnappers are total strangers. With limited information about Holly's abduction and murder, he said cases involving the abduction and killing of a child usually have common elements.

Levine concluded it was unlikely Holly was killed at the site she was found and by the time the body was found, little evidence was available.

"The child is usually sexually assaulted and killed somewhere else, perhaps in an automobile or house, then dumped in a predetermined secluded location," he concluded.

The police listened to the grim comments of the professor. If his theory were accurate, they would have little to no evidence, no fibers, no fingerprints, and no blood. In addition, if Levine was to be believed, the investigators had no crime scene.

However, the professor did agree that the victim usually knows or is familiar with the abductor. He suggested the police should be looking at neighbors, family and those close to the child. He doubted Holly was a victim of a serial killer, but strongly suggested it was someone within the community. He explained serial killers usually hold full time jobs, have a wife and children and 'kill for the fun of it'. He also stated few serial killers travel. Despite his description of a serial killer, the professor believed Holly's killer was more likely to be a sexually perverted member of the community who found an opportunity. He concluded his interview with,

"The last place to look is with total strangers."

The professor's observations were chilling, but the police directed their investigations based on Levine's expertise.

The police remained 'tight lipped' and released minimal information regarding suspects and any indication of how and where Holly was killed. They confirmed she had been killed not long after she disappeared, and they were confident the killer was familiar with the winding roads of Sturbridge and Brimfield.

State Police Lt. Peter Higgins delivered a statement to the press.

"No indication of a struggle. No indication of anybody being here and no witnesses saw anything. We can speculate that a vehicle had to be used to get her out of that area in a very quick and timely manner so that no witnesses saw it."

Higgins continued, "I believe her abduction took just seconds. There could be more clues in the woods where she was found and we are continuing to search for microscopic evidence on her body and clothes."

The investigators were sure the killer knew where to go with Holly.

It was unlikely the abductor would choose to travel Route 20 because it was thickly populated and heavy traffic being controlled by several police because of the construction being performed at the time. The traffic accommodating commuters and tourists was literally 'stop and go'.

The investigators believed Holly was taken from the corner of Allen and South Shore roads, where Holly's sneaker was found. After taking a right turn lies a 16-mile road that ends on an old railroad bed beyond blasted out stone walls in the Brimfield woods.

"It's very easy to get there and you don't have to use Route 20," replied Real Poirier when D.A. William Bennett paid him a visit. Poirier's house is directly across Five Bridge Road where Holly's remains were discovered.

Poirier added, "My opinion is it has to be a fisherman, not a hunter." He believed the killer might well be among the hundreds who hold state Fisheries and Wildlife sporting licenses in Brimfield and Sturbridge.

"A fisherman...he's going to be looking for a place. The hunters walk all over hell, but fishermen look."

Over the following several days, the family remained secluded.

Tina expressed relief that Holly was coming home.

Rick felt sorrow, not anger. He felt anger would do no good. He had held on to the hope that Holly would be found alive and not in a 'dumping ground'. Rick's sorrow soon evolved into anger.

As the family gathered, they shared their own memories of Holly.

Mary Cooper, Holly's maternal grandmother spoke of Holly's plans to become a marine biologist and live in Florida or California. She smiled as she reflected on fond memories.

"She's like a piece of my soul."

All agreed; Holly was an exceptional little girl. She was articulate and a budding perfectionist with an endless range of interests.

In addition to sharing Holly's memory, the family began the necessary arrangements for Holly's funeral.

The arrangements were particularly difficult because the burial date could not be determined until Holly's remains were released.

Mary Cooper took Andy and Zachary shopping for appropriate clothes for the service. On the way to the store, Andy asked his grandmother "Is it all right to be angry?"

Mrs. Cooper replied, "Whatever you feel is all right. Some days you will be mad, but Holly is in heaven now and you can talk to her whenever you want. She can hear you."

The family of Holly Piirainen was at odds with the Hampden County District Attorney's office. They'd received no information since Holly's remains were found five days earlier and were growing increasingly upset by a breakdown in communication. The D.A. discouraged callers from using a toll-free number established by the family's private investigator.

In addition, family members were angry that the District Attorney's office failed to notify them, before the press, that the remains found were positively identified as Holly.

Maureen Lemieux contacted the state police and demanded answers. Upon her insistence, a meeting was scheduled to meet with state police officials in an effort to bring the family up to date on any information and developments of the case.

It appeared the police were deliberately cutting the family out of the investigation.

William Bennett, District Attorney of Hampden County insisted the only number to call to be certain the state police investigators have all information was the police telephone number.

Holly's family had requested the public call the toll-free number for their private investigator Carl Westerman. The State Police publicly discouraged any contact directly to the investigator.

In response, Maureen Lemieux stated the toll free number would remain and people could use their own judgment about which number to call.

"It's more important to catch this person than to let egos get in the way."

Carl Westerman assured the family he would continue to staff the toll-free number for tips. At that time, Westerman continued to receive $1,000 a week, allocated from the fund set up for Holly's family.

He claimed he was receiving the same amount of calls he had received before the body was found, but would not disclose just how many that was.

Jeff Malone, the investigator from a Texas based non-profit organization had spent time in Sturbridge during the search. He learned of Holly's discovery and contacted the authorities.

Upon his return to Dallas, Malone created a profile of the killer and now offered it to Lt. Timothy Hackett of the Massachusetts State Police. Authorities would not comment on the profile, and it was doubtful they would make it available to the public.

arly in the investigation, Rick Piirainen was a suspect. He later said he was too concerned about helping the investigation to be offended. The authorities explained they had to question Holly's father in order to reply to those who would say, 'the father did it'.

Rick was surprisingly tolerant to what turned out to be an all-day interrogation by police beginning in Auburn, MA and ending hours later in Northborough, MA with the lie detector test.

The battery of questions and the ensuing tests were thoroughly explained to Rick. Once the tests were analyzed by the administrator, all law enforcement involved with the case were certain Rick Piirainen was not a suspect in the case.

He continued to have the guilt of letting Holly out of his sight and now believed it was bad judgment on his part. The police offered their understanding and assured him he was not negligent. They told Rick that he could not keep his daughter "on a string," and they believed he was a cautious, caring parent.

Upon learning what Rick had been subjected to, the family was outraged. Rick calmed them down by explaining the purpose and necessity of the questioning and subsequent lie detector test.

"They didn't want to waste any resources tracking down my alibis. It was understandable when you think about it. The only ones present when Holly was taken were Zach and Andy. I had no adult to back up my story."

Within a few days, Ed Lemieux, Holly's grandfather, along with Rick's two brothers-in-law would be asked to submit to a polygraph. They too were eliminated as potential suspects.

Another obstacle was thrown into the path of the grieving family.

Based on the timeframe they had been given, Holly's funeral was arranged to take place on the weekend of November 6, 1993.

Once again, the family was put off by the state officials. The family had been advised it would take 10 days from October 23 for Holly's remains to be turned over. Based on that information, Holly's funeral arrangements were scheduled to take place on Friday and Saturday at St. Phillip's Church. Another set back, due to what Lt. Hackett described as, "a little bit of conflict in communications."

The funeral arrangements were placed on hold pending the release of Holly's remains. Prolonging the inevitable served to keep the grievous wounds exposed, preventing any start of the healing process.

When each day ended, family members left the Grafton home that had become the gathering place.

Silence and the stillness of the night enveloped Rick Piirainen. The days kept him busy, but at night, the memories of Holly crept inside Rick's broken heart. The grief, fear and guilt that plagued him and dominated his emotions nearly every moment of the day seemed to subside in the late night and pre-dawn hours.

Rick pictured Holly, Zack and Andy when they had gone cave exploring at Purgatory Chasm in

Sutton. He smiled as he remembered how Holly loved riding his four-wheeler with him through the woods in Grafton and how she loved to swim.

Suddenly his visions would abruptly flip to scenarios of the abduction, and his mind became chaotic. The precious moments would be short lived and shift to horror of the present. He worried about the safety of his two boys, and the nightmare would play repeatedly in his mind.

Rick's persona changed from quiet, easy going, and fun loving, to suspicious, watchful and the inability to trust anyone. He looked at each friend and neighbor and wondered if that person murdered his child. He considered that abduction by someone Holly knew might explain why no one heard her scream.

Tuesday, November 9, 1993

Holly Kristen Piirainen's obituary ...

Holly Kristen Piirainen of Grafton died Aug. 5 in Brimfield. She was 10. Born in Worcester, she lived in Grafton since 1986. She was a fifth-grader at Grafton Intermediate School where she was a member of the school chorus.

Miss Piirainen was a member of St. Phillips Church and attended Confraternity of Christian Doctrine Education classes there. She received her First Communion in 1991 and the Sacrament of Reconciliation this year. She was also involved in the Girl Scouts of America in Grafton.

She is survived by her parents, Richard Piirainen and Christine Harrington of Grafton; two brothers, Andrew and Zachary; paternal grandmother and grandfather,

Maureen and Edward Lemieux of Grafton; maternal grandmother and step-grandfather, Mary and Stephen Cooper of Chatham; paternal great-grandparents, Maurice F. and Cecile Murphy of Worcester; maternal great-grandparents, Ovis Harrington of Brownsville, VT, and Elizabeth Grouke of Worcester, several aunts, uncles, and cousins.

A funeral mass will be celebrated at 10 a.m., Saturday at St. Philip's Church, corner of Church and West streets, Grafton. Memorial contributions may be made to the Holly Piirainen Memorial Scholarship Fund in care of Grafton Suburban Credit Union, North Grafton Shoppers Mart, North Grafton.

Burial will be private at the request of the family.

Grafton Police Chief Russell Messier put a plan in place to allow a smooth flow of traffic, making Church St. a one-way street to accommodate the anticipated traffic. State Police and police from other communities would assist with the traffic control. The police department would absorb the cost of the additional manpower.

The wake was scheduled to accommodate a large number who would pass through on their way home from work. The usual two hours were extended to four.

Mourners arrived at St. Phillip's Church to attend the wake of 10-year-old Holly Kristen Piirainen.

Outside the church, friends, family and even strangers placed pink ribbons in a wagon beside a sign "In loving memory of Holly Piirainen. May she rest in peace." Nearby a large photo of Holly urged prayers for her. The pink ribbons were handed out as a symbol of hope for the safe return of Holly.

Children wearing green Grafton school jackets to bikers wearing leather jackets were among the hundreds entering the church.

As they entered, they were greeted with a collage of photos of a Holly blowing bubbles and playing with her friends. In one, she was dressed in a white dress, and all reflected a happy, smiling 10-year-old.

Holly's parents, grandparents, aunts, and uncles received hundreds of mourners. They stood near a small white casket draped with pink flowers. Floral arrangements flanked Holly's casket.

Some mourners embraced the grief-stricken family; some simply lowered their heads and took a seat.

They came from around the state; license plates indicated Connecticut, New Hampshire, Vermont and New York.

As each somber visitor left, they were handed a pink carnation and a prayer card. The card read, in part, *"With deep gratitude for your support and prayers"* - The family of Holly.

The following day, under cold and gloomy skies, a white hearse, followed by three white limousines arrived at St. Phillips Church.

Holly's family were escorted to their seats. Hundreds of friends, relatives and even strangers bowed their heads as the family passed each pew.

Barbara Pryor sat close to the family. Her 9-year-old daughter, Sarah vanished while walking near her Wayland home in 1985. Beside Mrs. Pryor was Mark Russ of Frankfort, N.Y. Russ represented the family of 12-year-old Sara Anne Wood who was abducted from a rural area in New York State 13 days after Holly disappeared.

Neither Sarah Pryor nor Sara Anne Wood have ever been found.

Six men in gray suits wheeled the white casket as the entrance hymn "Wind Beneath My Wings" resounded throughout the crowded church. The coffin was placed before the altar.

The Mass began as tears were wiped from the eyes of the family, and all in attendance.

In a quavering voice, Father Marteka delivered a sermon.

"God did not will Holly's death. Man abused his capacity to love and chose to do evil. In the process we greatly suffered from this evil."

The cracked voice of the priest acknowledged faith would not wipe out grief. He continued, "The deeper our love, the deeper our grief will be."

He recalled Holly on the day of her First Communion three years before in the same spot where her coffin rested.

Following the sermon, Holly's two brothers, Zachary and Andrew followed by her cousins delivered the offertory gifts.

Holly's cousin, Leah Jolin stood before the hundreds in attendance. Leah was 13 and Holly's closest cousin. The young girl fought back her tears and addressed the mourners in a clear, precise tone.

Her Journey's Just Begun

Don't think of her as gone away-Her journey's just begun
Life holds so many facets-This earth is only one.
Just think of her as resting, from the sorrows and the tears
In a place of warmth and comfort, where there are no days
or years.
Think how she must be wishing that we could know today,
How nothing but our sadness can really pass away.
Think of her as living in the hearts of those she touched...
For nothing loved is ever lost and she was loved so much.

E. Benneman

The Mass ended and all stood as the six pallbearers escorted Holly on her final journey.The burial was private, and at least 40 cars followed the hearse and limousines to the burial. Several state troopers, dressed in plain clothes attended the funeral. Reporters were required to show identification.

The casket was completely covered with pink ribbons. Children had rested numerous ribbons on Holly's coffin as it was lowered into the ground.

Placed in the coffin with Holly's remains were her favorite porcelain dolls, letters from her cousins and friendship necklaces from two close friends who never had a chance to give them to her.

As the coffin lowered, the family embraced. Holly was finally at peace. She would never be forgotten.

A reception at the church followed the burial.

Rick Piirainen expressed he could try to forgive Holly's killer. He explained, "I would have to forgive if I want to go to heaven myself where Holly is."

"My personal belief is that Holly's killer is still in the area and could be right here among us."

Rick Piirainen's statement was chilling Two plainclothes State Police detectives watched for signs of a suspect amidst the throng of mourners.

Rich removed his jacket and tie and moved among those who attended the reception.

He seemed to be at ease when talking about Holly. He said Holly's grave was near a hill used for sledding.

"When the winter winds blow snow, I'll take Zach and Andy to visit the hill and remember Holly's laughter and delight in outdoor activities."

Rick's attention turned to the arrest of a prime suspect in the Polly Klaas abduction, murder in California. For a few moments he hoped the suspect in the Klaas case may have jumped around the country.

His hopes faded. He empathized with the Klaas family and sincerely knew exactly how they felt.

The search continued on a lead-to-lead basis.

Rick expressed the tragedy was far from over. "It still is a full-time job for us. I don't have the cards coming in and the phone calls as I did before. But, people are still out there looking for that missing link."

Friends of the Piirainen family set up a missing-children's foundation in Holly's memory.

The foundation would advise others on what things to look for, people to watch out for and how necessary it is to keep track of every detail.

On behalf of Holly's family, Rick expressed his sincere appreciation to all who helped with the search for Holly and all who offered emotional and spiritual support.

"Savor the moments you have," he advised. "People should think about how much they really have."

Angels from heaven, they make your life great... They've known you since you were born. They will be with you always...

-Holly Kristen Piirainen

The funeral of Holly Piirainen marked the one year anniversary of the disappearance of Jamie Lusher. There were still no answers. Driving to work each morning had turned into a haunting experience for Joanne Levakis and James Lusher.

The parents of Jamie Lusher traveled daily in two different directions but both spend at least a part of their daily drive coping with feelings of grief generated by the sight of teen-agers riding bikes.

One year had passed and the grief remained near the surface of his parents. Jamie had still not been found. The Westfield police acted on a lead-to-lead basis, but after a year, the leads were few, if any.

Jamie's father did most of his thinking about Jamie during the 40-minute drive to work. There was not a day that went by over the past year when he didn't think about his son and he anguished over his failure to confirm Jamie's whereabouts earlier.

Both James Lusher and Joanne Levakis had remained certain their son was abducted and did not run away.

Although a year had passed, both parents held on to the belief they might see Jamie safe and alive some day. Others did not share the undying hopes of Jamie's parents.

For the other members of Jamie's family hope was faint and they conformed to the belief that the worst had befallen Jamie.

The Jamie Lusher case continued to baffle detectives in Westfield. In almost a decade, there had been only one homicide and there had not been an unsolved case for as long as anyone could remember.

Jamie's parents were still struggling with the detective's reluctance to classify the case as abduction. The closest they would acknowledge a year later was that a kidnapping might be a possibility, though they still were not certain.

Lt. John Camerota was particularly interested in Jamie's case. He had made it a practice to look through Jamie's case file every day, but it was to no avail. Occasionally, Captain Avonti would discuss the case with the detectives.

"I've been here 21 years and this is the most baffling case I can think of. It continually plagues the department. I wish we could have found more."

Mr. Lusher often wondered what he could have done different. He lived with the guilt that if he had taken Jamie to his grandmother's house, Jamie would be safe today.

Memories of Jamie were evident in the homes of both parents. Jamie's room at his father's home remained untouched, after a year. On several occasions, James Lusher asked Jamie's sister Jennifer to help pack everything up, but Jennifer was hesitant to do it and it remained untouched.

Maybe, deep down, James Lusher did believe Jamie would return.

CHAPTER 7

Three years had passed since the Bernardo homicide. Jimmy's body was discovered in a wooded area of New York State, 200 miles from his home in Pittsfield, MA. The 12-year-old boy's murder remained unsolved.

In 1992, acting Police Chief Spadefero was relieved from the temporary position and Pittsfield Police Lieutenant Gerald Lee became the newly appointed Chief of Police.

The citizens of Pittsfield gradually returned to their normal lives. The Bernardo family lived with the heartache and anguish inflicted from the loss of their oldest son, suffering with the wound that would never heal. Jimmy's killer remained free, and the Bernardo family remained locked in a prison of agonizing grief.

On a blustery Friday morning, January 7, 1994 a 12-year-old girl walked quickly, through downtown Pittsfield making her way to school.

Suddenly, in broad day light, Rebecca Saverese was approached from behind by a gun-wielding stranger.

The gunman pressed a small handgun into the girl's side and told her to walk to his truck parked across the street.

"Just do what I tell you, and everything will be okay," the stranger whispered close to Rebecca's ear.

"You know I have a gun," he said.

"Yeah, I know, I see the gun," replied the girl.

Within seconds, Rebecca appeared to be hyperventilating and breathing became difficult. Her wheezing progressively worsened as she sat on the curbing.

Her armed attacker grabbed the girl's backpack attempting to force her to stand, but the fast thinking 12-year-old slipped out of the shoulder strap and ran up the street to a man shoveling snow at a bank parking lot. The man quickly led Rebecca to a telephone to call the police.

A bewildered, pudgy, scruffy-looking man, still clutching the backpack slid the pistol into his pocket and headed for his truck.

A motorist stopped at a traffic light witnessed the near deadly encounter.

Russell Davis hadn't seen the gun and assumed it was a father and daughter engaged in a disagreement. When Rebecca bolted, running down the street and her abductor scurried to his truck, Davis became suspicious and followed the truck long enough to obtain a partial license plate number and an accurate description of the vehicle. When Davis noticed the man driving the dark blue truck ran two red lights, he knew something was wrong and turned into a gas station where he spotted a police officer and reported the incident..

With the partial plate number and description of the truck, the police ran the information through their database. The number of 'matches' were abundant; however, when narrowed down to the greater Pittsfield area, they were able to determine the owner to be Phillip Shallies, Lanesboro, MA.

Russell Davis, using an Ident-a-kit, was able to create a composite of the man he saw trying to get the young girl into his truck.

Armed with the composite and the vehicle description, Detective Owen Boyington drove to the small suburb just north of Pittsfield. As he drove down Summer St. to the residence of Mr. Shallies, he spotted the dark blue pick-up truck parked in the driveway. Boyington continued up the road, turned around and as he passed the truck, confirmed the registration number.

Because Lanesboro is out of the jurisdiction of the Pittsfield police, Boyington radioed the local police and asked an officer to accompany him back to the Shallies' residence.

The two officers were greeted by Phillip Shallies. Mr. Shallies identified himself and confirmed he was the owner of the dark blue truck parked in his driveway. The officers offered the composite to Mr. Schallies who bared no resemblance to the man they were looking for.

"Sorry officer, I'm legally blind, and it's difficult for me to see what you're showing me here," said Shallies when Boyington handed the composite to the middle-aged man.

"Do you live here alone, Mr. Shallies?" asked the Lanesboro officer.

"No, my mother lives here. She too is blind," replied Shallies.

Just then, a man approached the inquiring officers asking, "What seems to be the problem here, can I help you?"

Boyington quickly glanced at the composite and back at the man approaching the doorway. It was uncanny; the composite was an identical match.

"What's your name sir," asked the Lanesboro officer.

"Lewis Lent, what can I do for you?"

The officer asked if Lent had been driving the truck parked in the driveway and Lent confirmed that he had. Next, Boyington turned to Mr. Schallies and asked if he would object to the officers taking a look inside the truck. Without hesitation, Schallies gave his 'ok'.

While the Lanesboro officer looked through the cab of the truck, Boyington stayed on the doorstep keeping a close eye on the two men in the doorway.

Lying on the front seat, in clear view, was Rebecca's backpack. Further search revealed a small firearm.

The officer returned to the house and asked Lent to step outside. Lewis stepped forward complying with the officer's request.

"We'd like to take you to the Pittsfield Police Station to ask you a few questions."

Lewis Lent was complacent and agreed to accompany the officers

Once Lent was inside the cruiser, the two officers talked privately beyond earshot of the small man seated in the patrol car.

"There's a backpack, a box of candy bars, and under the seat a gun, appears to be a .22-caliber handgun. Is that enough for you?"

"You bet it is," replied Boyington and with that, they headed for Pittsfield.

Once Lent was in custody, the detectives contacted Russell Davis and Rebecca Saverese. The 12-year-old was asked to identify her attacker in a police line up.

Rebecca was an exceptionally courageous girl. She arrived at the police department and positively identified Lewis Lent. In a separate viewing, Russell Davis also selected the 5'6 spectacled Lewis Lent without a moment's hesitation.

Detective Anthony Riello took the opportunity to talk with Rebecca.

"You must have been very frightened, how did you summon the courage you did to get away?"

"I learned it from the D.A.R.E. program, sir," the girl replied.

"I remembered what you told us; the three R's. *Recognize Refuse* and *Report*. Don't you remember?"

"I pretended I was having an asthma attack. As if I couldn't breath and sat on the curb like I was gasping for air. When he grabbed my backpack, I just slipped out of the straps and ran."

Detective Riello gave the girl a gentle squeeze and smiled,

"I'm very proud of you Rebecca. You have made the D.A.R.E. program worthwhile and you've proven how necessary it is to continue. You're a role model for all other children who might find themselves in a life threatening situation."

The detective was genuinely impressed with the fast thinking on the part of this young girl who had remembered his words. The D.A.R.E. session she referred to had taken place almost two years before!

Lewis Lent was read his rights, and officially under arrest for the attempted kidnapping of Rebecca Saverese. Without protest or opposition, he cooperated as the police proceeded with the arrest process. He was charged with kidnapping, armed robbery, and assault with a deadly weapon.

Lent was led to a small interrogation room to be questioned. Chief Gerald Lee, Detective McGuire, and Detective Owen Boyington were present.

It was around 4:30 p.m. when the three men joined Lewis Lent at the small table and began asking Lent about the event that had occurred earlier that day. Their questioning began as a casual conversation to enable the interrogators to get a feel for the manner of the accused.

"I'm hungry, can I get something to eat?" asked Lent.

"Sure, Lewie, what would you like? We'll send out for something."

"How about a Coke and some candy bars?"

The officers asked the curious looking man if he'd like a meal. He only wanted a Coke and candy bars. That would continue to be his diet whenever food was offered or requested.

Replying to the questions posed by the police, Lent showed little concern. He provided information concerning his employment, address, previous addresses, and all he could think of in between.

"What were you thinking when you approached the girl? What did you plan to do with Rebecca Saverese?" asked McGuire.

"Well, she fit into my master plan. I've been working on the plan for months, and the girl this morning was going to be the first."

McGuire pressed the suspect, "Tell us about your 'master plan' Lewie. Can you explain what it consists of?"

"Sure, I've been building these shelves, sort of like drawers, but they're shelves. I was going to collect young girls, with dark brown hair. Each would have their own drawer, well, shelf and I could keep them there. I wasn't going to kill any of them, just collect them."

The scenario Lent was offering to his interrogators was far beyond anything a rational mind could possibly comprehend. His 'master plan' was to collect young girls and keep them on shelves so they would be available to him whenever he experienced a fantasy, or some perverted desire.

Lent explained the plan of his as if it were totally reasonable, and commonplace. McGuire fell short of accusing Lent of 'playing with their heads'. What he was describing was far too outrageous. It surpassed even a Stephen King novel.

As the hours passed, the information offered by Lent was passed on to officers within the department and fed into the national databases. Inquiries were received from police departments in Vermont, New Hampshire, New York as well as Massachusetts all interested in any possibility Lent could be linked to their respective unsolved cases.

At one point, the Chief asked McGuire and Boyington, to join him in his office.

"Let's take a break Lewie," said Chief Lee. "Just relax, we'll be right back. You want anything?"

"Yeah, I'll have another one of these," he replied holding up an empty soda can. Lent was left alone in the small room. A police officer stood just outside the door.

The Chief addressed the detectives gathered in his office. He offered his thoughts concerning the unsolved murder of Jimmy Bernardo, which continued to baffle the task force for three years.

Considering information Lent had provided regarding his frequent visits to his parents home in New York State, Chief Lee believed delving into the Bernardo case would be appropriate.

Several neighboring states were interested in the past activities of Lewis Lent and the Chief believed the Pittsfield Police should also take a closer look into the Sara Anne Wood disappearance

Phone calls contacted the Mass. State Police, the FBI, and Captain Frank Pace of New York State Police. They were expected to arrive in Pittsfield within hours. Berkshire County District Attorney, Gerard Downing was on his way to the station.

The unassuming, peculiar looking suspect sat alone as the wheels churned just outside the door. In the next twenty-four hours, the task force members would arrive and Lewis Lent would be the focus of every law enforcement agency in as many as four states.

The interrogation of Lewis Lent would reveal the maniacal behavior of a complex, tangled mind. The most seasoned detectives were about to witness the revelations and admissions of a perverted predator.

The questions were posed in a casual nature, addressing the suspect as 'Lewie'.

When the Chief broached the subject of Jimmy Bernardo, Lewie began to respond in the third person.

"Well, if I were the one that killed him, I would have..." he would say, speaking hypothetically. This could not be considered a confession, but he was encouraged to continue. He needed little prodding from his interrogators; however, he would skirt potentially incriminating direct questions.

If the investigators were getting frustrated, it was not evident. They patiently listened to the rambling of Lent, hoping for an incriminating statement.

"Sometimes I do things, but I don't remember doing them. I have these, like blackouts and real bad headaches."

Lent tossed a new theory to the already complicated mix.

"I have this other person who is evil and tells me to do things and sometimes he takes over."

Was Lent implying he suffered from MPD, Multi Personality Disorder? The detectives were not buying the MPD Lent claimed to suffer and continued to give Lewie as much latitude needed.

Hours passed since their suspect was placed under arrest. Several members of the task force had arrived and each had opportunity to question Lent and witness his relatively demeanor attitude. Throughout the questioning, he never displayed a change in manner, which would be indicative of MPD if it actually existed.

The questioning ended for the day, to resume fresh the next morning. The information Lent provided would be the fodder to secure search warrants of his Hudson Street apartment, the theaters he worked as well as any vehicles he owned, or borrowed.

Detective Owen Boyington, accompanied by a Lanesboro police officer, returned to Lanesboro and advised Mr. Schallies his truck would be towed and impounded as evidence related to investigations being conducted. Boyington questioned the shocked Phillip Shallies about his friend Lewie.

Phillip Shallies said he met Lent about three years before. He said Lent would offer to drive him and his elderly mother on errands. He was always willing to lend a hand. Once he helped replace the foundation of his house, which was a two-year project.

"We all like Lewie," Shallies said. "He was always kind, polite and an even-tempered person."

Shallies' feelings for his friend changed once he learned of the arrest. "I feel like I've been abused and violated. He's just a Jekyll and Hyde. All the good he's done for us has been completely undone. I just don't know what else to say."

Shallies told the detective that Lent would sometimes drive the Oldsmobile belonging to the upstairs tenant. The 1983 Oldsmobile parked along side Shallies' truck belonged to Chester Forta.

As he spoke to the detective, Shallies recalled Lent being very concerned about cleaning out Forta's car, even vacuuming it, after using it. He said that was uncharacteristic of Lent who never even kept his own vehicle clean.

Shallies continued, "I never had an inkling of an idea that he was doing anything like this."

Phillip Shallies had spent time on a regular basis with Lent. "He was just a nice guy who was willing to help us around."

Phillip Shallies' mother offered her opinions of Lewis Lent.

Sarah Shallies stated, "We thought he was a great guy, a good friend. He was always willing to help or take us anywhere because both my son and I are blind. A person with a very nice character, very polite. He was well mannered and never gruff. I found him to be very even tempered, at least around us."

The elderly woman continued, "I've know him for three years. He used to talk about being a minister at some church over in Albany. I believed him when he said he had the license to marry and bury."

Mrs. Shallies concluded with, "Why, he didn't even drink or smoke."

Phillip Shallies told the detective about a conversation he had recently with Lewis during dinner.

"Somebody brought up the subject of Jimmy Bernardo's killing. An article in the newspaper reported that somebody else was being accused of killing the kid."

Shallies continued, "Lewie said, 'I hope they nail him.'"

"I should have suspected something by putting together the facts that Lewie worked at the theater and had relatives near where the Bernardo kid was found," Phillip Shallies concluded.

Boyington notified the owner of the Oldsmobile that it was being impounded as evidence. Mr. Forta had no comments to share about Lent. He was annoyed at the prospect of his car being removed but realized he had no choice. The two vehicles were towed and delivered to a secured impound yard.

An extensive search was conducted at Lent's apartment. Gaining access to the small apartment was simple. It was pitch dark when the officers entered. The windows were boarded with sheets of plywood preventing any light from entering. Feeling there way along the wall, they flipped the light switch. A dim overhead light barely illuminated the shabby living room area.

Unsure of exactly what they were looking for, the officers began looking around the cluttered room.

Floor to ceiling bookshelves displayed books of every subject. What was especially curious was the shelf reserved for an extensive collection of bibles.

Stacks of magazines and newspapers occupied every corner. The room was scantily furnished. The sofa, converted into a bed, was unmade.

Two locks secured the door leading to the bedroom. With the aid of a crowbar, the officers gained access to the mysterious room. In contrast to the first room, the intense lighting blinded the officers.

Approximately 30-50 plants were basking in the simulated sunlight provided by the high intensity lamps above them. Upon closer examination there was no doubt the thriving plants were marijuana. Plywood covered the one window just as the ones in the living room.

A plywood wall divided the room down the middle. Along the wall was a pile of 2x4's with a saw and sack of nails beside it. A partly constructed wooden box occupied the center of the room.

Under the bed, wrapped in a soiled quilt the officers discovered several firearms. Atop the dresser, various pieces of children's clothing were neatly folded.

The officers began filling evidence bags carefully labeling each with the date and location. One officer kept an inventory as the items were prepared for transport to the Police Station. Also noted were the items observed but too large to take into evidence.

Outside, curious neighbors congregated and could only speculate on the police activity. The accumulated evidence was loaded into two cruisers as a tow truck arrived and departed with Lent's vehicle on its clanging hook.

As the search was underway on Hudson St., North Adams, the Pittsfield Police Department extended their tentacles nationwide sending and retrieving information from as many as 39 states sharing information regarding Lewis Lent. Within hours, Lewis Lent's life was unfolding and a timeline of his whereabouts over several years began to take shape.

Townsend, Massachusetts, a small village located in Central Mass, near the New Hampshire border was among the cities and towns with unsolved abduction cases.

The small town had an unsolved case involving a 13-year-old. The girl's case dated back to 1977 and the circumstances of her disappearance were remarkably similar to that of Sara Anne Wood and Jimmy Bernardo. Countless unsolved child abductions were beginning to focus on Lewis Lent.

Eventually, many cold cases were brought to the forefront. Jamie Lusher, Holly Piirainen, and Sara Pryor were certain to be revisited.

Following the earlier interrogation, Lent returned to his cell. Chief Lee spoke to an officer who would be working the first shift. He instructed the officer to treat Lent with full cooperation and comply with any wishes he may express.

"Get him whatever he wants for breakfast. If he wants the paper, make sure he gets one, and I want you to be his 'new best friend'.

The officer looked a little puzzled as the Chief ordered this unusual treatment of the suspect in police custody.

"If he wants to use the phone, make sure you let him. We need him to develop a friendship with a cop, and you're going to be it."

The Chief had confidence in his plan. He believed Lent to be the type who had few friends, and perhaps he would be more talkative with his newly found 'cop friend'.

On Saturday morning, the police officer greeted Lewis Lent with an upbeat and pleasant, "Good morning, how you doing?"

"Not bad, I could use a more comfortable bed, but not bad. What time is it?" he asked.

The officer glanced at his watch and replied, "It's 7:35, we get up pretty early around here. You feel like breakfast?"

"Nah, I don't usually eat breakfast. I could use a soda though."

"You got it pal," replied the officer. "I'll be right back."

In a few minutes, the officer returned with a can of Coke and the morning edition of the Berkshire Eagle.

"Here you go. How they treating you? Should I call you Pastor? I hear you're a minister."

"No, just call me Lewie. What's your name?"

"Sgt. Cavanaugh*, but you can call me Charlie, nothing formal around here."

"Okay, Charlie, do I get to use the phone? I need to make a few calls. Can you find out when I get to use a phone?"

"No problem, I'll take you down myself. It's early; I don't think anyone's around that would object."

"Hey, thanks Charlie, I really appreciate that," replied Lent. Without hesitation, the officer led the prisoner down the hallway to the payphone.

"Got a quarter? They took all my stuff last night."

"Sure, here you go," replied the officer reaching into his pocket and handing Lent his change.

He walked a few feet back up the hallway, allowing Lent some privacy as he made his call. He admitted he would have liked to hear the conversation, but thought it would be wise to keep his distance.

Lent inserted a quarter and dialed. After a few moments, he slammed the phone down, muttering to himself. He glanced at the awaiting officer and turned his back to him. Again, he inserted a coin, dialed and soon began talking. The display of anger only a few minutes before dissipated and turned to a pleasant demeanor loud enough for the officer to detect a hint of laughter.

When the call ended, the officer escorted Lent back to his cell and started a casual conversation unrelated to the charges he'd been arrested for the day before.

Lent was responsive and appeared to enjoy the company of Sgt. Cavanaugh. After nearly an hour of 'chat', the officer announced he had to get some paperwork attended to. As he was leaving, he asked, "So Lewie, you going to talk today?"

"Yes," was the unexpected reply, "I'm ready to talk."

1994 was a winter of insurmountable snow. Law enforcement personnel traveling from New York to Pittsfield, MA was impeded and substantially delayed. Eventually, the three investigators arrived in Pittsfield and proceeded to the Allen Street station. They joined the awaiting members of the task force, Massachusetts State Police and Pittsfield Police detectives. In addition, Pittsfield's Chief Gerald Lee, Detective James McGuire, District

Attorney Downing, and Gerald Downs, of the FBI/ Springfield were present.

Requests for information regarding the arrest of Lent had been received throughout the last twelve hours. Authorities from as far as New Mexico as well as Florida had unsolved cases similar to the Bernardo murder and believed a connection to Lent was a possibility.

Not long into the questioning, Lewis Lent abandoned the "third person" dialogue.

His confession to the Bernardo murder and the subsequent rambling about an unidentified abduction of a child in Maine was chilling.

He detailed each step he took to accomplish his fiendish act. He described how Jimmy was 'just hanging around' the theatre on the night of October 22 and he (Lent) asked Jimmy to help him carry out the trash.

Once inside, Lent said he grabbed the boy, holding a small knife to his neck. He placed duct tape over his mouth because he was 'hollering obscenities' at me, and "I don't like that kind of talk."

He still had quite a bit of work to get done, so he bound Jimmy's hands and feet with the tape and kept him quiet while he finished cleaning.

As he brought the trash outside, he noticed Jimmy's distinctive Mongoose bike leaning against the building, and placed the bike in his van.

"The kid kept wiggling around on the floor. He was really trying to get loose, but I know how tight that tape is and no way was he going to get away."

The next statement sealed the validity of Lent's confession.

"Duct tape is really strong stuff, and I had the commercial strength tape, fire proof tape that I used when the seats in the theater got ripped. The fire code, you know in a public building."

The description of the type of tape used to bind Jimmy was never made known to the public. Only the killer could know it was fire retardant duct tape.

He told how he waited until all the Plaza stores were closed and the other theatres within the Cinema complex had emptied after the last showing. He described how difficult it was to pick up the bound and gagged 12-year-old.

"He wouldn't stop squirming, he just wouldn't give up."

He placed him in the van and drove directly to his Tyler Street apartment.

Struggling with the frightened boy made unlocking the door difficult, so he delivered a sharp blow to the boy's head which caused the boy to 'go limp' in his arms.

He carried the limp body of Jimmy Bernardo into the dark, dank apartment. No curtains hung in the two windows, but the sheets of plywood assured privacy from anyone attempting to see into the second floor apartment.

After he placed Jimmy on the sofa of the scantly furnished apartment, he removed the tape from his mouth. As Jimmy began to gain consciousness, Lent warned him to keep quiet or he'd replace the tape and put him into a closet.

The officers listened in disgust and anguish as Lent detailed his graphic depraved activity during the two weeks he held Jimmy captive in his apartment.

He finally recounted Jimmy's final day. Lent admitted to throwing the bike in the lake and proceeding to New York State with Jimmy bound and gagged.

Lent was familiar with the area and selected a road that led into the dense woods. He detailed the method he used to end the life of the young boy, there was no doubt; Lewis S. Lent was Jimmy Bernardo's killer.

"After I finished with the kid, I went to see my folks not far from there," Lent said.

Hours had passed, but nobody in the room seemed to be aware of the time.

A collective sigh came on the heels of the gruesome tale Lent had delivered.

A police officer wrote the confession on a yellow legal pad as Lent spoke. The officer quickly exited the room to get the hastily scribbled confession transcribed into a typed, word for word document to be presented to Lent for his signature.

Chief Lee suggested a break, and dismissed anyone who wanted to get something to eat. The stunned witnesses of the self-proclaimed child killer slowly exited and Lewis returned to his cell.

The case that had bewildered and frustrated an extensive task force for three years was brought to a conclusion and all because of an audacious act on the part of Lewis Lent.

If the incident with Rebecca Saverese had not occurred, it was anyone's guess how, if ever, Lent would have been apprehended.

All parties felt they were sitting on a time bomb. Would he 'give up' any others? What about Sara Anne Wood? Could the monster they had in custody be a serial child killer? The mere thought sent chills through the seasoned officers.

After a lengthy conference with all the departments represented, District Attorney Downing was prepared to conduct an additional interview with Lent with the hope he would confess to the disappearance of Sara Anne Wood.

Ample information was uncovered to tie Lent to Sara Anne Wood. They learned of Lewis Lent's frequent trips to New York to visit his family. The visits were in proximity to the location of Jimmy's body and the area where Sara Wood was last seen riding her bicycle.

Any preconceived notions of what a child killer and possibly a serial murderer should look like were quickly dispelled when the 5'6, curious looking man shuffled into the room.

His dark hair disheveled, he sported mutton chop sideburns and his hazel eyes were barely discernable through the thick lenses of his black rimmed glasses.

When all were seated, Lent was given his Constitutional rights, as he had been on several occasions throughout his previous sessions.

He spoke on his own volition and continued to waive his rights indicating that in Lent's mind, the game was up. He made it very clear he wished to discuss everything.

The investigator from New York began.

The self-proclaimed evangelistic minister reverted back to the 'third person' dialogue he had introduced in his initial questioning the night before.

He claimed to suffer from blackouts, and severe headaches.

"I think that's when the evil one comes out and takes over."

He called his alter ego 'Stephen'.

"Stephen makes me do bad stuff. He takes control over me, and sometimes I don't remember things. He's the evil one, I'm the kind one."

All present listened to the ramblings of the confessed killer. They suspected he was maligning because of certain types of reading material seized from his apartment the night before. One in particular addressed T*he Phenomenon of Multi Personality Disorder.* Another, *The Hillside Strangler*, the killer, Kenneth Bianchi claimed to possess a dual personality and referred to his alter ego as Stephen.

Once he concluded his explanation of the multiple personality disorder he claimed to be experiencing, Chief Lee posed a direct question.

"Lewie, what can you tell us about Sara Anne Wood?"

Lent thought for a few minutes, and replied,

"What about her?"

"We were hoping you could tell us if you had anything to do with her disappearance last August. She was last seen up in New York, around your neck of the woods. Not far from where your folks live. Does that help you remember?"

"Let me think, ah, let's see, last August. Yeah, I can tell you about her. I was up there visiting my folks in August."

All were silent in anticipation of a second confession in as many days.

District Attorney Downing interjected.

"Lewie, you understand your rights?"

"Yes, I've waived them a dozen times. I understand my rights."

An air of skepticism lingered throughout the room. How much credence could be paid to another voluntary confession? Was it possible they were about to listen to a 'false confession' from an unemployed high school dropout, who picked up odd jobs here and there; a little man who was nobody, but would surely enjoy the opportunity to be in the limelight.

Again, all listened intently for something that would connect Lent to the abduction and presumed murder of Sara Anne Wood.

Lent began his rambling assuming the 'evil one' named Stephen's personality.

Speaking in the third person, he recounted his activities of August 18 in New York State. He described how hot the weather was that day. How he had intended to visit his parents, but decided to 'drive around for awhile'. He had his 'murder bag' with him, which he never left home without.

He told how he had 'up-graded' the bag just before that hot August day, purchasing a pick and shovel at a local hardware store. He carried his tools in his van at all times. Also added to his 'murder bag' was a small handgun. The one he had threatened Rebecca Saverese with the previous morning, in broad day light.

"We (referring to 'Stephen') drove around and were getting pretty bored. We spotted this girl with bluish shorts on and a pink shirt. She was by herself picking up a bunch of books and papers she dropped on the ground."

He paused for a few minutes seemingly to refresh his memory of that day. When he continued the story, he dropped the 'Stephen' personality and continued in the first person.

"I just pulled over and helped her pick up her stuff. She asked me if I could fix the chain on her bike. I looked at it, it would have taken a couple of minutes to fix it, so I told her I had to get my tools from my van."

The New York investigator shot a glance at Chief Lee, then interrupted Lewis to ask, "Lewie, she wasn't riding her bike when you first saw her?"

"No, I told you, the chain was broken. She couldn't ride it."

That was it! The information withheld from the public. Even Sara's family was unaware of the broken chain on Sara's bicycle.

"Okay, Lewie, and then what. What did you do next?"

"Well, she walked over to the van with me. Boy, it was hot that day. I remember because I had the windows down and had to roll them up when I put the girl in. She was a lot easier to handle than the boy was.

"Did you tie her up too?" The investigator asked, keeping an even tone. "She must have given you some resistance."

"I did tape her wrists. She couldn't do much with her hands bound. Then I showed her my gun and she started to cry. I guess the gun really scared her. After that, she just whimpered and sniveled."

"I was just going to ride around for awhile, you know, just keep her with me for company. I think that's when 'Stephen' said to kill her and bury her."

"Stephen? The evil one?" asked Chief Lee.

"Yeah, I don't remember exactly."

"I took her back to my apartment overnight and then drove her back and killed her."

Keeping an even tone, which was difficult to do after listening to Lent's admission of the murder. The investigator asked, "Why did you kill her Lewie?"

Lent did not respond.

The investigator asked, "How did you kill her?"

"I hit her with a log," Lent replied.

The room became silent. Lent's elbows were on the table, his hands supporting his head. He removed the thick glasses and rubbed his eyes, appearing to be in pain.

"I'm getting a headache; I get them a lot lately."

"Can we get you something? You want to take a break?" asked Detective McGuire.

"No thanks, I could use a cold soda," Lent replied.

"Sure, we could all stand a little break. We'll take you back to your cell so you can lie down for awhile," the Chief suggested, gesturing to the officer posted at the door.

The officer escorted Lent to his cell. Questioning would resume later in the day.

Detective James McGuire visited the Bernardo family to inform them of Lewis Lent's arrest. The news they had waited to hear for three years was bittersweet.

Mr. Bernardo stated, "We are relieved after three long years we have some conclusion. More importantly, our Jimmy can finally rest in peace. We also hope that some other families can find the same sense of peace."

Sara Anne Wood's family was notified. Their immediate response was, "Where is she? Can we finally bring her home?"

The police did not have the answers to those questions.

CHAPTER 8

Sunday, January 11, 1994

SUSPECT HELD IN SLAYING OF CHILD

The attempted abduction of a 12-year-old Pittsfield girl led to the arrest of a North Adams man. During questioning of the attempted abduction, it has been reported, Lewis S. Lent of North Adams has confessed to the slaying of Jimmy Bernardo in 1990. His body was discovered a month later in New York State. Lent is suspected in the August disappearance of Sara Anne Wood, assumed dead but yet to be found...

The Pittsfield Police Headquarters would have been well served had they installed a revolving door to accommodate the influx of citizens arriving to offer information about the man they knew as Lewie.

Once the news of Lewis Lent appeared across the front page of the Berkshire Eagle, the police department was flooded with calls from concerned citizens wanting to know more. The police declined to offer any more than what was reported in the paper.

Once Lewis Lent was arraigned, further information would be available. Until then, the police remained silent.

Gerard Downing was a very seasoned, astute district attorney. The press was persistent and questioned repeatedly whether Lent actually confessed to the Bernardo murder. Downing was careful in the use of legal terms, and replied,

"He made statements in the nature of admission."

Captain Frank Pace of the New York Police had questioned the suspect. He too was cautious when addressing the media and stopped short of saying Lent confessed to the murder of Jimmy Bernardo.

Pace stated, "Certain statements have led us to believe he is the Bernardo boy's killer."

The Captain continued,

"Mr. Lent is the prime suspect in the abduction and presumed killing of Sara Anne Wood in upstate New York last summer."

"We are looking into links to unsolved cases."

A few days later, Jimmy Bernardo's grandfather appeared at a brief press conference in downtown Pittsfield. He thanked the Pittsfield police, the FBI and the New York State Police.

The elderly Bernardo made a statement to the citizens of Pittsfield.

"You picked us up when we were down and made us believe that justice would be done."

He addressed the press for their continued coverage of his grandson's disappearance and slaying but asked that the family be left alone.

"The whole family is tired, physically and emotionally."

He left the room without taking any questions.

North Adams, the smallest city in Massachusetts is located about 20 miles north of Pittsfield. A once thriving and industrial community, North Adams weathered the economical hardships a declining major industry often leaves in its wake.

In January 1991, Lewis S. Lent and his 16-year-old nephew, Jonathan moved from Tyler Street, Pittsfield to the second floor apartment at 18 Hudson Street, North Adams. As he unloaded his van and lugged his belongings to the second floor, Lent's young neighbor offered to help.

His neighbors on the first floor were a single mom and two children. Stephen Domenichini was 10 and his sister Monica was eight.

Stephen was a willing helper and spent most of the day assisting his new neighbor unload and carry personal belongings as well as a few pieces of furniture to the second floor. Half way into the day, Lewis ordered pizza for Stephen and Jonathan.

As they took a break and sat on the back stairway, Lewis and Stephen chatted and got to know each other. Stephen took an immediate liking to Lewis. Jonathan was also friendly, but quiet.

Lewis Lent spoke in a soft voice and connected with Stephen with his wit and ability to convey a sincere interest in the young boy.

When Stephen's mother arrived home, Stephen was pleased to introduce Lewis Lent as 'my friend Lew'. Linda Domenichini was cordial, but somewhat cautious toward the stranger taking residency upstairs.

Lewis was 5'6, disheveled-looking with thick glasses and heavy mutton-chop sideburns. His glasses often slid down his nose giving him a comedic appearance.

In a short time, Lewis Lent and Stephen became fast friends. Stephen looked up to Lewis as both a big brother and perhaps, at times the father he had never known.

Monica had very little to do with the tenants upstairs. She was only eight and had no interest in the company of Lewis Lent, Jonathan Wood and Jonathan's girlfriend Missy who lived nearby, but spent most of her time with Jonathan.

Over the months that followed, Lewis Lent won over the cautious mother and her suspicious concerns were dissipated. Linda Domenichini's attitude evolved into a trusting friendship. Stephen appeared to be happier; Lewis included Stephen in projects of interest to a young boy, and Stephen was eager to learn skills his mother was not equipped to offer.

Lewis was a skilled handyman and always available to help with any household repairs. He made it a point to include Stephen and instruct him as he performed any necessary repairs.

Linda thought of him as the all-American neighbor. Because he worked nights as a janitor at the Pittsfield Cinema Center, he was conveniently available to the needs of anyone requiring his skills.

Lewis began taking Stephen on day trips to visit friends and attend events in neighboring towns and frequent trips to Mt. Greylock. They would drive to the summit of the Mohawk Trail and Lewis was always enthralled with the panoramic view.

Longer trips would include attending various events offered at the Knickerbockers Arena in Albany, N.Y. Eventually, Lewis and Stephen began to travel to visit Lewis's family in Ithaca, New York. On those occasions, they would stay overnight. In subsequent interviews, Stephen would say he slept at Lewis's mother's house, but Lewis preferred to sleep in the van.

Linda came to depend on Lewis's help. On one occasion, Stephen had a doctor's appointment and Lewis, knowing Linda would have to take time off from work, offered to take Stephen to his appointment. On the way home, Lewis stopped at the local pharmacy to pick up the prescribed medication, and paid for it himself, never asking for reimbursement from Linda.

That was just one of many occasions Lewis Lent displayed his generosity and selflessness to the Domenichini family and others in the neighborhood.

Linda soon came to think of Lewis Lent, 'Lewie' as extended family. He spent holidays with her family and accepted the numerous invitations to join the Domenichini's for dinner.

The North Adams neighborhood was shocked upon learning the news of Lent's arrest. As they read the charges Lewis Lent faced, they were in total disbelief. Their thoughts immediately turned to Stephen Domenichini and the inordinate amount of time he spent with Lewis Lent.

Nobody could have been more horrified than Linda Domenichini as she stared at the Sunday edition of the Berkshire Eagle laid on the table before her. Her hands trembled as she lit a cigarette. She sat at the table and for a few seconds, stared at the incomprehensible headlines glaring before her. This can't be, it must be a mistake, she thought.

As a mother, Linda was guilt ridden over the devastating news and much more painful, was her son's sense of betrayal by his best friend. How could she have allowed Lewis Lent into her life?

The paper described Lewis Lent, 43, of 18 Hudson Street, North Adams. What followed caused Linda Domenichini to sob uncontrollably.

"Lewis Lent has admitted involvement in the 1990 murder of Jimmy Bernardo and is the prime suspect in the abduction and presumed killing of Sara Anne Wood."

She read those words over and over. Her thoughts of Stephen, alone with Lewis, were more than she could comprehend.

Was Stephen slated to be his next victim? Did Lent confide in Stephen about these murders? Her mind raced with questions, and concern for Stephen.

Stephen was a normal 12-year-old and described by his mother, teachers and neighbors as a 'good kid'. He excelled in school and was never a disciplinary problem.

As a single mom, Linda always felt Stephen was deprived of a male role model in his life. He had never known his father and Linda was pleased with the relationship that had begun two years ago believing Lewis was the perfect fit for Stephen. She hoped the close friendship that had developed would fill that void in Stephen's life; how could she have been so mislead?

My God! This child killer could have been plotting Stephen's death. The thought was more than she could bear. Her head fell into her hands as her tears fell onto Lewis Lent's picture staring at her from the front page of the newspaper.

In addition to the information offered by Lent himself, the police canvassed the residents of his North Adams neighborhood. As they spoke to neighbors, it was difficult to believe the neighbors were talking about the same man police were holding behind bars for the murder of two children.

One neighbor described Lewis Lent as, "very friendly, very social and eager to lend a helping hand. He got along with everybody on Hudson Street."

Up and down the street, the residents were all in agreement; Lent was a 'regular nice guy'.

The attitude changed substantially when Richard Baumann was interviewed. Baumann was the owner of the Cinema and employed Lent as a custodian up until November 1993.

Mr. Baumann replied to the investigators question, "Tell me about Lewis Lent. What sort of person was he?"

"He just wasn't one of those guys you could love. There was nothing about him that was personable, just one of those guys in a group that nobody would bother with."

Derek Baumann, Richard's son offered his comments regarding Lent.

"He would come in with friends all the time, little kids. I thought he was spending his whole paycheck on the kids. He would buy them popcorn, soda, candy and let them play the machines."

"He came across as a coward. He would never really talk back. It seemed you could tell him to do anything and he'd do it."

Richard Baumann interrupted his son and related the incident that led to Lent's dismissal.

"One day I complained to Lewie that a couple of the theaters in the complex were still messy. Lent argued and said they were clean."

Baumann said he showed Lent the mess and at that point he continued,

"Lewie said, 'I know all about your family. I know where they live'," the senior Baumann recalled.

"I asked him if that was a threat and he said yes."

Baumann said he walked off to call the police but the call never connected. When he returned, he found Lent's theater keys outside.

After the disappearance of Jimmy Bernardo, employees were questioned by police. Lewis Lent was not among those questioned. Lent had worked at the theatre for seven years. How could he have been missed?

Richard Baumann said it was his fault Lent was not questioned in 1990. He explained Lent had been working as an independent contractor and his name did not appear on the employee list.

"He slipped through; the police were not at fault at all."

In addition to searching Lent's apartment, the police were anxious to interview the family who lived on the first floor of the Hudson Street residence.

A Pittsfield Police investigator knocked on the door displaying a brass #16.

Wayne Rarick answered. The detective identified himself and displayed his badge.

"I'd like to speak to Linda Domenichini, is she here?"

"Yes, come in," Rarick replied.

Linda was sitting on the sofa watching the latest news reports of the child killer in custody. Also present were, Missy Benoit, Stephen Domenichini, Monica Domenichini and Linda's friend Wayne Rarick.

The detective began his questions and Linda willingly responded in an angry tone.

"I'm very angry and hurt," she said. "I trusted him with my children."

She told the detective she seldom saw Lent without his little bag. They knew he carried a knife inside. After he was arrested, they found guns in his room.

"He actually called me from jail. He said, 'I guess you know where I am, ha, ha, ha' and I asked him why he was calling me. That's when he told me to go into his apartment and remove a jar. He said it was stinking up the place."

She paused to light a cigarette and continued,

"I looked for the jar but didn't find one."

"I want to just kill him," Linda sputtered. "He befriended my son. I thought that was neat because I was a single parent. Lew would give us rides; do anything for the family."

She paused and took a deep breath,

"I'm feeling I'm a bad mother, but I had no idea. It could have been Stephen." she said and began to cry.

"When I saw him on TV, I wanted to kill the bastard. Lent might as well have stabbed me, the way I feel."

Wayne Rarick added, "I rode in his van once, he made me feel uncomfortable, he looked at me and scared me, and I'm not afraid of many people. Lew was giving me this look, like, 'don't touch anything.'"

Linda was concerned for her son's well being in the long run. She said she was seeking counseling for Stephen and believed he faced a troubled future.

"He's on a cloud right now," she said, adding that she feared her son would never trust a man again.

"After all this quiets down, who's going to be there for him when he comes crashing down? His best friend turned into a serial killer. It's so sad for him."

Stephen sat quietly beside his younger sister. He seemed to be disconnected from the conversations around him. The detective was anxious to hear what the boy had to say.

The detective walked across the living room to where Stephen was seated and pulled up the hassock placing it in front of the 12-year-old.

"Son, can you tell me about Lewis?"

The boy expressed how his life was turned upside down when he learned Lewie might be a serial killer who preyed on children his age.

Stephen appeared to be at ease when he spoke displaying high spirits and a high energy level.

Years later, when asked about the countless interviews, he would reflect and say,

"At the time, I thought I was like a rock star. I was on TV, 48 Hours, in front of cameras. Of course I was too young to realize the magnitude of emotional harm it had inflicted on me."

As Stephen spoke, his revelations stunned his mother. Stephen recalled Lewis Lent frequently talking about the murder of Jimmy Bernardo.

"I hate him. He hurt another kid," Stephen said. "He should have hurt himself instead of another kid."

Stephen went on to say Lent never told him he was the one who killed Jimmy, but he used the murder to caution Stephen and it was his way to make Stephen behave.

The young boy remembered being warned to beware of strangers who might do the same thing to him if he didn't obey Lewie.

As he delivered the tale of his life with Lewis Lent, he said Lewis would tell him how Jimmy Bernardo died. It was Lent's way to control Stephen when they were at the theatre.

Perhaps the most chilling portion of the young boy's account was when he repeated Lent's description of Jimmy's murder.

"He told me that a car was involved. Jimmy was hung and then stabbed or shot because he wasn't dead enough."

The investigator scribbled notes and repositioned the small tape recorder closer to the boy as he continued to tell of his experience with the child killer.

"At the theater, I wanted to go out into the lobby and sing and dance. He would point to the posters of Jimmy and Sara Anne and say somebody might break in and kill me and 'I won't be there to save you', so I didn't go out there."

When asked, Stephen said he was never harmed by Lent. He was just his close friend. He said he was aware of the canvas bag that his friend carried which contained a gun and 'medicine' for the migraine headaches he said he suffered.

"When he showed me the gun I got a little scared, but he let me hold the gun and said it was just protection and I shouldn't be scared."

"I was really upset when I found out I was hanging around with a murderer and a child molester."

The boy continued and the investigator attempted to mask his astonishment of Stephen's candid recall.

"He would act like a kid sometimes. Sometimes he would act like a grown-up. He had a bad attitude and he'd flip out over little things and blame other people if something got lost. He was always accusing them for stuff that wasn't true."

"I think the best day of my life was when he moved in the apartment upstairs." The excitement quickly diminished; the young boy's eyes cast downward as he spoke in a barely audible tone, "and the worse day of my life was when I came home from school and found out that my best friend, my very best friend was a child killer."

At the close of the interview, Stephen was asked,

"If you could say something to Lewis now, what would you say?"

Without hesitation, the boy replied, "I'd tell him he's a jerk."

At no time did Stephen request to, or did he ever see Lewis Lent again.

Stephen turned his attention to the television show he and Monica had been watching. The interview was over. Stephen had no more to say.

Missy Benoit, Jonathan Wood's girlfriend spent a lot of time at Lent's apartment over the past year. She said he spent a lot of time alone in his room, either sleeping or reading.

"He had a psychic book or something like that. He liked watching television shows about UFOs."

"He was a jovial, friendly guy but also had a temper. I remember one time; he tossed a couch over looking for the television remote control."

"He told Jonathan he knew he did something wrong, but said he couldn't remember what."

"Jonathan is so upset about the whole thing he's left. I think he went up to New York to Lewie's mother, or maybe with his own mother. I don't know where he is. I just know he's very upset."

The detective turned to Linda Domenichini, Stephen's mother. The 37-year-old single mother had listened to the experiences Stephen shared with the press. She was stunned as she was not aware of Stephen's knowledge of Jimmy's murder. She ached for her son.

The investigator asked Linda to comment on what she had just learned from Stephen's statements.

She expressed how she thought of Lent as a patient, kind man who doted on her son. Because Stephen had never known his father, she believed he helped fill that gap in her son's life.

"With Lew, Stephen had a big brother, somebody he could talk to. Anything Stephen wanted; all he had to do was holler 'Lew' and Lew would do it for him."

The investigator pressed the sobbing mother for more. Linda told when and how Lewis Lent came into her family's life. She was quick to assure her positive feelings were replaced with shock and fear when she learned what a monster Lent really was.

"It's startling to be in a position to hear your son tell you facts about a dead kid you never knew, some facts that were never in print. It's very scary."

"I know he would spend hours in his room because of overpowering headaches. I think he had medication for that."

The 37-year-old single mother paused and drew a heavy sigh.

"He's just destroyed all my trust. It's hard for my son to trust people, and now my neighbor is a serial killer."

She reached for Stephen's hand. "Unbelievable, he might as well have just killed me, because part of me died when I saw that animal on TV."

"I'm not sure if he touched Stephen or not," she said. "I want to visit Lewis in jail and have him look me in the face and say yes or no."

For seven years, Lent worked as a janitor in a Pittsfield movie theater. The investigators concluded that he used his contact with young moviegoers and frequent road trips to search for his next victim.

After Lent's confessions were secured, the Chief felt a further investigation of Holly Piirainen's murder in Sturbridge was certainly warranted. In addition to Holly, Chief Lee was prepared to contact the Westfield Police Department to look into 16-year-old Jamie Lusher's 1992 case more closely. The capture of Lent was surely an encouraging break in the unsolved murders of at least two children.

"His arrest is an enormous relief for the people in Berkshire County and all of Western Massachusetts," said Pittsfield Police Chief Gerald Lee.

Authorities from Pittsfield, Sturbridge, Westfield and New York State were about to take on an investigation of mammoth proportion. They would soon discover the many layers of Lewis Lent.

New York State Police had cases they wanted solved. Monique Santiago, age 11, disappeared in 1990 from Albany, NY and Tammie Anne McCormick, age 13, disappeared in 1986 from Saratoga Springs, N.Y; both had similarities to Bernardo and Wood, and possibly linked to Lewis Lent.

Col. Wayne Bennett of the New York State Police spoke with Pittsfield's Chief Lee.

"From what we can tell here, the method of operation is identical. It's a crime of opportunity. Whatever spurs him into doing it when the opportunity exists, he seizes it."

The Chief was in agreement with the Colonel's comments and replied,

"We have contacted Westfield and Sturbridge Police. We're interested in any link we can make to the Jamie Lusher disappearance and the Holly Piirainen murder."

He continued, "We've been inundated with calls from police departments in Vermont, Maine, and New Hampshire about Lent's possible involvement in unsolved children's slayings."

District Attorney Gerard Downing added, "There are very few people that commit the perfect crime. Sooner or later they make a mistake and police have long memories."

Captain Frank Pace of the New York State Police believed Lewis Lent could be responsible for the abductions and deaths of as many as eight children in New York, New England and Pennsylvania. The investigation could expand to Florida, Virginia and as far as New Mexico, where Lent lived at one time.

The four agencies conducting the Bernardo investigation formed a task force in an effort to trace Lewis Lent's activities beginning with the past three years. Twenty-five investigators from New York State Police, Massachusetts State Police, Pittsfield police and the FBI were assigned to the newly formed task force.

The Violent Criminal Apprehension Program (VICAP) was utilized. This database is provided by the FBI, to state and local law enforcement agencies. VICAP collects and stores information as far back as the 1950's. Cases examined by VICAP include homicides involving random, motiveless abductions suspected to be part of a series.

An arrested or identified offender can be entered into the VICAP system by any law enforcement agency for comparison and possible matching with unsolved cases.

As patterns develop, appropriate law enforcement agencies are notified and proceed using the information for lead value.

Police from across the country contacted authorities in Pittsfield to probe for any connection with unsolved crimes against children.

Pittsfield Police Chief Gerald Lee commented, "The phone does not stop ringing. We believe we're looking at Lent as a serial killer."

Based upon Lewis Lent's assertion he was suffering from Multi-Personality-Disorder, District Attorney Gerard Downing requested the FBI, Quantico, VA assign a behavioral specialist to interview and evaluate Lewis Lent.

Downing knew, once Lent attended his arraignment and entered a plea, an attorney would represent him. Further questioning would become more difficult.

Lent was read the 'Miranda' several times throughout questioning, and waived his rights each time, offering his confessions and other details voluntarily.

"It wasn't a 24-hour-a-day grilling by any means," said Chief Lee. "As a matter of fact it was quite casual."

At his arraignment, public defender, Richard LeBlanc entered a plea of "not guilty" of all charges on behalf of his client.

Lent's confessions, notwithstanding, the Commonwealth of Massachusetts prohibits a 'guilty' plea at arraignment. The burden to prove guilt lies on the shoulders of the Commonwealth.

Lent was held without bail, which negated the previous order of $200,000 cash or $2 million surety bail in connection with the attempted abduction.

When the arraignment ended, Berkshire County Sherriff's Department took custody and Lent was remanded to the Berkshire County Jail. He would remain there throughout his numerous court appearances, hearings and trials.

Robert Wood, Sara Anne's father requested a visit with Lewis Lent hoping he would lead him to his daughter's body. He pleaded with his daughter's killer to disclose where he left Sara's remains. He expressed the heartache his family had endured, and wanted to bring Sara home.

Both Massachusetts and New York Police followed Mr. Wood's visit. Under a relaxed questioning, Lent showed them a spot on a map where Sara's body could be found.

After searching the designated area, Sara was not found.

Over the following months, Lent would provide various inaccurate locations. Search parties would comb each area offered by Lent but none would yield the body of Sara Anne Wood.

Berkshire County Superior Court Judge Daniel A. Ford handed down an unprecedented court order.

On a Sunday morning, the court ordered Lewis Lent be transported from the Berkshire County

Jail to the Raquette Lake Region in New York State. Transportation to be provided by State Police helicopter.

The order was issued in the hope Lent would point out the location of Sara Anne Wood's body. The order was a compassionate effort on the part of Judge Ford.

After hours of 'wild goose chases' Lent was returned to the county jail.

In the months to follow, several attempts to convince Lewis Lent to reveal where Sara's body was would be futile. Lent would finally state,

"I don't want to tell you because there's another one there and I don't want you to find him."

Seasoned detectives cringed at the chilling statements Lent would offer throughout questioning and at his impending court appearances.

Lent's interrogators faced an evil, cunning albeit unassuming man with a severely tangled mind. Unraveling the various tales Lent would offer would be an onerous task.

A state and federal task force was formed to probe into a possible connection to other unsolved cases in the New England/New York region. The task force included the FBI, Massachusetts and New York State Police and Pittsfield Police.

Their first task was to compile and distribute a timeline of Lewis Lent's past whereabouts.

Sean Googin, 15, disappeared from Cazenovia Lake, N.Y. on July 3, 1992. His body was discovered the following day. The medical examiner determined the boy had died of strangulation.

The seemingly demure Lewis Lent told police, "I hunted for youthful victims, always prepared with my 'death bag' which contained duct tape, and sometimes a gun."

He added, "I'm a frequent road traveler, and I often used the road Googin walked when I traveled from Pittsfield to my parent's New York home." Apart from that, Lent offered no further comment regarding the Googin case.

Jamie Lusher's disappearance would be another consideration when authorities learned Lent frequently visited Westfield.

Jamie's case file disclosed statements from two witnesses confirming Lewis Lent was seen in Westfield on the day of Jamie's disappearance.

Westfield's Police Chief Benjamin Surprise did not agree with Pittsfield Chief Lee's perception. Surprise was reluctant to share the Lusher case file; however, other members of the Westfield Police Department were willing to consider Lee's exploration into the belief that Lent could be responsible for Jamie Lusher's disappearance.

After a thorough review, Jamie's file disclosed eyewitnesses who had offered information at the time the teen disappeared in November 1992.

The Pittsfield police dispatched personnel to canvas the area where Jamie's bicycle had been found. The residents of Bennett Road were questioned. None contributed any useful information.

The inquiring officers were interested in the statement of one particular resident on Bennett Road.

A commercial airline pilot made a statement early in the Lusher investigation. The witness was not at home the day Bennett road was canvassed by Pittsfield Police. He was expected to return the following day.

Upon returning the following day, they questioned the Bennett Road resident. They learned he had, in fact seen Lewis Lent seated in the passenger's side of his distinctive Ford Econoline van. The witness further stated the van was parked on the road, near the pond precisely where Jamie's bicycle was found and added, "There was a bicycle inside the van."

When asked what day, or date he had witnessed this, he said he didn't recall, but he could get an exact date by reviewing his flight schedules of November 1992.

The records indicated the pilot had no scheduled flights on the weekend beginning Friday, November 6 through Sunday, November 8, 1992. He confirmed he was at home the entire weekend in question.

Lewis Lent was asked directly about Jamie Lusher's disappearance, but continued to deny any involvement with the 16-year-old's fate.

While reviewing countless statements enclosed in Holly Piirainen's unsolved murder, the investigators discovered a statement taken from a young woman who had been jogging the morning Holly was abducted.

She described the vehicle as well as the driver; both fit Lewis Lent and his customized Econoline van. The jogger stated that Lent, driving his Econoline van slowed down and made lewd remarks toward her. She said she tossed a few 'suggestions' back at him and he drove away.

The young woman was shown actual pictures of Lent's vehicle along with several similar vans. She immediately selected Lent's van with the custom taillights. When shown a photo array, she identified Lent without hesitation.

Maureen Lemieux believed Holly could have been taken away in a van because of the sound Holly's 5-year-old brother Zachary described as a 'rolling thundery sound'. She believed the sound could have been of a van's door opening and closing.

"It's a process of elimination, and we haven't been able to eliminate Lewis Lent in any of the cases we've reviewed," stated Massachusetts State Police Lieutenant Peter Higgins.

Again, Lent voluntarily submitted to hours of interrogation by law enforcement officials. He admitted to stalking his victims but refused to admit or deny any sexual molestation had occurred. New

York State Police Capt. Frank Pace came away with this statement,

"If I were going to give a personal opinion, indications are that he is a pedophile."

Throughout the questioning, Lewis Lent's responses continued to baffle his interrogators. When asked if he was responsible for Holly Piirainen's murder, Lewis Lent reverted to his multiple personalities. He referred to them by various names.

The authorities speculated Lent was maligning, because of books on the phenomena of multiple personalities that had been confiscated when his Hudson Street apartment had been searched.

He said he didn't recall killing Holly, and claimed he just couldn't recall if he did or didn't.

Lent also claimed to have a girlfriend, however, those who lived with him, as well as his best friend Stephen Domenichini, stated, "He never brought 'Liz' to the apartment. I think he made her up."

The District Attorney faced a scheduling dilemma. On the morning of Lent's arraignment in the Berkshire Superior Court, the trial of Wayne Lo was scheduled to begin.

Wayne Lo, an 18-year-old student at Simon's Rock College of Bard, located in Great Barrington faced two counts of first-degree murder, and four counts of attempted murder.

On December 15, 1992, Lo set out on a shooting rampage on the campus of the serene college of the arts.

A request from Lo's defense council for a change of venue was granted and the trial was to take place in Hampden County Superior Court, Springfield MA.

Gerard Downing and his staff, which included several Massachusetts State Police, were expected to make the 70-mile trip to Springfield daily in order to proceed with the prosecution. The commitment to the Lo trial would surely handicap the District Attorney's efforts toward the investigation of Lewis Lent.

At the behest of District Attorney Gerard Downing, VICAP dispatched special agent Clint Van Zandt. The FBI behavior specialist arrived in Pittsfield on the Monday following Lent's arraignment.

Clint Van Zandt's expertise would be valuable when determining the mental state of Lewis Lent and his assertion he suffered from Multi Personality Disorder claiming to have an evil alter ego named Stephen who allegedly forced him to kill children.

Van Zandt would look for behavioral clues and behavioral traits evident from the crime scene and forensic analysis of the victims' remains.

There was no question; Van Zandt's credentials were beyond dispute. He had led task forces in past high profile cases. It is believed, the character portrayed by Jodie Foster in the 1991 smash hit, *"Silence of the Lambs"* was created from one of Clint Van Zandt's notable cases.

In addition to his expertise in behavioral science, Van Zandt was proficient in profiling, handwriting, fingerprinting, and virtually all aspects of investigation techniques.

In 1996, Clint Van Zandt would lead the task force responsible for the identification and apprehension of Theodore Kaczynski, the infamous Unabomber.

Van Zandt expended many hours reviewing Lent's files. Once he was able to 'fill himself in' with the information provided by the heavy file he met with Chief Lee. Van Zandt would partake in several interviews with those who had worked the Bernardo and Wood cases and the attempted abduction of Rebecca, which subsequently led to the arrest, and interrogation of Lewis Lent.

Clint Van Zandt wasted no time contacting all personnel necessary, and within 48 hours, he sat with Lewis Lent at the County Jail.

His interview was long and tedious. At the conclusion of his visit, Van Zandt felt a return visit would be necessary before he could draw any conclusions and submit a thorough report based on his professional observations of the subject. His report was submitted to District Attorney Gerard Downing. In short, it would state Lewis Lent was unquestionably mentally disturbed; however, he could not confirm the multi-personality-disorder Lent claimed to have plagued him.

Van Zandt advised the intelligent approach would be to look at all open homicide and abduction cases, then start from the outside and work in.

"You take the known characteristics, go back and look at all the unsolved cases. You look for similarities. There are a lot of cases, and we have to go through them all."

The investigators worked the recommended method. The timeline worked in reverse, the most recent cases and continuing back as far as 20 years. Reconstructing Lent's activities and travel over the past several years would become an enormous job.

Agent Clint Van Zandt would continue to work with the task force compiling information to develop a calendar of Lent's activities and travel over the past several years to compare with incidents of unsolved crimes against children. In the coming months, speaking on behalf of the task force, New York State Police Captain Frank Pace would report the force was able to compile a broad outline indicating possible criminal activities by Lent dating back to when he was 18 years old.

The New York Times picked up the story.

Captain Pace stated, "We would be remiss if we didn't consider Lent a serial killer."

The Captain continued, "It probably really starts to get going after his 18th birthday and goes up to the day he was arrested."

How could it be possible to go undetected for over 25 years?

CHAPTER 9

In January 1995, one year after the attempted abduction of Rebecca Saverese, Lewis S. Lent faced Judge Daniel A. Ford. Judge Ford sentenced Lent to spend 17 to 20 years behind bars for the attempted abduction to be served at Cedar Junction, Walpole, MA.

While serving his sentence, Lent would claim he feared for his life and reported he was beaten. Fear of other inmates affected Lent's behavior and he was often observed cowering under his prison bed, refusing to leave his cell.

Competence hearings resulted in a transfer to the Bridgewater Mental Health Facility for evaluation.

Prosecutors suggested that Lent was transferred to the psychiatric hospital because he was depressed about his imprisonment and terrified for his physical safety.

Lent had been attacked by other prisoners and suffered broken cheekbones.

In February 1996, Lent's case was reviewed.

A representative of the Corrections Department spoke at the competency hearing,

"The bottom line is that there is no change in his status. We continue to maintain he is not able to serve his sentence in a traditional penal environment due to mental illness."

The spokesperson continued, "He has potential to harm himself and others in the general prison population."

Lent's lawyer argued he suffered from a major degenerative disease in the frontal lobe of the brain. The exact cause of the ailment was yet to be diagnosed and the lawyer insisted Lent was unable to understand the charges against him. In Lent's case, whether he really suffered from the disorder would not matter.

In the Commonwealth of Massachusetts, a suspect may be found innocent by reason of insanity only if it can be proven a mental illness has incapacitated his ability to conform to the law or he is unable to tell right from wrong. Mental illness or a personality disorder does not rise to the level of insanity according to Massachusetts statutes. After correction officials argued Lent was mentally ill, the Brockton District Court judge extended commitment to the Bridgewater State Hospital for another year.

The following June, after repeated trial delays and arguments over Lent's mental competency the court made the decision; Lent would go to trial for the murder of Jimmy Bernardo.

The defense requested a change of venue. Request denied. The trial would take place in the Berkshire County Superior Court, Pittsfield, MA. However, Judge Ford made a compensatory decision in favor of the defense's request. The jury would be selected from the Hampden County jury pool.

With the jury selection to begin on June 4, 1996, the district attorney, Gerard Downing was astounded when Lent pled guilty.

Downing had not offered to soften Lent's sentence and stated, "I never saw the possibility of a guilty plea, and on a professional level I'm still surprised."

Following the surprise guilty plea, Lent was immediately given the mandatory sentence of life in prison without parole for first-degree murder. Judge Ford added an additional nine to ten years on the kidnapping charge to run concurrently.

The Bernardo family was present in the courtroom. Mr. Bernardo said, "Our family is very glad to be finally able to put this behind us. Perhaps we can now continue the healing process, knowing Mr. Lent is in prison for life and will finally be punished for his crime."

He concluded his statement with, "We are also praying for the Woods that they may reach this point soon."

Lewis Lent was remanded to Concord State Prison to serve out his sentence.

The court system had not seen the last of Lewis Lent. He still faced charges in the Sara Anne Wood case. Getting a conviction of first-degree murder in the Wood case would pose problems.

New York law is quite specific; it reads, "A person may not be convicted of any offense solely upon evidence of a confession or admission made by him without additional proof that the offense charged has been committed."

In a case of homicide, there must be evidence of the body. There must be proof there was a death and the violence that caused it.

Without Sara's remains, there was only proof she was missing, and if found, the authorities would have to establish cause of death. If the medical evidence were sufficient to establish death resulted from a violent act, then Lent would be charged.

Herkimer County District Attorney Michael Daley had an impossible task. He stated he would have liked to seek the death penalty against Lent but the charge for Sara's murder came before New York reinstated capital punishment. At best, Lent would receive an identical sentence to the one he was presently serving in Massachusetts, life without parole.

D.A. Gerard Downing considered a recommendation Lent be sent to a federal prison where he could be better protected from other inmates. Downing's counterpart, New York's D.A. Michael Daley adamantly opposed any plea deal of that sort.

"If he (Lent) wants federal prison, we are not giving him anything he wants until we get what we want, the body of Sara Anne Wood."

The angry D.A. continued, "We can put him in the last place he wants to be for the rest of his life. The deepest, darkest, smallest hole around is fine with me."

For more than two years, Sara's parents, Robert and Frances Wood carried on a crusade to bring Lent to trial in New York. They took their pleas to top officials such as U.S. Attorney General Janet Reno and New York Governors Mario Cuomo and George

Pataki. They walked and bicycled to Massachusetts to stir action. In the end they would say,

"There is a long road ahead, and we are confident in the district attorney of Herkimer County and the state police for what happens in the future."

Lewis Lent pleaded guilty to second-degree murder for the killing of Sara and received a 25 year to life sentence to run consecutive to the life sentence he was serving for the Bernardo murder.

During sentencing, the prosecutor offered a simple message to Lewis Lent.

"From all the people in this community who you hurt...the message to you, Lewis, is 'Burn in hell,'"

Herkimer County Court Judge Patrick Kirk stated that although Lent was not eligible for capital punishment, he often wondered if, as a judge, he would be capable of imposing the death penalty.

"You sir, have answered that in the affirmative."

Pastor Wood, Sara's father, told Lent, "You murdered her, she begged you to live."

"You lied to this day. You refuse to tell us where her body is; by those actions, you tell us your father is Satan, you are in league with the devil."

In the years to come, and in the wake of the prison slaying of a convicted priest, Lent would again express concern for his safety and be transferred from Concord, MCI to the Colonial Correctional Center, Bridgewater, MA where he remains today.

Police probing into other cases Lent has been suspected of frequently visited Lent hoping the confessed killer would take responsibility and enable other unsolved cases to be closed.

State Police Lt. Peter Higgins reported he had an ongoing dialogue with the convicted child killer.

"We have talked to him recently," Higgins acknowledged. He said conversations with Lent involved several unsolved cases in Hampden County.

"He pretty much has always been cooperative." Higgins replied when asked about Lent's demeanor. He declined to say whether conversations had been productive.

In the years to come, Lent would receive frequent visits by several members of the task force.

Today, the task force continues to be in effect and visits, although substantially less frequent, are in an effort to convince Lewis Lent to take responsibility for other murdered children, including Jamie Lusher and Holly Piirainen. He has never admitted to any other murders and refuses to disclose the location of Sara Anne Wood's remains.

Clearly, Lewis Lent is not a penitential man.

DANNY'S STORY
1972 Murder of an Altar Boy
1972

Chicopee Police cruisers raced to the riverbank beneath the Route 291 bridge. The call came into the station at 8:25 a.m. Saturday, April 15, 1972...

Daniel (Danny) Croteau was a 13-year-old boy, the youngest boy of the Croteau family.

Carl and Bernice Croteau raised seven children, five boys and two girls. The Croteau family lived in a middle class neighborhood of Springfield, MA. It was the only home the children had ever known.

Carl and Bernice (Bunny) Croteau raised their family enforcing strict Catholic beliefs and values. They were a devout Catholic family and each of the Croteau boys served the church as altar boys.

With his strawberry blonde hair, his face peppered with freckles and a fishing pole resting on his shoulder, Danny was a walking image of a Norman Rockwell creation.

Danny Croteau was somewhat mischievous. He was inquisitive and his rakish ways attracted him to some questionable friends. As the youngest boy, Danny was impatient to reach the appropriate age to participate in the activities of his older brothers. Many believed him to be a 13-year-old trying to grow up too fast.

Danny's friends described him as a fun loving kid, a little on the wild side and somewhat of a delinquent, according to standards of the early 1970's.

The young teen was not one to live his years in the shadow of his four older brothers, and his adventurous ways would often times place him in harm's way.

Danny Croteau was living a life of dark secrets he could not share with anyone. He was a prisoner within himself believing there was no escape.

He experimented with pot, smoked cigarettes and drank, long before his peers.

It would take a horrible, meaningless murder to reveal the agony of the demons that dwelt within the 13-year-old boy.

The death of Danny Croteau would free many from the same living hell he was forced to endure.

Officers exited their squad cars with the red and blue lights whirling. Small groups standing on the bridge overhead strained to see what the commotion was all about.

An angler leaned on one of the police cars, talking to officer Burl Howard who had just arrived. The shaken fisherman reported seeing a body floating in the Chicopee River under the Robinson Bridge.

When Danny Croteau didn't come home the night before, his parents began to call his friends. One friend was a parish priest; it would be likely Danny would visit.

Father Richard Lavigne received the call from the anxious mother and said he hadn't seen Danny.

By 2:00 a.m., Carl and Bunny Croteau panicked and reported Danny missing to the Springfield Police Department. Mrs. Croteau reported she had not seen Danny since he went outside around 4:00 p.m. Friday afternoon.

On the last day of his life, Danny attended Our Lady of Sacred Heart School. He returned home that afternoon, played kickball in a neighbor's yard, and went out the door heading toward Wilbraham Road. Mrs. Croteau never saw him again.

The police retrieved the small body from the river and identified Danny Croteau. The tentative identification was based on the yellow exam paper found in the pocket of the boy's suede jacket.

Carl Croteau was at work when he received the agonizing call. He rushed home and instructed to go to the Chicopee police station.

Mr. Croteau headed for the Chicopee Police Department, stopping at St. Mary's rectory hoping for emotional support from the family friend, Fr. Lavigne.

"They found Danny murdered," Croteau blurted to the priest in the doorway.

Without any questions, the priest asked, "Do you want me to come along?"

The two arrived at the station and were informed Danny was taken to a nearby funeral home. Father Lavigne embraced the grieving father and offered to accompany him to identify Danny's body.

Father Lavigne returned to the rectory where Croteau had left his car. Croteau returned home to his grieving family.

Sunday, April 16, 1972

BOY, 13, FOUND SLAIN
IN CHICOPEE RIVER

The headlines were gruesome, but the article that followed was brief. The police did not disclose the details of Danny's murder. They reported evidence of a struggle. It was evident Danny fought for his life but lost.

Chicopee Patrolman Burl Howard discovered Danny Croteau at 8:20 a.m. The fully clothed body was floating a few feet from shore where the river flows under the Interstate 291 bridge.

The detectives stated they were working without a significant clue and without a sure motive for the crime. They appealed for public help in solving the murder of 13-year-old Daniel Croteau.

Danny's death occurred at a time when news was abundant. The newspaper accounts of his murder were overshadowed by other events.

- B52s were bombarding North Vietnam.
- Apollo 16 was nearing the moon
- Sen. George McGovern toured the U.S. Envelope Co.
- Protesters were marching against Westover Air Force Base.
- "All in the Family" nominated for 11 Emmys.
- "Clockwork Orange," "The Godfather," and "Dirty Harry" were vying in the box offices.
- Springfield police shot "Snowball," the Forest Park polar bear after he mauled a girl who tried to pet him.

Chicopee police were searching for evidence at the riverbank and surrounding areas where Danny was discovered.

Chicopee Police Lieutenant Edmund Radwanski was on the scene. An area was roped off with yellow crime scene tape in an effort to prevent contamination of any potential evidence.

The Lieutenant noticed Fr. Lavigne walking along the riverbank. The priest was dressed in his cleric garb and the officer became curious. Radwanski was not acquainted with Fr. Lavigne and thought perhaps the priest was there to "bless the scene" or something of a religious nature. However, the officer would interview the priest.

The location Danny was found was a popular fishing area and in the evening, a popular 'parking spot' for teenagers. It would be difficult to determine evidence that related to the drowning. Debris and tire marks were abundant.

During the subsequent interview with Father Lavigne, Lt. Radwanski noted several inappropriate statements and questions from the priest, which the officer considered notable in his report.

Fr. Lavigne asked, "If a stone was used and thrown in the river, would the blood still be on it?"

The autopsy on Danny's body was yet to be performed. The cause of death had not been determined at the time of the interview. The priest posed another curious question.

"In such a popular hangout with so many cars and footprints, how can the prints you have be of any help?"

As a seasoned police officer, Lt. Radwanski believed further questioning of Father Richard Lavigne would be appropriate.

Radwanski asked about the relationship between the victim and the priest. Fr. Lavigne told the officer he was, in addition to being a parish priest at St. Mary's; a family friend to the Croteau family. He visited their home regularly and often took the Croteau boys fishing.

"All five boys were altar boys at St. Catherine's."

"When was the last time you saw Danny?" asked the officer.

The priest thought a few minutes and replied he could not recall.

"Did you see him last Friday?"

"No, I did not," replied the priest.

Throughout the interview, the priest made it very clear that he was never alone with any of the boys.

"Whenever I took Danny anywhere, it was always with his brothers or a gang of kids," he stated.

At the conclusion of the interview, Lt. Radwanski wrote a report and brought it to the attention of the State Police Lieutenant James Fitzgibbon. Radwanski expressed his concern to the investigator.

Lt. Fitzgibbon visited the Croteaus at their home. He asked Carl and Bunny about the relationship between Fr. Lavigne and their family. The Croteaus confirmed that Fr. Lavigne was a parish priest and a family friend.

Mrs. Croteau told the Lieutenant how Father Lavigne came into their lives.

After he was assigned to their parish, the new priest arrived on their doorstep.

"He just popped up here all of a sudden. We didn't invite him...He said he wanted to help us."

Mr. Croteau continued from where his wife left off.

"He knew we had a big family. Things were tough. I'd be laid off sometimes. Fr. Lavigne would raid the freezer at the rectory and bring us steak or a roast. He offered to look after the kids, to baby-sit them."

Soon after, Father Lavigne became a regular visitor at the Croteau home.

It was a time when having a priest come to dinner or take the children for sleepovers was a status symbol.

From the start, Lavigne was charismatic. He spoke out against the Vietnam War and at times his views made some parishioners uncomfortable.

In addition to his cleric duties, the young priest was a political figure, very popular among left-wing activists. He would march up front of their protest rallies, his collar giving moral prestige to their causes. He wove his way through the Democrat politicians and established political connections.

Sleepovers at the rectory or at Lavigne's Chicopee home was commonplace. Often times, the priest took the boys in the neighborhood for rides in his Mustang convertible.

"He would round up the boys and take them fishing. The kids thought he was a 'cool priest', and we believed him to be a positive influence on them."

To the younger members of the parish, the arrival of Father Richard Lavigne was a refreshing change. The young priest took the 'starch' out of the traditional collar.

Stephen Burnett, Danny's best friend served Mass with Danny for Lavigne.

"When we served funeral masses, Father Lavigne would take us out of school and afterward, Danny and I would share a chalice of wine." Burnett would state.

"We cruised with him in his Mustang convertible. I remember there were Playboy magazines under the seat in the convertible. Father Lavigne encouraged us to look at them."

The Burnett family eventually moved from the Springfield area.

Several similar accounts would not be forthcoming for years to come.

Funeral arrangements were made. The Croteaus requested Rev. Richard Lavigne officiate.

Relatives from various parts of the country flew in to attend Danny's funeral. One in particular, Bunny Croteau's sister Betty flew in from California.

Father Lavigne greeted her at the Croteau's home. Shortly after her arrival, the priest took her aside and told her he had identified the body. He advised Betty to convince Carl and Bunny to keep the casket closed for the wake. Lavigne told her Danny's face was mangled and his mother shouldn't see him that way. Betty convinced the grieving parents to have a closed casket. Bunny and Carl complied.

The Chicopee police wasted no time initiating an investigation into the death of Danny Croteau.

State trooper James Mitchell asked the Croteaus and those close to the family to alert them if they noticed anyone acting strangely at Danny's wake.

The friends and relatives of the Croteau family began arriving at the funeral home.

Danny's closed casket was draped with a blanket of white flowers tied with a golden ribbon with one word written across it, "BROTHER." The casket was surrounded with an array of floral arrangements and among them placed atop the closed casket, the image of 13-year-old Danny.

Father Lavigne was noticeably absent from the wake. The only priests in attendance were Father Griffin, pastor of St. Catherine's and a priest from the Franciscan Order, Father Barnabas Keck. The Franciscan priest displayed behavior quite puzzling to the Croteaus. A stranger to the family and having no official function at St. Catherine's or St. Mary's church, the priest sobbed uncontrollably at the wake.

When Father Lavigne was transferred to St. Mary's, all assumed it was because of the friction between him and Father Griffin.

Father Griffin, the pastor at St. Catherine's disapproved of Father Lavigne's political positions and radical tendencies.

After the funeral, State Police Lieutenant James Fitzgibbon visited the Croteaus to offer his sympathies and make a few inquiries. Lt. Fitzgibbon asked if anyone at the wake seemed to be peculiar. Carl Croteau told him of the Franciscan priest. Fitzgibbon made note to would follow up with a visit to the Bridge Street Chapel.

He asked Carl Croteau why the casket was closed. Carl explained he acted on the advice of Father Lavigne.

"Father Lavigne identified Danny's body and wanted to spare Bunny and I from viewing Danny's mangled face."

Fitzgibbons shook his head in disbelief.

"Danny's face wasn't disfigured at all. The wounds were to the back of his head," the officer replied.

The police had received the preliminary autopsy report. It had not been published. The manner of death, homicide. The cause of death, a blow to the back of the skull.

Also included in the notes and observations of the coroner, Danny's blood alcohol level was .18 – more than twice the legal limit for driving. Danny was drunk when he was killed.

Lt. Fitzgibbons pressed the parents for more information.

"Was Father Lavigne ever alone with Danny, or any of the boys?"

Carl replied, "Yes, on several occasions. Sleepovers at the rectory were common." Carl paused and appeared to be hesitant.

"Is there anything else you can add regarding Danny and Lavigne?"

"Father also had the boys stay with him at his parents' Chicopee home. One day Joe, my 14-year-old boy came home after a sleepover. He appeared to be hung over. Father Lavigne told me that Joe had gotten into his parents' liquor cabinet without his knowing."

Mr. Croteau sheepishly added, "I chastised Joe."

Bunny Croteau sat by her husband's side. She began recalling several incidences involving Father Lavigne and her family. At the time, she had no reason to question any of the circumstances. Upon reflection, her point of view slowly began to change.

Lt. Fitzgibbons told the Croteaus about a report the police had received from a Chicopee woman.

According to the woman, a week before his death, Danny knocked on her door at 10:30 p.m. He claimed to be lost and asked to use her phone. About five minutes later, a maroon Mustang arrived and picked up the boy.

The police questioned Father Lavigne about the evening of April 7 and the priest admitted he had picked up Danny and taken him to his parents' house in Chicopee and called Danny's parents. Danny spent the night at Lavigne's parents' home. The priest contradicted earlier statements he was never alone with Danny.

Bunny Croteau replied, "Yes, I remember Danny arrived home the following morning and said he felt ill. Later he threw up repeatedly. When I asked Father Lavigne about it, he believed Danny might have gotten into his parents' liquor cabinet."

As Danny's parents recalled 'incidents' relating to Father Lavigne's interaction with the Croteau family, Lt. Fitzgibbons determined a thorough investigation of the parish priest was appropriate and would be initiated.

Each account, standing alone had little significance and appeared to be of no consequence. When compiled they began to create a profile reflecting a popular, well-liked parish priest who had a dark side capable of deceit and violence.

Despite their interest in Father Lavigne, the police were cautious and careful to avoid 'tunnel vision'. Other persons of interest would be interviewed and investigated to the satisfaction of the authorities.

Fitzgibbons passed the information regarding Father Barnabas Keck's behavior at the Croteau wake to State Police Investigator James Mitchell.

Mitchell met Father Keck at his chapel office in downtown Springfield.

"Why did you go to the wake, Father?" asked Mitchell. "Do you know the family?"

"No," replied the priest.

"Do you always go to wakes of people you don't know?"

The priest replied the murder of the boy moved him so deeply he felt he should pay his respects.

The detective noticed the newspaper story about Danny's murder was posted on a bulletin board behind the priest.

Mitchell was careful not to exceed his boundaries while questioning the priest. He believe Keck to be Lavigne's confessor, but Massachusetts law protects priest-penitent confidentiality.

At a later visit, Father Barnabas stated no one had ever confessed to him about the murder of Danny Croteau. He confirmed that many Springfield priests used the St. Francis chapel for confession, but that he never saw their faces.

"I knew of Father Lavigne, but I never met him face to face. I wouldn't have recognized him."

A produce manager at a nearby supermarket was interviewed. Danny had recently visited his house and painted a bedroom. Lt. Mitchell questioned the manager and ruled him out as a suspect.

A man who led the Boy Scout troop Danny belonged to was also questioned. After checking out his alibi, which provided his whereabouts during the time of Danny's absence, Mitchell stated the Boy

Scout leader did not rise to the level of suspicion and ruled out as a suspect.

As the investigation continued, all leads consistently brought the police back to Father Lavigne.

A short time after the investigation began; Father Lavigne became a prime suspect.

The priest called Mrs. Croteau and in the brief telephone conversation stated, "Under the circumstances, I don't think I should come around for awhile."

They never spoke again.

Within the week following the funeral, the Croteau's could not comprehend what had happened to Danny. They couldn't bring themselves to the conclusion Father Lavigne could have played any role in their son's death.

The abrupt phone call prompted the Croteau's consideration of the police's suspicions. They were prepared to give the police their full cooperation.

Before long, rumors became rampant. Father Richard Lavigne was under investigation in connection to Danny Croteau's murder.

Two weeks passed. A high school student contacted the State Police offering a statement about what happened to him when he stayed overnight at St. Mary's rectory with Father Lavigne.

The police learned Lavigne gave the boy alcohol and fondled him. After one of the sleepovers, the boy said, Lavigne took him to the St. Francis Chapel saying they needed to go to confession.

The boy's statement fit perfectly into the information previously gathered. The reference to St. Francis Chapel was particularly of interest. The Chapel on Bridge Street, Springfield, served as a confessional for priests throughout the diocese, assuring priests would be unknown to their confessors.

The boy was credible and his story was consistent with the theory that Father Lavigne provided alcohol to the boys he molested. They had no idea how many abuse victims would come forward.

Lt. Fitzgibbon visited Danny's parents and shared the information he had received from the high school boy. He asked to interview Danny's brothers.

The Lieutenant talked to each brother separately in one of the bedrooms. Carl and Bunny waited in the living room.

Fitzgibbon delivered the devastating results of the Croteau boys' interviews. Fitzgibbon told them their sons said Lavigne had sexually abused some of them. It was a hurtful, cruel blow to the couple. They couldn't believe it. Their world began to crumble around them.

As the words of the investigator began to sink in, Bunny and Carl reflected over the past five years. It wasn't long and their suspicions grew.

Mrs. Croteau's first reaction was anger. She searched the house for photos of her sons with Lavigne, ripping them to shreds, attempting to destroy any memories, any reminders of the priest she had trusted and admired. She was unable to rid the indelible memories deep inside.

Carl and Bunny were faced with a difficult decision. Should they betray their trusted friend, a Catholic priest? After careful consideration, their loyalties rested with their sons who had suffered abuse at the hands of Father Richard Lavigne. The possibility Lavigne was involved with Danny's murder was a struggle the Croteau's believed needed to be considered.

Mr. Croteau accompanied by his wife and son Joe drove to the Chicopee police station. Danny's parents signed a complaint for the murder of Danny and Joe signed a complaint for sexual assault he had experienced naming Father Richard Lavigne the molester.

Lt. Fitzgibbon advised Carl and Bunny Croteau to refrain from discussing the sexual abuse allegations of their sons. The Lieutenant said it might prejudice a future trial of the criminal case against Father Lavigne.

The Croteaus complied with the advice and for decades would not discuss the circumstances, surrounding incidents the boys had experienced.

Shortly after the complaints were filed, Father Leo O'Neil visited the Croteaus at their home. Father O'Neil was a parish priest at St. Catherine's and an acquaintance of the family for several years.

The usual cordial demeanor of Fr. O'Neil transformed to a nervous, trembling man in black.

The shaken priest sat in the front room; he slumped in a chair and asked, "Do you think Father Lavigne is capable of murder?"

Mr. Croteau replied that the police had informed him Fr. Lavigne was their chief suspect. Croteau also added they had discovered Lavigne had molested their boys as well as other kids whose parents were reluctant to come forward. The priest listened to the accusations coming from Mr. Croteau.

"Father O'Neil saw how tense I was and suggested I go out and get a couple of beers to calm down."

Carl Croteau believed his friend; Father O'Neil would surely inform the Bishop of what he had learned regarding the molestation of the Croteau boys. He was sure O'Neil would be compelled to do the right thing. A week passed and a more composed Father O'Neil walked to the front steps of 106 Ferncliff Ave., the home of Carl and Bunny Croteau.

When Carl answered the door, Father O'Neil greeted him and said,

"Here is some spending money. We're sending you and your family on an all expense paid trip to visit Bunny's sister."

"We thought it would help you with all the pressure of the investigation," said the priest, handing Carl an envelope containing a hefty wad of bills totaling $700.00.

Carl was dumbfounded, and thanked Fr. O'Neil for the generosity of the parish and diocese toward his family. Mr. Croteau has maintained the 'gift' was a sincere, personal offering from Father O'Neil and the pastor, Father Thomas Griffin.

Over the years, Carl continued to dispel any rumor the gift was a payoff or bribe on the part of the church.

During their absence, the investigation into Danny's murder continued.

The police reviewed all evidence collected at the scene.

Two types of blood: Type O and Type B. Danny was Type O, and Father Lavigne was Type B. It was noted only 9 percent of the population were Type B.

A straw and piece of rope with traces of Type B on them were collected. In 1972 DNA testing to link blood samples to particular individuals had yet to be developed. Nearly twenty years would pass before the evidence could reveal additional information.

In addition to the evidence collected, the investigation turned to the statements implicating Fr. Lavigne. Each statement was carefully reviewed.

Joe Croteau confirmed the priest was familiar with the spot where his brother was found. He stated Father Lavigne frequently took several boys fishing at that spot as recent as the previous summer.

His suspicious inquiries reported by Lt. Radwanski the day after Danny's body was found were also reviewed.

Upon their return from California, the Croteaus had another visitor. Attorney James Egan came to the door, unannounced. He introduced himself as the attorney for the diocese.

Mr. Egan was not one to skirt an issue. He asked bluntly, "What do you want out of this? Is there anything you want?"

Once Carl was able to overcome his astonishment of the attorney's questions he replied, "What do you mean, what do we want?"

After a few moments of hesitation, Attorney Egan answered, "Well, if you ever decide you need something, let us know." With that, he left and never contacted the family again.

Father O'Neil became a regular visitor to the Croteaus. During one visit, O'Neil told Mr. Croteau he too had heard about allegations of sexual abuse of boys in the parish.

He told Mr. Croteau on more than one occasion he had received reports from Annie, the housekeeper at St. Catherine's. The housekeeper informed Father O'Neil Father Lavigne frequently persuaded kids to skip school and stay with him in his private bedroom.

Adhering to the directive of Lt. Fitzgibbons, the Croteaus refrained from discussing the molestation with their boys. What they failed to understand was why Father O'Neil or anyone else from the diocese never asked to interview his sons to confirm their allegations against Father Lavigne.

After three years, Carl Croteau was frustrated with the investigation. Despite the promise, "we'll nail him" offered from Lt. Fitzgibbon no indictment had come down against Father Lavigne. The priest had not been charged with molestation, and there was no indication he would be charged with Danny's murder.

Mr. Croteau arrived at the District Attorney's office. He asked Matthew Ryan why the case was not proceeding.

The District Attorney replied, "How can I ever convince a jury of twelve men and women to find a priest guilty of murder?"

Mr. Croteau shot back, "What about the abuse case involving my other boy Joe?"

In a patronizing tone, Ryan said he couldn't push that case because it might screw up the murder case.

It was an impossible journey. The Croteau boys were victims of abuse at the hands of a Catholic priest who had befriended the family. Their youngest boy was murdered and the same priest, Father Richard Lavigne remained the prime suspect, yet nothing was being done.

Over the next two decades, statements would be taken from former altar boys claiming abuse at the hands of Father Richard Lavigne. Many claims would be submitted directly to the diocese, naming Father Lavigne to be the molester. The diocese would be non-responsive, and when asked, would deny any knowledge.

The Danny Croteau murder would reveal the tangled web protected beneath the umbrella of the hierarchy within the Catholic Church. The Croteau's faith in God never wavered. They reflected upon the words offered by Father Leo O'Neil,

"You must not allow man to come between you and God."

Canon Law *vs.* Civil Law
1991

For two decades after Danny's murder, Lavigne continued to work quietly within the church until 1991.

Saturday, October 19, 1991

CATHOLIC PASTOR HELD
ON RAPE CHARGES

A Roman Catholic priest from Shelburne Falls was arrested on a warrant charging him with two counts of rape of a child. The priest was being held at the Shelburne State Police barracks.

A warrant was issued out of Greenfield District Court and Father Richard Lavigne was arrested at his parent's home in Chicopee. His bail was set at $10,000 pending his arraignment in Greenfield District Court on Monday.

In 1975, Father Lavigne was transferred from St. Mary's Church, Springfield, MA and assigned to St. Francis Church in North Adams, then to St. Thomas Church in Palmer.

In 1982, Father Richard Lavigne was assigned to St. Joseph's parish in Shelburne Falls.

Lavigne was the sole priest serving 600 members. He was responsible for all the elderly, the sick, performed all weddings, and officiated at all funerals

The reaction of the St. Joseph's parishioners was disbelief.

"He's very much loved. He's the most beautiful man, and the news of his arrest almost killed me," said a 74-year-old parishioner. "He's being treated like a serial killer."

A nine-year-old altar boy who served Mass for Lavigne cried when he heard the news. "It's not fair," he said to his father.

His father commented, "My son has been alone with Fr. Lavigne on many occasions. This is a travesty. My son has been crying for over an hour."

At the arraignment, Father Lavigne entered "not guilty" pleas to all charges.

Several parishioners attended the arraignment supporting their pastor.

Shelburne Falls Police Chief Mark DeJackome said he was aware of the warrant prior to Lavigne's arrest. He made it a point not to become involved and avoided being caught in the middle. The Chief was the head of the Church Council.

The Assistant District Attorney, Sandra Staub was asked several questions regarding the charges. She stated they involved a "series of events" that took place over a period of time.

When asked how many victims, she replied, "more than one."

Following the arraignment, Father Lavigne was released on $5,000 personal bond with a condition he was not to contact any of the alleged victims.

The court officers would not disclose the identity of the accusers. They confirmed there were two counts of rape of a child under 16 and one of indecent assault on a child under 14.

The incidents all took place on or before August 29, 1991. Applications for the warrant identified the victims' ages were 9, 18, and 20 years old. According to the ages of the 'victims' and the date of the incidents, it appeared the incidents occurred four years before.

As the news spread throughout the community, parishioners were stunned the diocese knew about the charges and did nothing. They expressed shock by the arrest.

As the news unfolded, the small town of Shelburne Falls learned of Lavigne's involvement with the murder of an altar boy over two decades before.

The murder of a 13-year-old altar boy remained unsolved. In 1972, Danny Croteau was found floating in the Chicopee River.

At the time, Father Richard Lavigne, a family friend of the Croteau family became the prime suspect.

Although his non-conforming ways were sometimes frowned upon by the older priests, Father Lavigne was charismatic and won the trust and admiration of all he became involved with.

When Danny was murdered on Friday, April 14th and found the following morning, the investigators uncovered a dark side of the good father. As the investigation intensified, all leads came back to Father Richard Lavigne. He became the prime suspect, the only suspect.

The District Attorney as well as State Police Lt. James Fitzgibbons were frustrated. Although they believed the priest was responsible for Danny's murder, they failed to get sufficient evidence to obtain an indictment.

Despite written complaints from Carl Croteau, stating he believed Lavigne killed his son, the District Attorney failed to seek an indictment.

In addition, Joe Croteau, one of Danny's brothers filed a complaint of molestation, naming Richard Lavigne as the molester.

The chief investigator, State Police Lt. Fitzgibbon was confident Lavigne was responsible for Danny's death. He assured Mr. Croteau Lavigne would be apprehended and an arrest would be soon. "We'll nail him," said the Lieutenant.

Representatives from the diocese stated that the church leaders were aware Fr. Lavigne was the chief suspect in the 1972 murder of Danny Croteau. The spokesperson continued to comment stating that while they were aware of the suspicions, they failed to take action against him.

"Former Springfield Bishop Christopher J. Weldon was aware Father Lavigne was a suspect in the earlier case but decided not to relieve him of his religious duties after the district attorney declined to prosecute," replied Rev. Gonet of St. Catherine of Siena's Church.

Rev. Gonet continued, "The late bishop interviewed Father Lavigne, and he maintained his innocence before the police and his bishop. The Bishop dismissed the charges against Lavigne 20 years ago."

The Reverend admitted, today, things would be done differently.

"I'd insure the priest received some kind of medical attention or psychological counseling to determine whether or not there was a problem."

"In most instances, the priest would be relieved of his duties whether or not he was ever prosecuted."

The parishioners were stunned that the diocese knew about the charges and did nothing.

A source from the Chicopee police department stated that after a week into the investigation of Danny's murder, Lavigne took a polygraph test. The test was inconclusive, but it did indicate Lavigne was a homosexual. The test could not determine guilt or innocence in the murder.

The officer who worked the case said Father Lavigne had been with Danny in the early part of the evening, but they were unable to put him with the boy later in the evening. The lead investigator, State Police Lt. Fitzgibbon died in 1985.

As the coffee shops buzzed with the news of St. Joseph's pastor, Danny Croteau's murder was resurrected and brought to the forefront.

The unsolved, 20 year old murder became the No. 1 topic throughout the Franklin County town of Shelburne Falls, in addition to the greater Springfield area and throughout the state.

Information was published that had not been at the time of the murder. The current charges against the 50-year-old priest in addition to the charges that loomed over him for the past 20 years dominated the news.

Father Richard Lavigne would be only one facet of the scandal within the Catholic Church. The charges he faced in 1991 would spread and infiltrate every parish and diocese throughout the Commonwealth for years to come.

As Father Richard Lavigne awaited his trial for the current charges that he sexually assaulted three minors, District Attorney William Bennett (successor to Ryan) began reviewing the Croteau murder case.

Several police officers, who worked the case, came forward offering information pertinent to the 20-year-old case. Most were retired, but their memories were keen.

Staff members of the former D.A. Matthew Ryan stated Ryan was convinced a Roman Catholic priest had murdered the 13-year-old altar boy, but did not seek an indictment because a key piece of evidence had been washed away by rain.

A sudden downpour washed away a tire track investigators believed came from the vehicle used by Croteau's killer

A former prosecutor said, "Throughout the years, Matty (Ryan) would use that case as a reference point for the need of better forensics. He really felt that if those tire tracks were preserved, he would have had a case."

"I remember Matty was convinced the priest was the killer. He'd say, 'I know it's him.' He was really frustrated that he couldn't go for an indictment, but in good conscience, the evidence just wasn't there."

Amidst the optimistic atmosphere, law enforcement officials suggested that unless investigators uncover a previously unknown witness, it was unlikely they could proceed with a murder case against Father Lavigne.

Within a week of the arraignment, Bishop Joseph Maguire of Springfield proclaimed the church's support of Lavigne's plea of innocence.

Just at the time the Bishop publicly announced the church's loyalty to their own, new allegations surfaced.

A 32-year-old man from South Hadley contacted the district attorney's office and gave a sworn statement.

Lavigne had molested him when he was a boy. He detailed the incidents he claimed occurred at the rectory of St. Mary's Church in Springfield in the late 1960's.

He said his brother also slept over at the rectory, but not at the same time as he had.

"When my mother found out, we never went to the authorities. Everything was hushed up, which was normal in that era."

Mr. Chevalier continued recounting his experiences with Father Lavigne, "I came forward because I found out that other kids were involved. I feel I'm doing my part, he's a sick man."

About three weeks had passed since Father Lavigne's arraignment. Father Lavigne was admitted to the Institute for Living, a psychiatric hospital in Hartford. He was unavailable to the media, but aggressively sought a top-notch attorney.

Lavigne, not the Catholic Diocese of Springfield, would pay for his defense. Max D. Stern, a high profile

Boston attorney was retained to represent the tainted priest at a pre-trial conference.

The pre-trial conference was delayed and re-scheduled from November 18 to December 20. The delay was requested by the district attorney's office to allow additional time to obtain further discovery to present to the defense.

Max Stern wasted no time preparing his defense. He met with the district attorney's office and consented to allow police to take pictures of the rectory where Father Lavigne resided.

The pictures were to show the physical layout. The district attorney's representative stated, "It's really no big deal in terms of evidence. If we thought the rectory itself contained any direct evidence, we would have gotten a warrant for a search of the premises right away."

Once dismissed from the Institute for Living, Lavigne would not return to the rectory. He had been replaced at the church. Lavigne took residence at his sister's home in Tewksbury.

As the defense prepared their case, and the D.A. gathered evidence to present on December 20, the community was split in their opinions regarding pending charges against the priest. All were strongly opinionated, some positive, some negative, but few were 'undecided'.

Lavigne wrote a letter to the parishioners of St. Joseph's church. He maintained his innocence and opined savage bludgeoning received in the press. He closed with, "The Lord is by my side."

One of Lavigne's strongest supporters, a 74-year-old woman, claimed, "Everything that could possibly be happening, they're trying to connect to him. I think the press has been unfair."

The woman appeared angry. "I have given quite a bit of thought to the fact that there might be a conspiracy to destroy him. He is a good man."

A former altar boy from St. Mary's parish in Springfield, described him as "An incredible guy, an artist, a man who built his own house, and who helped me with my homework. He challenged me to be a better person."

The supporter was a grown man with a family of his own.

"I have a son of my own now. He never took advantage of me and he had plenty of opportunity. We went away together, to his parents' house in Chicopee, and Vermont. I saw the good side of Father Lavigne and the good side is very good."

When detractors were contacted, they commented, "I don't want to be identified as a friend in case he is guilty of everything."

A priest who asked not to be identified said, "It's a tragedy. I don't want to prejudice the case. I know he's innocent until proven guilty, but 'Dick' Lavigne was an accident waiting to happen."

Another priest described his colleague as "a misunderstood, moody, artist, an enigma."

Many recalled Father Lavigne in his days as a young priest. They told of incidents revealing the priest was quick tempered and often displayed his anger.

He had no patience with crying babies in church. One woman recalled a time he flung a missal across the church when she couldn't quiet her small child.

Father Lavigne relished his exploits and shared them with parishioners. One story in particular reflected his arrogance.

In one parish, the house rule was no one could be seated at the dinner table after the pastor said grace. He walked in after grace and the housekeeper told him he couldn't be seated.

Lavigne boasts that he walked over to the stove and announced, "If I can't eat, no one will." He then emptied that night's super on the kitchen floor.

Similar stories were numerous. Some folks favored the non-conforming ways of the young priest. Some feared him. He was no stranger to controversy.

It was not surprising, after interviewing hundreds, the subject of Danny Croteau was broached.

The five Croteau boys were altar boys. Father Lavigne was a regular visitor to the Croteau home. He took the boys on overnight trips.

It was a friendship so close that the first person Carl Croteau reached out to after he learned of Danny's death was his friend, the parish priest. Lavigne identified Danny's body and made the decision to keep the casket closed. Within days, the Croteaus learned from police the priest was a suspect in their son's death.

Lavigne professed his innocence. He claimed he was doing errands that night. He was home when Danny's mother called looking for her missing son.

Bishop Weldon wouldn't allow him to talk to police.

He ordered the priest to "get in the rectory and stay there."

One friend added, "He could relate to hurt and suffering. He had no use for beer-guzzling jocks, but if you were in trouble, he wanted to help."

Included in the never-ending stories and recollections from acquaintances of Lavigne, new allegations were mounting. An area patrol officer reported he witnessed molestation. He said the boy told his parents, but they chose not to do anything.

"It's been going on a long time," the officer concluded.

Hampshire County District Attorney's office declined to say how many people had come forward with statements alleging Lavigne molested them. The D.A.'s office did confirm they had more than just the three boys.

Once again, the pre-trial hearing scheduled to take place December 20 was pushed to January, 1992.

Attorney William Flanagan, representative for the Roman Catholic Diocese of Springfield made statements in support of Father Lavigne. He disputed the claim from a police officer that the polygraph test determined the priest was homosexual.

"I was a witness to the polygraph test and Father Lavigne passed. That's why the investigation stopped. He wasn't the man."

The attorney added that a member of the state police, two Chicopee detectives and the specialist who conducted the test were in the room.

State police rebutted stating the tests were easy to beat. You can beat them with tranquilizers. He described the tests as psychological and complicated. A series of questions are asked that can determine deception or no deception.

The retired officer continued, "The only way anything would come up about someone's homosexuality would be in the pre-test interview. If properly done, it is very effective."

Boston attorney Max Stern was contacted and asked how the defense was prepared to proceed in the January hearing. Attorney Stern said the defense would contend that Lavigne was 'set up' by a Catholic cult from the town of Heath.

The Holy Trinity Lay Community Inc., claiming to be part of the St. Joseph parish had a parting of the ways the previous year. After several name changes, the sect eventually settled in Somers, Connecticut and at one time had close to 100 families within.

After investigations into allegations that members engaged in homosexual acts, Bishop Reilly, of Norwich Connecticut declared the sect was no longer permitted to operate under his diocese.

Additional 'black eyes' were sustained by the renegade defunct Catholic organization. Misappropriations of funds were contended and a lawsuit ensued, naming Charles Shattuck, president of the sect and a Heath resident.

The suit charged "unallocated vacation and severance pay" was allotted for corporate directors and employees. The suit was dropped when restitution was paid.

The January 17, 1992 trial date was rapidly approaching. Supporters of Lavigne were being interviewed by the defense.

One of Lavigne's strongest supporters, Most Rev. Joseph F. Maguire, Bishop of the Roman Catholic Diocese of Springfield, announced his retirement. Most Rev. John A. Marshall of Burlington, VT was to succeed Maguire.

Maguire insisted his health was good and that he asked Pope John Paul II to accept his resignation over 10 months earlier. He denied rape charges against Lavigne and the subsequent revelations that Lavigne was a suspect in the murder of Daniel Croteau had anything to do with his decision.

"I just had a feeling it was time for me to step aside," Maguire said. "When the time comes, you sort of know it." Maguire did say sorrowfully that he had been deeply wounded by the Lavigne case.

"It has been my darkest hour as bishop."

Maguire described his successor as one of the most highly regarded prelates in the country.

"He (Marshall) and Bishop Thomas Dupre will make a great team."

1992

Nearing the January 17, 1992 trial appearance, Father Lavigne rented a post office box in the town of Westford to receive monies for his legal defense.

The local office of the newspaper received a five paragraph letter signed *"Friends of Father Richard Lavigne."*

The letter stated that defense costs could run into six figures.

When the attorney for the Diocese of Springfield learned of the letter, he was quick to state the diocese had nothing to do with it.

A portion of the letter said, "To defend his name and his life, he has retained the services of a prominent Boston attorney. The process of a competent defense requires a great deal of time, labor and money. A priest's salary is hardly sufficient to defray these costs."

It was a lengthy letter that concluded with,

"As you consider your gift, please remember that in many ways, Father Lavigne's burden has been our cross as well as it is our responsibility to help him carry it. Won't you help? Any amount in single or multiple gifts now and at any time in the next few months will show you care."

At that time, priests earned $900 a month, which included car allowance. They had opportunity to earn extra money by officiating at funerals, weddings and baptisms. They were allowed to keep any gifts received from parishioners.

On January 18, 1992, the Greenfield District Court convened and Father Richard Lavigne was noticeably absent.

Attorney Stern informed the Assistant D.A. David Angier his client had signed a waiver of appearance.

After about 15 minutes in chambers, all parties agreed to continue the case until February 7, 1992.

Max Stern addressed the media asking the public to reserve judgment until the legal process had completed its course.

When Assistant D.A. Angier was asked why the case had not gone to the grand jury yet, Angier replied, "I'm not going to comment on the grand jury."

Max Stern requested to try part of the case in a lower court, but District Court Judge McGuane denied the request.

Stern argued, "We believe he has the right to have the case heard separately because it involves a different person, a different time and a different incident. The judge ordered all parties to court on February 26 for a probable cause hearing. The result of that hearing could put the entire case in the Franklin County Superior Court where Lavigne would face greater penalties if convicted.

It was a valid argument on the part of the defense. A District Court could send a convict to prison for no more than 2 ½ years. The Superior Court could sentence a maximum of life imprisonment on the rape charges and a maximum of 10 years on the indecent assault charge.

As Lavigne prepared for his court appearance, another priest faced charges of raping a girl from Poland and indecently assaulting another.

Father Julian Pagacz, pastor of St. Valentine's Church, Northampton, MA and part-time at another Polish National Church in Chicopee, MA entered pleas of not guilty at his arraignment in Greenfield District Court.

The charges the Polish priest faced were one count of rape of a 16-year-old girl and two counts of indecent assault and battery of a 17-year-old girl. According to documents, the incidents occurred sometime between 1989 and May of 1991.

The priest held the passport belonging to the Polish girl and threatened to have her deported if she reported the incidents.

Upon his release, Fr. Pagacz was ordered to turn over the girl's passport. In addition to the court order, the priest was ordered to surrender his travel documents allowing him to leave the country. The Polish priest had dual citizenship between United States and Poland.

The case was scheduled for a pretrial conference and possible additional charges.

The Polish National Church is a separate sector from the Roman Catholic Church and is not under the supervision or governed by the Catholic Diocese.

The Polish National Church consists of nearly 200 parishes in the United States, Canada and Poland.

It was founded by Polish Americans who believed the Roman Catholic Church failed to recognize Polish traditions and culture.

The bishops and priests in the Polish National Church are permitted to marry.

The charges similar to the ones Lavigne faced provided evidence the sexual abuse behavior was not confined to the Roman Catholic Church. It infiltrated many religious denominations.

By mid February, Rev. Richard Lavigne faced charges contained in five indictments. Each indictment represented a different victim. In addition to the original charges brought forth by two men, three new individuals charged him with rape, indecent assault and battery occurring over the last 10 years. The charges mounted to a total of 12.

The case was continued to March 17 in Franklin County Superior Court.

The hearing attracted a crowd filling the gallery and included Carl Croteau, the father of the murdered altar boy twenty years before.

Max Stern spoke to the media waiting outside the courtroom.

The Boston attorney stated one charge involved a person who, "as recently as December, told us categorically that nothing had ever happened between himself and Father Lavigne."

Stern stated the person changed his story after being put under pressure, but declined to say who applied the pressure.

In his first public statement, the accused described the proceedings as "the most gut wrenching experience of my life."

The priest showed signs of distress.

"The people who have leveled charges against me know them to be untrue. I just hope to one day be vindicated and return to my work at St. Joseph's where I belong."

Max Stern characterized the case against his client as a "witch hunt."

Rumors began to spread that some of the alleged victims were members of the Holy Trinity Lay Community, known to have been denounced by Lavigne.

Closed pre-trials were held between defense and prosecution teams. Max Stern advised he would argue in Superior Court on March 17 that the trial should be moved out of Franklin County. Lavigne's attorney argued vehemently that his client had been subjected to a witch-hunt.

The Catholic Church was about to experience another blow. Allegations of rape raised its ugly head once again.

On April 25, charges were filed at the Hampden County Superior Court.

An employee in the rectory of St. Mary's Church, Westfield, MA charged the Rev. Gary LaMontagne with rape, indecent assault and battery and assault with intent to rape.

The indictment stemmed from charges that the woman, a church worker was sexually assaulted on February 18 in the rectory.

Westfield's Police Chief, Benjamin Surprise said the woman delayed reporting the rape because she was embarrassed and worried that she would not be believed because of the man's connection with the church.

Detectives Boldini and Burns conducted an investigation. Surprise said they had knowledge of the situation and were able to verify some of the information supplied by the victim.

The newly appointed Bishop Marshall was not aware of the charges until John Egan, the diocese attorney, told him. LaMontagne would be placed on administrative leave pending the outcome of his case.

"The leave is the usual procedure for any priest charged with any misconduct because people have a right to worship God without distractions," said Marshall.

The Westfield priest was charged with digitally raping a church worker and attempting to have sexual intercourse with her.

Reverend LaMontagne would be the third priest facing charges of indecent assault.

The pastor of St. Mary's, Fr. Anthony Crean, addressed the parishioners.

"It is with a deep sense of sadness, pain and sorrow that we have learned the news about Father Gary LaMontagne."

The pastor said he had never seen any difficulties or anger between Fr. LaMontagne and the worker.

He offered a prayer for Fr. LaMontagne and his accuser. In support of LaMontagne, Father Crean described him as, "a good worker, really loved by a great deal of people."

Despite earlier comments by Bishop Marshall, Fr. LaMontagne was moved from St. Mary's, Westfield to Holy Family Parish in Holyoke. The reassignment came in March.

The allegations were said to have occurred in February but not reported until April.

After several rescheduled court hearings, requests for a change of venue, proved to be a win on the side of the defense of Father Richard Lavigne.

After presenting voluminous reports including media news tapes, and newspaper articles to buttress her arguments claiming the defense's case was contaminated, Patricia Garin, a member of Lavigne's defense team was certain a change of venue would be granted.

Franklin County Superior Court Judge John Moriarty granted two pre-trial motions. The five indictments would be tried separately and not in Western or Central Massachusetts. Newburyport in the far northeastern corner of the state was the chosen site.

The judge urged both sides to prepare for a trial quickly. Max Stern said he didn't think he would be ready to go to trial until September. Assistant District Attorney Angier said he expected to be ready in July or August.

Judge Moriarty ordered the attorneys to report to the court on the following Monday with a decision on a date and which indictment would go first.

The following week, as instructed both the defense and the prosecution faced Judge Moriarty and set a tentative trial date of June 22.

Assistant District Attorney Ariane Vuono could not say which indictment would be brought to trial first, but papers would be filed with the court soon indicating that.

J ury selection began as scheduled on June 22 in the seacoast town of Newburyport, MA. The jury was selected from Lawrence, Essex County because it had a larger pool. Once selected, the jurors would be bused the 23 miles to court. The trial was expected to last a week. Judge Guy Volterra would preside. The first case would not be among the first three people who came forward.

Since Lavigne's arrest in October, as many as 19 people had come forward with sworn statements to the State Police and District Attorney's offices stating the priest either raped or sexually abused them.

The District Attorney's office commented they had statements from alleged victims dating back more than 30 years and through the present.

Judge Volterra denied a prosecution motion to include past acts in the trial. Max Stern submitted a motion to continue the case. He argued the case against his client would be prejudice because of the publicity surrounding Fr. James Porter.

Porter, a former priest from North Attleboro, appeared on television stating he molested dozens of children in Massachusetts in the 1960's. The judge denied Stern's motion for a continuance.

One hundred and forty potential jurors gathered in the courtroom. Father Lavigne wearing his cleric collar and donned in a black suit stood and addressed the courtroom of strangers, 12 of who would decide his fate.

"My name is Father Richard Lavigne and I'm the pastor of St. Joseph's Church in Shelburne Falls..."

After introducing himself, Lavigne sat beside one of his lawyers and nodded as Patricia Garin spoke on his behalf.

Customarily, the individual "voire dire" is conducted in open court. It was held in private because of the lengthy list of questions and their personal nature.

Each side was allowed 16 peremptory challenges, that is, passing a juror without offering reason. The questions were not published, however one excused juror said she was asked if she had heard about the case and was dismissed when she said she had.

By the close of the day, the jury was in place. Including three alternates, the jury consisted of eight women and seven men. Opening arguments were scheduled to begin the following day.

Included in the lengthy list of questions asked at voire dire were:

- Do you currently practice or identify yourself with any religion? If so, which religion?
- Have you or any member of your family ever been a member of a religious order?
- Do you think Catholic priests have any problems that are particular to Catholic priests?
- The complainant is a 20-year-old college student. The defendant is a 51-year-old Catholic priest. Would you tend to believe the testimony of one over the testimony of the other?

The judge addressed the jury.

"This trial has received some media attention, and as a result it is going to require sequestering. You're going to be guests of the Commonwealth." The judge proceeded to read the charges.

"A 20-year-old Greenfield man has brought accusations dated back to 1983 or 1984 when he was a 12-year-old boy. He stated that Lavigne fondled him twice."

"Father Lavigne denies these allegations, and states that he is innocent," the judge said.

The victim's mother, brother and father were expected to testify according to the witness list. The man's father was also on the list of possible witnesses for the defense along with Lavigne and two other men.

Questions arose concerning the cost of Lavigne's defense. *The Friends of Richard Lavigne Fund* had been set up and donations from many supporters in Franklin County were received daily. Estimates for Lavigne's defense team ran as high as $100,000. One attorney familiar with Max Stern commented, "Somebody's paying some big dough for this case."

The trial was set to begin. It was expected to last about a week with a sequestered jury. Lavigne entered the court accompanied by his sister, brother-in-law and nephew. He greeted parishioners with warm hugs. As he made his way through the over 33 supporters, he broke down and cried.

Just as the court was called to order and the trial was about to begin, Father Richard Lavigne pleaded guilty to charges of assaulting one of the victims now

20. He also admitted to molesting a 15-year-old altar boy in 1987 or 1988.

Following his reversed plea, Lavigne made a statement, "I'm sorry for the harm I caused and I ask for their forgiveness."

Some of the thirty-three supporters began to weep.

Superior Court Judge Guy Volterra sentenced Lavigne to a suspended four-to-six year jail sentence, 10 years probation and ordered him sent to a psychiatric hospital in Maryland that specializes in helping clergy.

Lavigne agreed never to serve again as a parish priest.

In addition to the plea agreement, the state agreed not to pursue the more serious charges of child rape. The prosecutor said it was imperative to get Lavigne to admit guilt in open court.

Six charges of molesting a child under the age of 14, two charges of molesting a child over 14, and 2 child rape charges were dropped.

Also stipulated in the terms of probation was Lavigne never work alone with children under the age of 16 and never live in the same house as a child under the age of 16.

He would serve no jail time. The convicted child molesting Catholic priest's confession avoided a four to six year Cedar Junction prison sentence.

The court ordered him to be admitted immediately to the Maryland facility.

The judge rejected the prosecution's request that Lavigne serve six months of an eighteen-month jail sentence.

The judge blamed the media for giving the case more attention than he thought it deserved. He also suggested that Lavigne might have won an appeal of a conviction because the statute of limitations had run out, but was extended retroactively by the legislature.

One of the victims in court replied, "What you did to me was wrong. Sometimes it's difficult to forgive but being a Christian in my heart, I forgive you."

A second victim's prepared statement was read to the court.

"This is a man I didn't have to learn to trust," Angier read. "A man of the cloth is someone you can always depend on. When I was little, I thought it was my fault. Not only did he choose to do what he did, he chose to hide it. As a result, I have lost all interest in the Catholic Church."

Speaking in support of Lavigne, Michael Slowinski stated, "I work construction so I have this bad right ear, so I shifted my seat and leaned in and I tried to listen real hard. I couldn't believe I heard right."

Slowinski contended his friend; Richard Lavigne was not guilty of anything. He believed the guilty plea was an effort to avoid five trials and the emotional as well as financial expense. He believed it was Lavigne's way to put an end to this and get on with his life.

The victims and their families were outraged. One woman called the sentencing a joke, a farce.

"If he wasn't a priest, he'd be going to jail, not some country club."

TV cameras and reporters surrounded the priest with his attorney at his side as they tried to leave the courthouse. Lavigne would not comment and his attorney referred to the press as "vultures."

The attorney would not give reason why his client changed his plea.

"There were many, many factors that went into it. I think this is a very sad day in a man's life, a life he's known for 25 years. His undying love for a parish is over. The sentence enables him to walk away with dignity and start a new page in his life."

At the closing of the day's proceedings, one supporter of the priest stated, "He's been a great inspiration to our family. He's been our family's best friend."

Many of Lavigne's supporters found the guilty plea hard to believe. Some thought the surprise plea was an effort to spare the church further and undue publicity.

In contrast to that theory, Raymond Babeu who had known Father Lavigne when he was a priest at St. Francis Church, North Adams stated,

"I'm really thankful that he came clean...There are many others who should come clean by repenting and confessing." He continued, "This goes on in a lot of churches, both Catholic and Protestant.

Bishop Marshall expressed sadness. "This series of events has truly been a tragedy for all concerned." He called for prayers to hasten the healing process.

"It's been a roller coaster of emotions in the Shelburne Falls Parish."

Some believed, until the confession, the complaints against the priest may have been motivated by a quest to sue for money.

Although several parishioners of St. Joseph's maintained support for their pastor, others expressed distain and claimed the conviction came as no surprise.

One resident described Lavigne as "an oddball character." A 12-year-old said, "Personally, I think he's disgusting."

The conviction was of no surprise to a local construction worker. "I knew someone who had an incident with him," he said.

In the ensuing weeks, and months, 'tragic' would be the most accurate description of all the circumstances surrounding the Fr. Lavigne incident.

Tragic for the victims of Lavigne's actions, and in the eyes of steadfast friends of the convicted priest, tragic for the man who did so much good work as a priest.

Sympathetic supporters believed the priest was merely a man, subject to disorders that led him to abuse the trust of vulnerable children.

The matter of celibacy would surely come into question. The Vatican would be asked to reconsider the restriction required of all Roman Catholic priests.

"Flesh and blood needs flesh and blood."

Most believed Lavigne would be subjected to the most severe punishment, that of his conscience. To live forever knowing he committed the crimes he had confessed to and the lives he damaged would be the pain he would endure the rest of his life.

Cardinal Bernard Law announced he was looking into the personnel records of all priests in the archdiocese to see if there were other cases. Cardinal Law believed every step should be taken to avoid tragedies in the future.

The public was asked to remember who baptized their children, who buried their dead and who made visits all hours of the day and night to hospitals. They were reminded that priests had walked through the pain of others, now; they must walk through his pain.

Father Lavigne was serving his time at the Maryland facility. Occasionally, he spoke to the press however; his words were always self-serving.

"I have been crucified by the press." He believed he was misunderstood.

"Now I'm paying the price. Very few people really know who I am. They know me from working with me, or my sermons, or the jokes I tell, but few people know and understand me."

Through his public statements, never was there any indication of remorse or sorrow for the pain he'd inflicted on his numerous victims.

"I'm a very, very trusting person, and I know if I go to the press with my story at this point, I could create problems for my defense. Being too trusting has always been one of my problems."

He believed he was the victim. The words were chilling to the true victims.

The cost of Fr. Lavigne's defense was being tallied. The numbers were astronomical. Some say as much as $200,000 was paid to Max Stern for his legal services.

A large portion was paid by the diocese. Lavigne used his personal property consisting of his personal home in Ashfield, MA as security. The home was valued at $133,500 for fiscal 1992.

Allegations of sexual abuse throughout the dioceses of Springfield/Worcester Church were beginning to dominate the news on a daily basis.

Msgr. Leo Battista, St. Leo's Church, Leominster, MA - having sex with a nun from 1972-1977.

Rev. David Holley, E. Douglas, MA - oral sex with two altar boys in the early 1960's.

Rev. Victor Frobas, St. Rose of Lima, Northborough, MA – rape in 1978.

Msgr. Kelley, Gardner, MA – assault 1983-1985.

Rev. Joseph Fredette, Worcester, MA – molesting residents of a halfway house, 1972-1974. (Fredette fled to Canada to avoid prosecution.)

Rev. Ronald Provost, Barre, MA - photographing nude boys – September 1992.

The manifest continued to grow. Some would be dropped because of the statute of limitations, some would be brought to trial, and others would be quietly settled by the diocese.

One 19-year-old victim spoke out. He was among the over 500 staunch supporters of Fr. Lavigne, assisting with tag sales to raise money for the defense of the convicted priest, and defending the rumors and negative comments that had become rampant.

Dana Cayo turned from ally to animosity. A soft-spoken 19-year-old spoke freely to the press. He was frightened and said he felt relieved the priest was being charged and convicted and believed the priest would be incarcerated and put away for a long time.

During his confinement at the St. Luke's Institute, Maryland facility, Father Lavigne made repeated telephone calls to the young man.

"Let's make plans to get together when I get out," he would say when he called Cayo.

"He wanted to know if I missed him," Cayo said. "I'd say no." Lavigne ignored Cayo's response and asked, "Let's plan a camping trip to Mount Washington?" Cayo reported. He expressed his fear.

The 19-year-old said he hadn't come forward before because he thought the easiest thing to do was to hope Lavigne would just go away. He described the relationship he had with the priest.

He described the behavior of Lavigne's visits between the time of his arrest and the trial. Lavigne would regularly visit Cayo's sister's home.

"He would come in disguise, hide out in the bathroom when visitors came, nervously watching cars driving down the rural road and basically acted like a haunted, hunted man."

"I think he thought he was going to jail and he was scared." Very peculiar behavior Cayo commented.

"He could be moody, too. You just never knew what to expect. He would ask me if my girlfriend was as nice as he was. He's a very sick man who should be in jail, not allowed to walk the streets."

Cayo sold his van and drove to Florida with his mother to start a new life. He was included in the dozen alleged victims to be represented by Michael Wiggins, a Boston attorney. The attorney for the victims was negotiating with the Diocese of Springfield for damages.

In late 1992 following Lavigne's conviction, Bishop John A. Marshall appointed a commission to investigate complaints of sexual misconduct by priests.

The Commission for the Investigation of Improper Conduct of Diocesan Personnel consisted of nine members appointed by the diocese.

The panel was to interview the accuser, the accused, any witnesses and consultants. All information was to be kept confidential until the commission's recommendations were presented to the bishop.

It was a sincere effort on the part of Bishop Marshall; however, to some it appeared as the church policing their own.

The accounts and sworn statements of accusers were monumental, and would be the beginning of the downward spiral of the Catholic Church for years to come. Every diocese throughout the country would be called to task. No cleric was immune. The accusations would range from the newly ordained priest, pastors, monsignors, bishops and cardinals. Eventually, the Vatican would take action.

1993

Father Lavigne was released from the Maryland facility late in January of 1993. He remained secluded at his Ashfield home. However, his life would be anything but secluded. The day of his release, he faced an additional eleven charges of abuse.

His legal battles would accelerate as William Bennett; District Attorney of Berkshire County continued to investigate the 21-year-old murder case of Danny Croteau.

Carl and Bunny Croteau were encouraged and cooperated with the District Attorney's office. After two decades, it appeared Danny's murder would be resolved, and his killer would be brought to justice.

The Croteaus were watching a press conference on television when they heard statements from the new victims.

Brian and Michael McMahon, brothers and nephews of the retired D.A. Mathew Ryan detailed their experience with Father Richard Lavigne.

They described an incident that occurred during an overnight stay in Goshen.

During a bit of horseplay, the 37-year-old McMahon said he pushed Danny to the floor.

"Lavigne saw this and struck me in the face so hard it knocked me down. He was enraged. I was shocked, hurt, embarrassed and confused for I had never seen him exhibit such rage. "

"I went to sleep that night without saying anything to him. Father Lavigne, got into bed with me, awakened me in the middle of the night. He molested me that night."

The McMahon brothers stated they contacted State Police and the District Attorney's Office in 1991.

They blamed their molester for subsequent problems with drugs and violence and concluded their interview with, "I think it's an atrocity that Lavigne had free rein on young boys with no one to stop him."

"It seems the Catholic Church decided to turn its head while young boys have had their lives psychologically scarred. I feel the Catholic Church owes the community, the victims and the victim's parents an explanation of why it allowed this to happen for so long."

Countless victims came forward delivering their unimaginable experiences with the parish priest. Each account revealed the dark side of Father Lavigne

Some brought forth the priest's propensity for violence. Some described the cunningness, manipulation, and the ability to instill fear in his young prey. Many accounts indicated Danny Croteau's presence.

"When I heard Danny's name on television during the press conference, my body went numb. To make that connection…I wasn't expecting it. I've lived every day hoping something would break in Danny's case," said Bunny Croteau.

Carl Croteau added, "The 11 victims are just the tip of the iceberg. We've been hearing things for years, now we have the faces behind the whispers."

William Bennett communicated with Danny's family and assured them that he was aggressively doing everything possible in respect to Danny's murder.

"It's a 20-year-old case and that makes any investigation pretty difficult."

The blood found near the site where Danny's body was found had been sent to a laboratory in California for testing.

In late January 1993, as part of the investigation, the District Attorney requested a court order requiring a blood sample from Lavigne.

F. Michael Joseph, a Springfield attorney represented the Croteau family, vowed to prove who killed Danny.

After two months passed, the District Attorney continued the battle to obtain blood samples from Lavigne for the purpose of comparison with the samples obtained 21 years before.

Lavigne's attorney continued to appeal to the courts, blocking the state's repeated requests for blood samples. The defense proclaimed taking blood from his client would be an invasion of privacy.

The court continued to take the matter under advisement.

As the courts continued considering motions from the District Attorney and the defense, the Croteau family was far from silent.

At a March interview, Greg Croteau offered his recollections and experiences involving Father Lavigne.

Greg Croteau stated that in 1988, he told Father O'Neil of his obsession with killing Lavigne and of the night Lavigne plied him with orange juice laced with vodka and tried to lure him into bed in a Vermont motel.

Greg said O'Neil appeared to be surprised to hear him say that Lavigne was a child molester.

"He told me it was the first he's heard of it," Greg Croteau said. "He said he would look into the matter and looked me in the eye and said if there was any evidence that Lavigne was involved with children, he was going to personally make sure Lavigne would never harm another child in his position as a Catholic priest."

O'Neil was elevated to Most Reverend Leo O'Neil, Bishop of Manchester, N.H. in 1989. After the interview with Greg Croteau, the media attempted to interview the New Hampshire Bishop at St. Francis of Assisi Church.

Bishop O'Neil's comment, "I'm not going to talk about it." He referred all questions to the bishop of the Springfield Diocese, John A. Marshall.

The months passed and there appeared to be no progress in the Croteau murder investigation. The battle over blood samples continued.

Finally, on September 9, 1993, state police took Lavigne from his home and transported him to Baystate Medical Center where blood samples were obtained. It was the first step but not one without restrictions.

Judge Moriarty ordered the sample, but placed a restriction on whether the blood would be analyzed and compared to blood found at the Croteau murder scene.

The judge would rule on the district attorney's motion to test the blood and Lavigne's motion for return of his blood. The ruling was expected within a few days.

While the attorneys argued the issue of Lavigne's blood, Carl Croteau sat with his son, Joseph, and daughter-in law, Pat.

"If he's got nothing to hide, why is he hiding?" Croteau asked. "If I knew a blood test could clear me of a murder, I know I would bring a gallon of it in."

Again, the court would take both sides under advisement. Another three weeks passed.

On August 31, 1993, Lavigne lost his efforts to reclaim his blood.

Judge Moriarty rejected the motion to reclaim the blood sample. He added the defense would have one week to appeal the ruling to the Court of Appeals in Boston.

If the ruling were upheld, the blood would be turned over to the district attorney's office and sent to California to be compared with DNA analysis of blood found on the drinking straw discovered near Danny's body. Test results were expected within three weeks of receipt.

D.A. Bennett was pleased with the favorable ruling and stated, "This is one step on a very long road."

Danny's parents shared the optimistic tone of the district attorney.

"It's been tense, but today it's worth the wait. We've been waiting 21 years for the truth. Today we're a little closer to it." Bunny Croteau stated her opinion with a smile. She rarely smiled when interviewed. The favorable ruling was one of her rare bright moments.

Carl Croteau added, "After 20 years of nothing, this is something. We're still hopeful that someone out there who may know something will come forward."

The judicial rollercoaster was set in play.

Less than a week after the favorable ruling to obtain a blood sample of Lavigne, investigators were notified the judge extended his stay order until October 20 to allow the priest time to appeal.

Another month passed. On November 2 Max Stern, the attorney for the defense announced he would file an appeal to a three judge panel of the state Appeals Court, or the Supreme Judicial Court to order the blood sample returned to his client.

Until the 'bloody decision' was handed down, the blood would remain at a western Massachusetts hospital.

Stern claimed reasons for fighting the blood tests. He claimed the district attorney refused to drop the investigation if the tests cleared his client.

"He doesn't think he should be a suspect because he didn't do it," said Stern.

The district attorney faced the obvious question of motive.

An investigator working with the D.A.'s office expressed his belief the killer wanted to silence Danny Croteau.

"I believe Danny Croteau was either going to blow the whistle or blackmail his killer and the killer decided to shut the kid up."

The investigator stated that Lavigne became a suspect when several altar boys, including at least one of Danny's brothers told police Lavigne had sexually assaulted them.

Early December, 1993 rolled around bringing a surprising turn of events.

Father Lavigne claimed indigence.

He submitted an affidavit to the Public Counsel Services stating,

"I am unable to pay the fees and costs of this proceeding without depriving myself of the necessities of life, including food, shelter and clothing."

Max Stern who charged Lavigne nearly $200,000 to defend him for over two years and easily charged hundreds of dollars an hour for his services would receive the public defenders' rate of $25 per hour out of court and $35 per hour in court. This rate would apply to felonies and misdemeanors. In a murder case, the rate would increase to $50 per hour.

A defense lawyer is obligated to represent an indigent client or be on the list of lawyers available for appointment.

The decision by the state Appeals Court was not expected until early 1994.

Lavigne remained on the diocesan payroll despite being banned from ever serving as a parish priest again.

Bishop Marshall said Lavigne would receive an undisclosed stipend until he found employment.

Lavigne was no stranger in the courtroom.

He faced a judge in Franklin Superior Court. Once again, he entered an innocent plea to charges of child rape

Franklin County grand jury indicted Lavigne on November 4 for statutory rape for a single incident that occurred sometime between September 1984 and February 1985 in Shelburne Falls. The maximum penalty for a child rape conviction, life in prison.

At the five-minute court appearance, Lavigne's usual pallor revealed a healthy tan. He wore a tweed sport coat, gray slacks and a mock turtleneck. His beady eyes peered through the metal framed glasses that balanced on his beaklike nose. When accused of the child rape, he rose and answered "Not guilty" in a firm tone.

As they exited the courtroom, Stern replied to the reporters, "He has not committed a rape on this person or any other person."

The alleged victim had come forward after Lavigne pleaded guilty to two counts of child molestation in June 1992.

Assistant D.A. David Angier stated, "Some people just for whatever reasons can only come forward when they're ready."

Negotiations with the diocese were ongoing. Dozens of victims continued to seek compensation for damage done to them and their families by Lavigne.

A separate complaint was filed. This time, Rev. Richard R. Lavigne would face a familiar accuser.

Joseph Croteau, one of Danny's brothers filed the suit charging Lavigne with molestation when he was 13 years old.

The complaint charged the priest with fondling his genitals and masturbating in his presence 24 years before. The incidents occurred at the priest's Ashfield home, a church rectory and at Lavigne's parents' home.

The molesting continued for more than a year.

Joe stated following the 1991 arrest of Lavigne he was questioned by the Massachusetts State Police. He was asked to review the complaint he had issued 20 years before. While reviewing his statement he began to experience flashbacks of his molestation.

Joe had purposely waited for an opportunity to file just in case the courts did not rule in favor of Lavigne's blood to be tested.

"I love my brother, I love my parents, I couldn't live with myself if I did not go forward again."

Carl Croteau informed the press that his son had given a statement to Chicopee detectives and the District Attorney's office in 1972.

"Nothing ever came of Joe's statement from what I can see."

Representing the Croteau family, Attorney F. Michael Joseph spoke on their behalf.

"The whole Croteau family has been severely hurt by this man. We could have come forward earlier, but we did not want to interfere with District Attorney Bennett's investigation into Danny Croteau's murder. This suit is not about money. It is about justice."

Joseph Croteau's complaint made no mention of monetary damages.

Following Joe Croteau's allegations, another of the Croteau boys spoke to the press.

Greg Croteau was the second oldest of the Croteau's seven children. He was a body builder and a recovering drug addict.

Greg grew up with the notorious "Circle Gang" in the Sixteen Acres section of Springfield. He admitted to being involved in "really insane things."

"I've done some bad things, but I'm not a bad person. I'm grateful I'm not spending my life in jail."

Greg Croteau remembered Lavigne as a 'different kind of priest'.

"He didn't have the mystery like Father Griffin. He never seemed priestly to me."

The 38-year-old man recalled a trip to Vermont around 1967. He said the priest pulled into a parking lot of a motel and slipped his clerical collar on before he registered, claiming the collar would get him a discounted rate.

"When we got to the room there was one bed and he handed me a container of orange juice. I was a street kid and had drinks before. I knew there was vodka in the juice. He said it must have fermented in the refrigerator. I said, 'Yeah, it fermented a lot.'"

Croteau did not indicate whether Lavigne molested him.

1994

As the New Year began, the Roman Catholic Church was close to finalizing monetary settlements for 17 people who claimed they were molested by Father Lavigne.

The settlement took almost a year of negotiations between Attorney John J. Egan, who represented the diocese and Attorney Michael Wiggins representing the victims.

Mr. Wiggins stated an official announcement of a settlement was expected next month.

The victims would be required to sign an agreement not to talk about specifics of the monetary settlement or risk losing a portion of it. It was disclosed each victim would receive $40,000 to $100,000 depending on a psychiatric assessment performed as part of the negotiations. Most were undergoing psychiatric counseling at the time of the negotiations.

Lavigne was arrested in October 1991. Three years later, he continued to be entangled in the judicial system

Father Richard Lavigne remained the central focus of controversy. The pending trial for one count of child rape was another issue.

In exchange for the guilty pleas in the 1992 trial, prosecutors dropped two child rape charges and eight molestation charges. At that time, Angier had agreed not to prosecute as the result of any investigations then already in place. The two sides argued the period of the rape allegation Lavigne was facing two years later.

Defense attorney Max Stern claimed the prosecution knew about the charges before the June 1992 agreement was struck. Angier claimed the victim, a 20-year-old Pittsfield man, revealed his rape allegations after the guilty plea.

A pretrial conference was scheduled. Angier would file his report in the Greenfield court within the week.

In addition, Lavigne still faced a lawsuit filed by Joseph Croteau. Court appearances for Lavigne were ongoing.

Max Stern opposed Joseph Croteau's complaint claiming the three-year statute of limitations on complaints of assault, battery, negligence and infliction of emotional distress had taken effect. In the case of a youth, the statute begins to run at age 18.

Repressed memory can delay the limitation. The statute could begin when the memory was recalled.

Michael Joseph, the attorney representing the Croteau family stated,

"You do not start a lawsuit and draft a complaint in a vacuum. It starts with damage. The damage was not identified to a cause until a later date."

The arguments became heated as each side made their points and their interpretation of the law. The judge faced another complex decision. After lengthy arguments, the case was continued.

Again, the issue was argued regarding returning the blood samples taken in September 1993. Although the District Attorney was able to obtain three vials of blood from the priest, they were unable to perform DNA testing, subject to objections of the defense..

Hampden County District Attorney William Bennett continued his efforts to test blood from Lavigne, the prime suspect in the Danny Croteau murder case.

The question of whether the blood was illegally seized from Lavigne and should be returned, or would the prosecution be allowed to test the blood against a sample recovered from a drinking straw found on the banks of the Chicopee River 22 years before . The Supreme Judicial Court expected to hold a hearing later in the year.

Over nine months after the samples were obtained; three vials of Richard Lavigne's blood were still chilling on a shelf at the lab of Baystate Medical Center waiting for the ruling of the state's highest court justices

Patricia Garin, assistant to Max Stern offered the prosecutor a 'deal'.

The defense claimed the only reason her client had balked at the testing was that no promises had been made to cease scrutiny of him if the test indicated innocence.

"We firmly believe the blood will prove our client's innocence. We have no guarantee from the prosecutor that they will cease the investigation."

Garin continued, "We would like a guarantee… We may well turn it over. We want this case to be over."

At the time of the controversy, DNA evidence was not considered reliable enough to be introduced in state court.

The District Attorney was perceptive, and proceeded because he expected it would soon be allowed.

The judge supported the D.A.'s contention.

Danny's father, Carl Croteau was confident the blood would prove guilt.

"I think they'd like to have the blood as a spike in Lavigne's coffin. My family would like to see this come to a conclusion and see Danny rest in peace for sure."

On July 3, 1993, 66-year-old Bishop John Marshall died of cancer. A few months before, the bishop had announced to his parishioners he suffered from metastasis adeoncarcinoma.

Under Canon Law, an administrator must be appointed within eight days.

Cardinal Bernard Law, archbishop of Boston and head of the New England province would forward three names to the Vatican's ambassador to the United States. The ambassador would research the candidates' backgrounds.

While waiting for a decision from the Vatican, Auxiliary Bishop Thomas L. Dupre would be named administrator.

I n early July, Judge James Dohoney dismissed two of the five charges contained in Joseph Croteau's suit. He stated that Joe had filed the suit 16 years too late.

Despite arguments from the Croteau's attorney, the judge gave credence to the defense's argument presented at the March hearing.

However, Judge Dohoney compensated and delivered a split decision. He contended that Joseph Croteau did not realize the effects of the alleged attacks until recently. The charges of negligence, infliction of emotional distress and civil rights violations were upheld.

Over the past three years, Richard Lavigne had appeared in four state courthouses to answer criminal charges. His lawyers had appeared in at least three other courts to squelch accusations.

In addition, the Diocese of Springfield paid $1.4 million to 17 plaintiffs who suffered at the hands of Lavigne. Lavigne continued to receive pay from the church. There was no question; Richard Lavigne was somewhat of a liability to the Roman Catholic Diocese.

Months passed without mention of the pending cases Lavigne was facing. To date he was expected to address the following:

- One charge of rape of a child, filed by a 20-year-old Pittsfield man (defense assertion the charge should not be prosecuted because of the deal made at the time Lavigne pled guilty in 1992.)

- Three charges filed by Joseph Croteau. (Two charges were dismissed, however three remained.)
- Decision regarding DNA testing of blood samples.
- Potential charge of the 1972 murder of Danny Croteau (murder has no statute of limitation)

In mid November, the Supreme Judicial Court presented a divided decision. They cited the common law rule. There must be probable cause for believing the person whose blood is sought by the prosecutor has committed a crime.

The defense believed the ruling would lead to the vindication of her client because prosecutors would be compelled to go into court and detail what evidence they had linking Lavigne to Danny's death.

The State Supreme Court came to further conclusions. The state's highest court approved the use of DNA evidence. The ruling would have future ramifications for the guilty and innocent.

The ruling allowed DNA to be used as a tool to clear or convict a suspect. The decision was not total and carried restrictions. It stated DNA tests could be used for comparison but population statistics were not reliable and could not be included.

State Supreme Court determined the blood samples were obtained illegally. Judge Moriarty issued the warrant; however, Bennett failed to show probable cause. The Supreme Court ruled that the search warrant for Lavigne's blood violated his rights.

In order to get another court ordered blood sample, investigators would be required to reapply for a search warrant and schedule a court hearing at which the defense could challenge any evidence showing probable cause that Lavigne killed Danny Croteau.

After 15 months of challenges, Richard Lavigne offered his blood to the District Attorney declaring it a sign of innocence in Danny Croteau's murder.

D.A. William Bennett agreed to close the murder investigation if Lavigne's blood failed to match the sample found at the scene of the crime.

Bennett was pleased with the voluntary offer and stated, "Without evidence from the blood, there is insufficient evidence to proceed with charging anyone in this investigation. That would conclude our investigation."

The defense exhibited an optimistic point of view.

"What has happened to Father Lavigne shouldn't happen to a dog," replied Max Stern. "The man has made some mistakes in his life for which he has taken full responsibility. The fact of the matter is that this man has been hounded, and I mean hounded, out of Western Massachusetts."

Stern added, "That is why we are here today in order to establish the man's innocence and basically to establish his right to live in this state as any other citizen."

Dr. Edward Blake a highly regarded DNA expert whose services were retained by O.J. Simpson's defense team commented,

"DNA can only eliminate a suspect to an absolute degree of certainty. However, if the DNA does not match, it does not exonerate Lavigne," Dr. Blake said. "It would just indicate that his blood was not on the straw."

The blood samples were submitted and the waiting game began. Richard Lavigne's fate rested with the DNA testing and reports of the experts.

1995

Both sides waited for test results. The Croteaus believed the results would trigger an indictment and subsequent conviction of Richard Lavigne for the murder of their youngest son after 23 years. Each day brought them closer to receiving the call delivering the long awaited news.

Five months passed.

On October 25, 1995, the D.A. dropped the investigation of Danny Croteau's murder. The tests proved inconclusive.

The small flicker of hope extinguished with the closing of their son's case. Carl Croteau said, "The smoking gun just went away. Bennett called me and said…not that he wanted to drop it, but he couldn't go forward with the case at this point."

William Bennett had fought over a year to clear the way for the blood tests to be performed. It was a devastating blow to Bennett. The District Attorney had no choice; the Danny Croteau murder case was officially closed.

Judge John F. Moriarty stated he would continue to impound all police documents, evidence compiled against Richard Lavigne along with sections of court decisions. The records were sealed by order of the court.

1

1996

Although Lavigne would not be prosecuted, the case of Danny Croteau remained open.

There was no other suspect and technically, a murder case always remains open without an arrest because there is no statute of limitations.

An attorney representing the newspaper opposed the decision to impound material, police reports, court decisions and affidavits, claiming that the public interest in the case was not mere curiosity. He claimed the public had a right to see the documents to understand the justice system.

Judge Moriarty took the stand that the impoundment order was to protect Lavigne's right to a fair trial and the names of any witnesses contained in the reports should not be available to the public. The impoundment order would be automatically dissolved at the close of future criminal proceedings.

The prosecutor allied with the defense in support to continue the impoundment. Each had their own agenda, but ultimately the same end.

The prosecutor said releasing the records would have a "chilling effect" on potential witnesses and may prevent them from coming forward. He also expressed concern that disclosure would jeopardize ongoing probes.

The prosecutor broached the possibility of a "deathbed confession."

"If all is disclosed, there will be no way to corroborate information if such a confession is made."

Investigators often hold back key details in a case from the public to verify whether a confession is factual since only someone with an intimate knowledge of the crime could possess the information.

The defense argued that a convicted child molester would not get a fair civil trial in Hampden Superior Court. The defense pointed out that the impounded records included hearsay statements, speculation and unproven evidence.

Although Judge Moriarty ordered civilian witnesses' names be censored from the records, the prosecutor and the defense claimed that other information could lead to their identities.

The Croteau family became frustrated by the contradictory nature of a closed case that is said to be ongoing.

"What they've got, the world should know about. It's public documents."

After hearing arguments from all parties, the judge would take the matter under advisement.

Three weeks later, a decision was handed down.

Court papers were made public for the first time in 24 years. The judge, to protect civilian witnesses, heavily censored the documents released. The released material would disclose why police investigators suspected Richard Lavigne in the Danny Croteau case.

While the papers gave some insight into why Lavigne was suspected, they withheld a great deal which prosecutors felt would jeopardize future police work.

They contained Lt. Edmund Radwanski's report of his interview with Lavigne the day after Danny's body was discovered. Also included were statements regarding Danny's frequent visits with the priest up to and including the week before his death.

A report from the Croteaus was also included. One in particular, referred to a phone call two days after Danny was found.

Carl Croteau Jr. answered the phone and heard a familiar voice say, "We're very sorry what happened to Danny. He saw something behind the circle he shouldn't have seen. It was an accident."

Carl's father said his son had recognized the voice as Lavigne's. Lavigne was associated with *"The Circle Gang,"* a notorious group of youths named for the area where they hung out behind the library in the Sixteen Acres neighborhood.

Pages of the documents provided a profile of a child molester – someone who used ritualistic patterns to seduce and sexually assault young boys.

Examination of the released documents revealed incidents where victims claimed Lavigne had threatened them with a knife if they revealed the sexual abuse. The victim continued his allegations.

"He took us fishing and became so upset about something he threw rocks at me."

The Croteaus also contributed statements. They offered many incidents involving the priest and Danny's relationship, including the matter which occurred a week before Danny's death. According to

344

Lavigne, he dropped Danny off at the corner of his street the morning of April 8 and that was the last time he saw Danny.

A week later, Danny was found dead.

The question never answered; where was Danny the day before his body was found floating in the Chicopee River?

The medical examiner was only able to determine the time of death as between 4:30 p.m. on Friday and 8:25 a.m., Saturday, when the body was found.

Disclosure of the censored documents shed a glimmer of new light for the Croteau family. In addition to the memory of Danny, they had an image of Richard Lavigne standing on the riverbank where their son was killed. The fact remained, after 24 years; they were no closer to resolution.

In late September, a civil lawsuit was resolved. Richard Lavigne would have to testify for the first time in a courtroom about allegations that occurred 25 years before. Danny Croteau's brother Joseph brought the allegations forth.

Michael Joseph, the attorney representing Joseph Croteau stated the settlement agreement contained a non-disclosure clause.

The Diocese of Springfield had washed its hands of any involvement and it was expected Lavigne would satisfy the monetary portion of the settlement.

Previous settlements amounting to $1.4 million came from insurance funds from an unrestricted account. The late Bishop John A. Marshall said, "The payments were made in a spirit of justice and charity."

Throughout the years, Carl and 'Bunny' Croteau would not lose faith.

Bunny Croteau believes, "I don't think people can go to their graves knowing what happened. I really don't. All we're looking for is justice to be served, a chance for some closure. We still pray, every day, that someone will come forward that knows something. Twenty-five years is a long time, but not long enough to forget what happened to Danny."

Carl Croteau, Danny's father, frequently serves as altar boy at St. Catherine's where Danny had once served.

"It makes me feel closer to Danny."

2002

Apriest stepped forward and delivered a haunting, sorrowful account of his experiences as a child, and later his reasons for becoming a priest.

His words were chilling, as he recalled the abuse he suffered at the hands of his mentor, Richard Lavigne. In part, Rev. Kevin Sousa claimed the priest who inspired him as a boy inflicted something far darker on him too.

He admired Lavigne so much that he joined the priesthood, but Lavigne also became the reason Sousa left the priesthood.

In 1991, Sousa watched television and listened to Chevalier's description of his boyhood overnight visits with Lavigne. "I was paralyzed. I was shocked because he was telling my story. The oversized T-shirt...it was all the same." Sousa detailed numerous incidents including witnessing the volatile side of Lavigne. Sousa was a junior in high school at the time.

He recalled playing a Mass entrance hymn on the organ. Lavigne began screaming at him and rudely shouted instructions to play another song.

"I was so embarrassed and hurt. After Mass, I went to him crying and saying that when I became a priest I would never treat anyone as he just treated me."

Lavigne's response was, "You're the one crying. That's your problem. You deal with it."

Sousa was interviewed by the police. In five hours of interviews, Sousa could not bring himself to reveal what he remembered about the abuse.

Before the deposition, Sousa informed Bishop Marshall about the questioning.

"After I told him about the deposition, I said to him, 'By the way, Bishop, if you're wondering about this Lavigne and whether he is an abuser or not, he is.'"

Bishop Marshall responded, "Thank you very much."

The Bishop said, "I haven't been here that long, and I have only met the man once...You have just given me the piece of information that I needed."

A few days later, Bishop Marshall announced to priests and the media that Lavigne was banned as a priest for life.

Bishop Dupre responded saying, "I was very saddened to hear about these tragic circumstances. I offered him my help and assistance and that of the diocese."

Sousa was disappointed in the Roman Catholic Church's response to sexual predators among clergy.

"The church has not responded to these issues in a pastoral way...It has only responded in legal ways."

Although Sousa is still a priest in good standing, he is not in active duty. He lives in New Hampshire and teaches in a regional school system.

He no longer goes to church.

Over a decade had passed since Richard Lavigne confessed to two counts of child molestation.

In April 2002, two months before the expiration of the 10-year probation sentence two more abuse charges were filed.

The charges were filed by two brothers, altar boys from St. Joseph's parish. The accuser was a 22-year-old from Greenfield. The younger brother, 19 was not included in the suit pending investigation by the district attorney's office for possible criminal action.

The brothers stated the abuse took place in the sacristy, a room where they dressed and prepared to serve Mass.

Lavigne corresponded with families who later would join those accusing him of molesting children. The letters offered clues to his psyche. In his letters, Lavigne compared his plight to the agony of Christ in the garden of Gethsemane on the night before his death.

John J. Stobierski, the lawyer representing the alleged victim obtained the letters. They were written during the investigation and prosecution a decade before. In part they read,

"I, for one, have given up on convincing anyone of my own situation. People will believe what they will, one way or another...I have suffered, yes, but Gethsemane is at the heart of ministry. Jesus wasn't killed because He was popular. He was killed because He spoiled the party for some people."

The letters were written to the parents and boys who were 12 and 9 at the time.

Another letter written by Lavigne was directed to the two most recent accusers. It was dated August 5, 1992. In the letter, he thanked the boys for helping with the tag sale held to raise money for his legal expenses. The letter continued.

"Few priests can boast of having such great kids in their cheering section. I miss you all very much. It's not the same here in Maryland."

He referred to the Maryland facility as a "summer camp" and complained about the weather.

Bishop Thomas Dupre replied to the new accusations.

"The Misconduct Commission and the Diocese have received several new complaints about misconduct since January 1, 2002. All such complaints are directed to the Commission for review. That process is still ongoing and no recommendations for action have been given to the bishop to date."

The chairperson of the commission, James Bell stated, "Neither of these new allegations have come to us and I don't know why. I think those individuals decided to go directly to the civil authorities."

After Cardinal Bernard Law turned over the names of 87-suspected pedophiles in the Boston area, other diocesan leaders followed.

Rev. Thomas Dupre, the bishop of the Diocese of Springfield stated he would not release the names of priests accused of molesting children in the past.

Bishop Dupre confirmed that six priests had been removed from full-time parish ministry as a result of misconduct complaints over the last decade. He added that since the six priests were removed in 1994, the diocese had not faced a lawsuit in more than five years.

Through examination of the records, it was learned that although six priests had been removed from churches throughout Western Massachusetts they maintained positions within the church.

The Rev. Edward Kennedy was one of the six barred from ministry. His records indicated he was "on sick leave." The diocese sent him for psychiatric treatment and then on to canon law school.

After he was able to receive his Master's Degree in canon law, he returned and became an assistant judicial vicar on a diocesan council that grants or rejects requests for annulments which includes the examination of applicants' sex lives.

In addition to the position on the council, he was allowed to fill in at Sunday Masses when priests were sick or on vacation and assigned to serve as chaplain at a Holyoke retirement community. He was restricted from appearing at the Northampton parish from which he was removed.

Rev. Richard Meehan was listed among the six removed priests. His records indicated he took a "leave of absence."

He was assigned to conduct archival research for local churches.

Revs. Donald Dube and Alfred Graves personnel files also indicated the two 'removed' priests had taken a "leave of absence."

Rev. Donald Desilets was barred for misconduct and retired to Montreal where he died in 2001.

Rev. Alfred Graves resigned abruptly and he too was listed as 'on leave of absence'. He disappeared from the directory altogether.

The late Bishop Marshall, who created the Misconduct Commission in the wake of Lavigne's conviction, refused to let priests found to abuse children back into the church. Marshall's replacement, Bishop Dupre created a re-entry system that allowed ousted priests to request new assignments provided they didn't involve children.

Out of the six 'ousted' priests, Richard Lavigne was not among those who held re-entry positions.

To date, Richard Lavigne had a conviction of two charges of molestation, was ordered to a treatment center, and now was only weeks away from completing his 10-year probation.

During the previous decade, Lavigne continued to receive monthly payments from the church, and no steps toward defrocking were initiated.

Throughout the decade, he had appeared in court on countless charges involving allegations of child abuse, rape and molestation.

Although the file was sealed concerning suspicions of his involvement in the Croteau murder over two decades before, the D.A. continued to review the case.

Adult men continued to come forth with new allegations of abuse they had suffered at the hands of their parish priest.

Cardinal Bernard Law was an advocate of Bishop Marshall's policy that barred priests from any assignment at all.

Bishop Dupre would not publicly release the names of the six priests who had been accused of sexual abuse over the years, but when the news media were able to obtain the list through other sources, the bishop confirmed the names.

Dupre said that priests who were under treatment for sexual misconduct were usually classified as 'on leave' but the classification also applied to priests who were totally unscathed by allegations of any misconduct.

When asked about payments being made to the 'removed' priests, the bishop said it was canon law, which dictates that ousted priests are to be provided with minimal stipends, and health insurance even if they are never allowed re-entry, provided the priest has not been defrocked. "That is a measure rarely employed by the Vatican."

Cardinal Law agreed to release the confidentiality clause from the settlements within the Boston Diocese.

Bishop Dupre refused. The secrecy clauses prevented victims from speaking with prosecutors who would determine whether criminal charges should be brought.

Most parishioners were outraged upon learning of the ousted priests' assignments.

"How on earth can priests who have shown themselves to be sexual abusers sit in judgment of married couples?"

"This shows a diocese that while holding itself up as a model for others really needs to look in the mirror and get over its arrogance." Were outcries of angry parishioners.

In Amherst, the parishioners of St. Bridget's had even more reason to be confused and doubtful of the treatment their pastor had received five years before.

Rev. Bruce Teague had noticed Lavigne hanging around the church. Having knowledge of Lavigne's past, and concern for the children, the pastor sent word to his superiors at the Diocese of Springfield.

At one point, Lavigne tried to assist another priest who was hearing children's confessions. Teague ordered Lavigne to leave.

Bishop Dupre did not respond on behalf of the diocese so Teague took the next appropriate step. The pastor went to Amherst police who issued a trespass order, threatening the convicted child molester with arrest if he came back.

It wasn't long and Teague felt the wrath of Dupre. He was reprimanded for going outside the church, which led to his eventual dismissal as pastor.

Upon hearing of the removal of Rev. Teague and the reason behind it, the parishioners unsuccessfully sought meetings with Dupre to argue for Teague's reinstatement.

One individual representing the group stated,

"Here you have a good priest who blew the whistle on a bad priest and it's the good priest who gets punished. Father Teague was driven out of here because he protected children and dared to challenge Bishop Dupre."

"Priests continue to socialize with Lavigne and the diocese continues to coddle him, a convicted pedophile. It's an absolute disgrace."

Rev. Teague said that after clashing with his superiors, "it was very clear that the diocese didn't want me there." He was informed that he would not be reappointed as pastor and has been on leave ever since.

Rev. Teague was labeled a "whistle-blower." The transgression was...he turned in another priest. The parishioners of St. Brigit labeled him "brave and heroic."

According to Bishop Dupre, Teague reported Lavigne had been seen in the office of a layperson in the parish center.

The Bishop denied the incident had any bearing on his decision not to reappoint the pastor. He further stated that Teague was granted a leave of absence "for personal reasons" based on his own request and was not reassigned to St. Brigit because of the needs of the parish and his performance as pastor.

At a hearing in the Hampden County Superior Court, Judge Peter Velis allowed the accuser to use a pseudonym to avoid identity. He would be referred to as simply, 'John Doe.'

The suite charged Lavigne with sexually abusing John Doe for four years starting when he was seven and ending only when Lavigne was arrested.

The suit also included charges against the diocese for negligence, claiming officials knew about Lavigne's tendency to abuse children and did nothing to stop him.

The diocese continued to hold back Lavigne's personnel records from the prosecutor. While some of the local priests were very helpful, the Catholic Diocese repeatedly refused to provide information. Not only did the diocese fail to explain why Father Lavigne was moved from parish to parish, but also it refused to identify other victims.

Lavigne's personnel file would disclose his sexual tendencies all the way back to 1958. Lavigne was a teen-ager working with the Chicopee park and recreation department. He was discharged for being 'undesirable' to be around children.

Judge Peter J. Velis ordered the affidavits filed by John Doe be impounded to protect his identity. The accused indicated through his therapist he feared personal harm if his allegations were disclosed.

Stobierski attached Lavigne's real estate holdings in Ashfield as security for the lawsuit. Lavigne moved into his home in Chicopee to protect it from seizure in a lawsuit, and if John Doe prevailed, he would receive money only if the priest sold his home, moved or died.

The church refused to assume any liability.

In the wake of the new allegations, Most Rev. Thomas Dupre, bishop of the Diocese of Springfield announced Richard Lavigne could possibly face defrocking.

Dupre said he anticipated bishops would work in Rome on defrocking procedures that would simplify the current cumbersome judicial process.

In 2002, a new ruling came down from the Vatican. The ruling required all new child sexual abuse cases by priests to be reported to the Vatican's Holy See. From there, the dioceses would be advised on how to proceed with cases. This was an enormous change from the previous manner in which cases were handled within the dioceses.

The bishop said the church had been reluctant to the "defrocking" process against 'notorious and serial' child sexual abusers because the process was too cumbersome.

"When I became bishop in 1995, I saw no reason to defrock Father Lavigne."

Once laicized (defrocked) a person can no longer present himself as a priest. He is stripped of all responsibilities and rights of a priest.

Ten years after his conviction, Richard Lavigne continued to receive financial assistance from the church. Dupre stated it was minimal food and shelter expenses to keep him off public assistance.

Still another suit was filed. This suit accused the Rev. Robert W. Thrasher of witnessing Lavigne's abuse.

Stobierski filed the newest charge on behalf of two 41-year-old Springfield men.

Steven Block charged Thrasher with negligence during the summer of 1972 at the rectory of St. Mary's.

He walked into the room and left after seeing Lavigne abusing Block. According to Block, Thrasher never reported the incident.

Rev. Thrasher denied the charge, claiming it never happened.

"I know it didn't happen because I have no recollection of the fact. Something of that nature, you don't forget," he said.

Thrasher added, "If it had happened, I would have spoken to Lavigne at the time."

In addition, Thomas Martin cited the Diocese of Springfield for liability.

Martin was not an altar boy, but claimed he was abused from age 7 to 13, usually on church grounds after Mass and occasionally at his own home when Lavigne visited Martin's family.

"I never told my parents because you have to remember how highly a priest was regarded back then. I felt if I said something I would have been accused of doing something wrong."

The diocese acknowledged the three new suits and advised they would be forwarded to the diocese's insurance carrier for an appropriate response.

John Doe in a signed affidavit expressed his feelings and the life he was living as a result of the abuse inflicted upon him.

In part, it stated, "He ruined my life. I have not been able to hold a job and cannot function in society. I have been homeless and live on a subsidized income."

Stobierski continued on the part of his client.

"Richard Lavigne used a number of sinister methods to try to keep my client from telling anyone what was happening to him. One was the use of the confessional and invoking God to keep him quiet."

The bombshell came when a therapist stated,

"He had indicated clearly in our first meeting that it was his conviction that this priest had murdered a former altar boy because this altar boy had or was going to talk."

Both Block and Martin accused the diocese of negligence and liability.

Block said he was abused several times in the St. Mary's rectory.

Lavigne once told him, "God wanted it to happen, and that even if it hurt, Jesus had suffered on the cross, and so he could suffer a little also."

Steve Block and Tom Martin were friends of Danny Croteau. They claimed the parish priest had a motive for the murder, to hide a dark secret that Danny was threatening to tell.

"He told me he hated Father Lavigne and he hurt him," said Martin. "I knew exactly what that meant."

Martin charged Lavigne was sexually abusing Danny, just as he had molested Martin and other boys at the church.

"He forced me into oral sex on him twice," said Martin. "I was only eight years old."

Steve Block told his story.

"He actually invited me over to the rectory to make breakfast. At that point he took the initiative to move me into another room and sexually assaulted me." Block said this happened when he was 12.

The two young men were asked if they were aware of other boys being abused.

"The only time I ever spoke about it was with Stephen (Block) and the only thing we ever said to each other was 'is he doing the same thing to you?'" replied Martin.

"The only other person that ever said anything to me about Father Lavigne was Danny Croteau."

Both men left the church because of the abuse.

In the March 29, 2002 issue of the Catholic Observer, the Most Reverend Thomas L. Dupre, bishop of Springfield Diocese addressed the public in a column entitled, *"Setting the Record Straight."*

In the article, Bishop Dupre addressed many controversial subjects that had besieged the church over the past several years.

The issue referring to laicization was of particular concern. On that the bishop said, "Laicization is only granted by the pope in Rome and only after an extensive process."

He did not address why Lavigne was not defrocked. Dupre said Lavigne did not seek laicization.

"The process can be complex and cumbersome as in any judicial procedure."

Warren Mason, a Springfield resident wanted the diocese to take action. He took his concerns to his local parish, St. Michael's church in East Longmeadow, MA. To his surprise, he found a receptive audience.

Sister Mary McGeer replied to Mason's concerns.

"Molestation of children is evil and there's no other name for it. When we cover it up, it's evil. The people covering it up are evil."

Mason took a bold step. He met with the Rev. James Scahill, pastor of St. Michael's.

He proposed the congregation withhold funds from the Springfield diocese until Father Lavigne was defrocked and removed from the payroll.

"As long as Father Richard Lavigne is receiving any sustenance from the diocese, I will not give any money to the church."

Rev. James J. Scahill listened patiently to his angry parishioner. Mason pushed the envelope a bit further, "Hold back the bishop's money."

The pastor was noticeably surprised at Mason's proposal, but agreed to submit it to the head of the Springfield Diocese, Bishop Dupre.

Fr. James Scahill described the bishop's reaction as furious.

"He said what? I repeated the proposal and he said, 'You cannot do that. There's no conversation relative to this matter. You absolutely cannot do that.'"

At that point, Dupre threatened the pastor with suspension.

Sister McGeer noticed other local priests treated Scahill as a traitor.

Scahill would not be intimidated.

"The church must become accountable. The church must change."

Fr. Scahill received encouragement from his congregation and Warren Mason sent countless letters to newspapers demanding Lavigne be defrocked.

Father Scahill urged parishioners to write to Bishop Dupre and urge him to bring about laicization. In addition, he urged they express their dismay that Richard Lavigne was being paid by the Springfield Diocese.

The parishioners seemed to be waiting for the approval of their pastor, which was indicated by the applause after the announcement following Communion.

The parishioners of St. Michael's expressed gratitude that a priest spoke about the church's current sexual abuse scandals.

"It's about time that someone addressed it. You can't make believe it didn't happen," said a parishioner of 45 years.

It was a bold step for the 55-year-old pastor of St. Michael's. Father Scahill had become pastor only five weeks before.

Scahill said, "Canon law has nothing to do with Jesus Christ, and Jesus Christ has nothing to do with canon law."

Rev. Scahill spoke from the pulpit.

"I will make sure there will be no chance whatsoever that even one cent of anything you offer within the sacred Mass will go to supporting Lavigne."

He explained to the congregation how the collection money is allocated. 9% is assessed. Of that, 3% supports local parochial schools and 6% goes to the bishop's office.

He stated St. Michael's would retain the 6% from their parish in a separate account that the diocese would not have access to. He concluded the money would be remitted once the diocese was restored.

He expressed his feelings beyond the opposition to the financial matter. He told the parishioners that it was his belief Richard Lavigne was not reduced to lay status thanks to the immobility of the church hierarchy over the past 10 years.

The congregation was in favor of the rebellion their new pastor had sparked. They were somewhat surprised because they believed that priests pretty much conform to what the bishop dictates.

"I applaud Father Scahill for taking the initiative. He is a strong leader, and other churches should take note of what we're doing here for justice's sake," commented one of the outspoken parishioners.

Others called their pastor courageous.

Charges against Richard Lavigne continued to mount.

After Lavigne's 10-year probation had been served, a North Adams resident joined 'John Doe' and petitioned to open the 1992 file in which Lavigne admitted to molesting two boys.

They believed it would prove Lavigne was part of a ring of priests that passed children around and the Diocese of Springfield knew Lavigne was a sexual abuser as far back as 1986.

Paul Babeu stated there was a ring of priests who passed children to each other. He accused Lavigne of passing him along to another priest who abused him in Vermont.

The accuser was able to produce a copy of a letter he received from Bishop Marshall saying he had never heard any rumor, innuendo or complaint directly or indirectly that Lavigne possessed pedophilic tendencies.

Because of the agreement struck in accordance with Lavigne's guilty plea, Babeu was barred from filing any criminal charges.

Babeu believed the diocese should have stepped forward and acted on the knowledge it possessed at the time, prior to the 1992 agreement.

Babeu encountered Lavigne while he was assigned to St. Francis of Assisi Parish in North Adams.

"He told me there was nothing wrong with homosexuality and there were passages in the Bible to prove it"

In rebuttal to Babeu's statements, the diocese spokesperson issued a statement claiming one individual came forward in 1986.

Subsequently, Lavigne was ordered to undergo a mental health evaluation, which determined the priest was no threat.

Two clergy members stepped forward in 1986 and informed Bishop Leo O'Neil that Babeu was being abused by Lavigne. O'Neil died in 1997 and no records were discovered to substantiate the statements

The two supporters of Babeu said they were led to believe that Lavigne would be removed from parish ministry, but that didn't occur until criminal charges were filed in 1991.

"I'm here not only to support Paul, but as part of the institutional church I need to take responsibility and I need to hold the church accountable."

The nun, speaking in defense of Babeu said eight people had come forward to say they were molested by Lavigne since 1986.

Amidst all the new scandals, Richard Lavigne's probation ended. On June 16, 2002, Lavigne would be required to register as a sex offender. A hearing was set by the state Registry of Sex Offenders to determine which of four levels Lavigne would be registered under.

He continued to live in his Chicopee home.

Victims of the disgraced priest continued to endure the emotional pain; some would find it impossible to live with.

Raymond Chelte Jr. fatally overdosed on drugs four years after he was one of the 17 who settled a suit with the diocese in 1994.

His death was a suicide ending years of drug abuse and failures that began when he was abused as a pre-teen. For years, acts of misconduct within the Roman Catholic Diocese of Springfield focused on Richard Lavigne, the priest convicted of child molestation.

By June 2002, many local Catholics were not pleased with the Most Rev. Thomas L. Dupre, the bishop of Springfield Diocese. They were discovering their bishop was less than frank when discussing matters of concern to the parishioners.

In the matter of defrocking Lavigne, they learned other bishops had successfully sought to defrock child-abusing priests in a matter of months. Dupre claimed it to be a "cumbersome and complex process." The general opinion was it was just too much effort on the part of Dupre.

David Angier, prosecutor in the case against Lavigne in 1992 said he faced uncooperative church leaders who refused to hand over information about the priest's history. He said going after the diocese criminally was never on the table.

Attorney General Thomas Reilly considered indicting Cardinal Bernard Law and other clerics in a criminal case. The indictments would claim conspiracy charges and accessory after the fact.

These charges would state the church hierarchy ordered the destruction of documents or evidence in trying to conceal their knowledge of criminal conduct.

The charges would be brought forth claiming the Cardinal and other church leaders continued to reassign priests after repeated allegations of sexual abuse, and failure to adequately supervise priests who they knew abused children.

Bishop Dupre said repeatedly that they sent Lavigne for an evaluation after they received the complaint and assured by a therapist he was cleared for future assignments.

Dupre made it clear his views on the laicization process for any priest who sexually abused one child in the future and for any priest who sexually abused two or more minors in the past.

Dupre favored the "two strikes" policy on past abusers. He believed zero tolerance was a bit harsh especially if a priest had reformed his life and had done a good job in the last 20 to 30 years.

2003

In January the Massachusetts Sex Offender Registry Board rendered a decision on the appropriate level Lavigne would be classified under.

The 61-year-old ousted priest would be classified a level 3 sex offender regarded as a high risk for re-offending. The board would make a 'community notice' to the city of Chicopee where Lavigne resided and required to register with the police annually. In cases of level 3 offenders, public notification is required.

The notice provided Lavigne's residence, 86 Haven Avenue, Chicopee. His description, 61-year-old white male, 6 feet tall, 170 pounds with blue eyes and brown hair. Following the description was a brief description of the conviction. It also stated that he was not wanted by police. The level 3 offender's notifications are distributed to schools, and Boys and Girls Clubs.

The decision to classify Lavigne as a level 3 offender was challenged by Max Stern, on Lavigne's behalf.

The obligation to register as a sex offender was 'stayed' pending an appeal. The appeal pertained to legal documents that had been 'impounded'

Immediately following the appeal the Springfield Diocese challenged the First Amendment.

The Diocese would seek dismissal of all sexual abuse lawsuits claiming the First Amendment prevented civil courts from interfering with the relationship between church leaders and their priests. If the diocese prevailed, and the motion upheld 19 suits would be thrown out.

John Stobierski, the attorney representing 14 of the victims appealed to Judge Sweeney who was in the midst of reviewing similar arguments brought by the Archdiocese of Boston.

The Diocese argued that the First Amendment of the U.S. Constitution stated in part, "Congress shall make no law respecting an establishment of religion, or prohibiting the free exercise thereof..."

Also cited in their argument was the U.S. Supreme Court ruling.

"The First Amendment prohibits civil courts from intervening in disputes concerning religious doctrine, discipline, faith, or internal organizations to establish their own rules and regulations for internal discipline and government."

Michael Callan and Phillip Callan Sr., the attorneys representing the diocese were able to cite a precedent.

"Of course, there is no protection, criminal or civil, for any abuser. In 1995 a similar suit involving another religious denomination was dismissed on constitutional grounds by the Superior Court."

The diocese claimed they sought the same constitutional protections.

Stobierski disagreed, stating,

"The First Amendment doesn't reach so far as to prevent a church's internal policies and procedures from providing a basis to award damages to those who have been victimized."

The administrators of the church feared the insurance companies would abandon the church if it failed to explore all possible legal defenses.

Stobierski also filed a motion to consolidate the 14 pending cases.

"As time goes on and more and more victims come forward, it makes sense to have them all taken care of in one forum."

He added, "I have sent two specific demand letters quite some time ago requesting settlement of cases, and I have received no response from the diocese other than they were referring the letters on to the insurance carriers."

"There has been some general talk, but nothing specific. The talk is always initiated from the plaintiffs' side."

As the arguments continued within the court, Rev. James Scahill addressed his congregation.

"Bishop Dupre has accused me of being disobedient and I've told him there's no virtue to obedience that requires one to suppress one's conscience."

"The kind of obedience he's looking for is the obedience of the soldiers of Hitler – blind, myopic obedience."

Scahill ended with, "I've lost friends, but that's a minor cost."

Dupre insisted the financial aid to Lavigne was mandated by canon law.

Scahill held strong to his convictions. He would not be convinced that the will of Jesus Christ would endorse a manmade canon law to protect an abusive cleric, and not protect innocent children.

The 'renegade priest' was supported by the parish. They expressed fear that their courageous pastor would be suspended or removed from the diocese because of his views.

Rev. Scahill responded to the parishioners' concerns.

"At a recent retreat, several priest shunned me and the bishop threatened to suspend me."

He accused the Catholic clergy of being too quick to go along 'to get along' and protect the institution at all cost.

"I think there needs to be other voices out there. A healthy church requires change."

On the heels of the numerous court motions, which required complete review of the First Amendment new allegations, were filed.

The lawsuits came from two women. The suits added two more to the more than two dozen filed against Lavigne.

One complainant, a 45-year-old Greenfield woman described Richard Lavigne as a family friend. Her mother looked to the priest for help with her daughter. She would drop her daughter off to spend time with the parish priest.

The accuser stated she was raped and molested beginning at age 8 and continuing until she was 17.

The second female accuser, a 46-year-old woman from East Longmeadow, named Richard Lavigne and Monsignor John F. Harrington.

The Monsignor was implicated because he failed to supervise priests during the time the abuse occurred.

'Jane Doe' #1 claimed she was first molested by Lavigne at Sacred Heart Parish in Easthampton. Later the incidents occurred at Precious Blood Parish in Holyoke, St. Catherine's and St. Mary's both in Springfield. Other incidents occurred at Lavigne's Ashfield home.

Jane Doe #1 resided out of state given the option of filing in either federal or state court.

Jane Doe #2, a resident of East Longmeadow filed in Hampden County Superior Court.

Both retained John Stobierski for representation, joining the over 22 clients of the Springfield attorney's case load.

The co-defendant, 93-year-old Rev. Harrington was retired and living in Springfield.

The Springfield diocese refused to comment on the two female accusers but stated neither the diocese nor its insurance carrier were notified of the complaints.

After the court reviewed the allegations filed by Jane Doe #1 and #2, the court decided the women should have filed their lawsuits sooner.

"A reasonable person should have been able to make a connection much earlier between the abuse and the emotional harm she said she suffered."

State law required sexual abuse lawsuits to be filed within three years of the person's 18th birthday or within three years the victim discovered emotional problems were linked to the abuse.

The ruling appeared favorable to the defense for impending cases.

The battle between diocese and complainants would be ongoing. The church evoked an 'immunity clause' stating the church was 'immune to mandatory reporting sexual abuse of a child.'"

This clause was actually in effect up until September 1971.

The matter of defrocking continued to be in the forefront and Bishop Dupre was pressed for answers.

Canon law obligating a bishop to support a laicized, needy priest presented a challenge to church officials as well as laity.

Since his removal from public ministry, it was calculated Lavigne had received more than $100,000 and health insurance benefits from the diocese.

Bishop Dupre intended to continue support of Lavigne even after laicization. He claimed he was obligated to do so by canon law and his desire to keep Lavigne off public assistance.

Rev. Dupre was a canon law lawyer. He cited Canon 1350, which stated, "...the ordinary bishop is to take care to provide for a person dismissed from the clerical state who is truly in need because of the penalty."

Dupre continued to defend his actions, or lack of action. Lavigne had been directed by the diocese to seek a job but the ousted priest claimed he was unable to do so because of his circumstances and the continued media attention.

The large majority of the church congregations disagreed with the sympathetic defense of Lavigne.

"Lavigne abuses untold numbers of children over 30 years; costs the diocese millions; is a continuing danger to the community, an embarrassment to the diocese, yet the payments go on. What's it going to take for the bishop to do the morally right thing? *Is Lavigne going to have to kill someone?"*

The poignant question resounded throughout the area. The parishioner believed Dupre was misusing canon law.

Other victims of Lavigne would come forward in various forums to tell their personal experiences of abuse at the hands of their trusted priest.

'Peter' met with a reporter who covered the lengthy trials and transgressions of the Catholic Church over the past decade.

The compassionate reporter listened to the pain in Peter's voice. He appeared scared and his voice 'communicated a lot more than what he was actually saying.'

The 40-year-old victim, appeared down trodden, but as he revealed he had been sober for the past nine years, his demeanor portrayed a sense of pride. He was really proud to state his accomplishment. A difficult one, but one he was extremely proud to share.

Lavigne had given him his first drink at age 8. The effects of the alcohol on an 8-year-old provided the priest easy access to the young boy. Peter says the molestation continued until he was 13.

He discovered painkillers in the family medicine cabinet. It wasn't long before he learned the affect of alcohol and painkillers would produce.

"Pills and booze can kill a lot of pain and even make you forget Richard R. Lavigne."

As he delivered incident after incident to his silent listener, the soft-spoken man had something else to tell.

"I have leukemia, I'm dying."

Before the reporter was able to reply, Peter asked for a favor.

Peter's conversation turned to Father James Scahill.

Peter had met Rev. Scahill 11 years before when his father was dying. Because the presence of the priest gave his mother comfort, Peter allowed the priest to visit his father's sickbed.

Despite his efforts to ignore Father Scahill, the priest did his best to open a line of communication.

Eventually, Peter spoke with the priest and Father Scahill offered his hand in friendship. Peter still maintained despise for priests.

He says he doesn't know why, but he accepted the priests offer to meet for coffee. Peter made sure it was a very public place. He had been tricked and manipulated in the past and he was not about to take any chances.

After several encounters with Fr. Scahill, Peter began to tell the priest of pain that started from the time of his First Communion when he approached a priest about wanting to be an altar boy.

As he spoke, he came to believe that he had found a friend in Jim Scahill. He told the concerned priest that his adulthood became a downward spiral.

Addictions, suicide attempts and confinements in psychiatric wards. Three divorces and loss of custody of his kids, now living in Florida. He was arrested for writing bad prescriptions. His pain accelerated as he told of the suicide of a cousin, more like a brother, also a Lavigne victim. He expressed regret, and felt overwhelming shame.

He received settlement money from the diocese for what Lavigne had done to him and used it to by a house for his family. He eventually lost the house.

Peter spoke freely of his friendship with Father Scahill.

"What he did was care. One priest took from me; this one was trying to give something back."

Peter continued to deliver incredible stories to the reporter. He described Father James Scahill with a sense of indescribable admiration of the genuinely caring priest.

The generosity he showed when Peter was in total despair and faced Christmas penniless; unable to deliver gifts to his kids. A charitable organization had promised to buy gifts, but they didn't come through. After a detailed account of what happened next, his story ended with Fr. Scahill's unselfish, caring act.

Peter was instructed to pick up an envelope left outside the rectory door of St. Michael's. The envelope contained $500.

"I don't know how he knew."

He said his hands trembled as he counted the five crisp one hundred dollar bills. He wept as he boarded the bus that delivered him to the nearest Western Union service.

He wired the money to his kids in Florida.

If this was to be his last Christmas, Peter Bessone knew it would be his best.

With tears in his eyes, he asked the man across the table, "Will you do a story on Father Scahill? Will you?"

Tom Shea knew this might be his last visit with Peter.

Springfield Bishop Thomas L. Dupre was beginning to be seen in a less favorable light as each accusation became public and his handling of the matter of defrocking the ousted priest. He failed to support the unscathed priests within his diocese while he defended those who had been removed and/or convicted.

According to Rev. James Scahill, Dupre attended a council meeting at which he was present. Scahill reported a disturbing comment he heard from Bishop Dupre.

The priest contended Dupre said, "Fortunately, for the church of Springfield, many personal and personnel files were destroyed. He said it with glee in his voice and glee in his eye, almost gloating about it."

Dupre made the statement referring to action on the part of Bishop Christopher Weldon who retired in the mid 70s then died in 1982.

Fr. Scahill later confronted Dupre about the remarks; the bishop denied making them.

He described Scahill's account as "an oversimplification of a complicated conversation." Dupre continued, "Father Scahill has exaggerated many facts in Springfield. He is prone to wild speculation."

In his defense, Fr. Scahill stated his willingness to make his allegation under oath and said he hoped Dupre would be questioned under oath also.

Stobierski, representing the victims, scheduled depositions from both Scahill and Dupre citing that destruction of records would carry serious civil ramifications, including a finding of liability.

Fr. Scahill explained his concern for the statement of Dupre. In light of the diocesan lawyers citing acts before 1971 when charities were exempt from legal action for abuse suits. He believed in good conscious Judge Sweeney should be aware of this as she made her decisions regarding the 'exempt clause'.

In dioceses other than Springfield, lawyers were able to uncover records that showed church leaders protected abusive priests and covered their crimes. No paper trails were available in the Springfield Diocese.

The Springfield Diocese was seeking to have five cases dismissed on the bases of the immunity law. Without documentation, it would be impossible to prove the cases were filed after 1971.

The Boston and Providence dioceses settled. Worcester diocese also settled. The Springfield Diocese refused to follow the example of their counterparts throughout the state.

A diocesan leader close to the late Bishop Weldon said multiple accusations against Lavigne were made in the 1960's. He also confirmed that the late bishop O'Neil was also aware of accusations against Lavigne at least by the early 1970s.

Dupre defended his comments, "What I said was Weldon destroyed 'personal' files, not 'personnel' files."

Father Scahill responded, "I had to break my silence in light of the diocese's statement that it had no knowledge until 1986 in regards to multiple offenses of a pedophile who had already been a priest for 20 years by 1986."

John Stobierski countered, "It wouldn't surprise me if records were destroyed, especially since they had someone suspected of killing an altar boy. It is consistent with the pattern of secrecy and concealing misdeeds to protect the reputation of the church."

Court records revealed that many dioceses kept two sets of personnel records. One set was the 'official' records, the other 'secret' records. The secret set of records often detailed accusations of abuse.

The Diocese of Manchester N.H. (which was the late bishop O'Neil's diocese) was one of those that kept 'secret' records.

Sworn affidavits were filed confirming the diocese was aware of misconduct by priests long before 1986. The affidavits stated officials knew more than 30 years ago that Lavigne was believed to be a sexual abuser when he was a suspect in the murder of Danny Croteau.

The diocese fought to have the affidavit removed from court records.

The affidavit was written and sworn to by Maurice DeMontigny, a Bishop Weldon confidant.

A portion of his lengthy affidavit stated, "Given the fact I knew Bishop Weldon to be quite close to Father Griffin and the fact I was part of the process of passing along information during the Croteau murder investigation, I am sure that Father Griffin would have directly reported to Bishop Weldon any allegations of sexual abuse."

The affidavit painted Lavigne as arrogant and unafraid of the questions being raised about his behavior. On one occasion in the 1970s, Lavigne told DeMontigny that Fr. Griffin had admonished him concerning boys in his bedroom.

"Lavigne was contemptuous of the pastor's attempt to exert his authority over him. He said something to the effect that 'they can't do anything to me, and laughed about it."

Years later, DeMontigny, a Chicopee resident would say he completely stands by his statement.

The battle between Scahill and Dupre accelerated. Scahill accused Dupre of verbally assaulting him and threats to suspend him for protesting financial support of an ousted priest.

Scahill stated to Dupre, "I know you can suspend me but so convinced am I of the correctness of what I am doing I am risking that suspension." Scahill went on to say that in front of all the priests attending a meeting, he verbally assaulted him and raped his character.

Just about that time, Bishop Dupre announced he was seeking the defrocking of Richard Lavigne.

The bishop expressed sadness within the church and the priests throughout the diocese.

"People are hurt, and the priests are affected by the scandal." He hoped that ultimately what the church learned from its own clergy could be used to prevent sexual abuse outside the church, specifically in the home.

He stated the initiation of the defrocking mechanism against Lavigne was in place. His efforts went unnoticed when he delivered this statement, "I think the whole thing will be a sad loss of opportunity if we just consider this a problem of the church and its ministers. Unless we realize this is a systemic problem throughout society, and that most of it occurs in the home.

Until we realize that and we start dealing with that, then we really are not going to be protecting our children."

The bishop's claim the children were suffering sexual abuse inside the homes was a foul call and was not well received by the infuriated majority.

Bishop Dupre announced the Springfield diocese had been audited. The bishop reported the diocese developed a structure to review misconduct complaints, hired a professional to work with victims of abuse and is taking preventative measures to end the sexual abuse of minors within the church.

"We are trying to do whatever we can to prevent this from happening again. We can't undo what happened, but we certainly can help prevent it from happening again."

The Bishop made several efforts to gain the confidence of the angry parishioners and cast a more favorable light upon himself.

Protestors waved signs, and shouted what the signs already displayed. One read, *"Bishop Dupre, you are no longer our shepherd. You have deserted your flock."*

Another, *"We have been quiet for too long. Our children have suffered enough."*

Dupre offered explanations to the St. Michael's parishioners.

"Just as in our own American legal system, there is a great emphasis in church law on due process to protect the rights of all parties involved, as well as a thorough and fair review of all relevant fact."

In October, Father Scahill received a phone call from a concerned mother. She had been following the news about Scahill's battles with Dupre and had something Scahill needed to know.

The woman claimed that her son and one of his friends had been abused by Bishop Dupre.

Scahill met with the two men, who repeated the charges.

The pattern fit. The mother of the alleged victim described the relationship she and her family enjoyed with the bishop.

"I never, never suspected," said the woman. She became friends with Dupre because he and her son were such close friends.

Her son met Dupre through a friend who belonged to St. Louis de France Parish in West Springfield. Her son was a freshman in high school and she believed the sexual relationship lasted far into her son's college years.

Dupre introduced him to the arts, museums and opera. He took both her son and his friend camping and swimming at various lakes in the area.

Dupre was a frequent dinner guest in the family's home.

According to the mother, her son met with the bishop at a Sturbridge restaurant where her son expressed his anger to Dupre. Dupre apologized to him, she said.

His manipulation was unique and disturbing to say the least.

Dupre showed the boys pictures of men dying with AIDS to scare them so they wouldn't have sex with anyone else. He would say, "This is what could happen to you; therefore you come to me."

A Boston Law firm spoke of their client being a refugee who came with many members of his family in 1975. The family was sponsored by a parish in Springfield and lived for a time in a convent.

The boy's father was unable to come with the family. The boy submitted a statement to his attorney, which stated in part that one of the priests in the parish was Father Thomas Dupre. The priest offered to teach the 12-year-old boy English.

Dupre took the boy's hand and proceeded to masturbate himself with the boy's hand. The abuse progressed to sodomy, which continued until the boy, an altar boy, started dating a girl in high school.

The second of the two victims was also an altar boy. His father had died when the boy was young and the abuse continued after his loss.

According to the two men, the bishop (then a priest) was in his early 40s at the time.

The statement included claims the bishop took one of them on various out-of-state trips, including to Canada.

He was taken to Connecticut to purchase gay pornography. The men stated the first victim showed the pornography to a friend who was attending a parochial school. That was when Dupre started abusing both. The abuse of the second man continued until he was approximately 20.

When the boys 'balked' at what was being inflicted upon them, Dupre told them, "The alternative is a promiscuous gay lifestyle involving bathhouses."

Dupre showed pictures of people dying of AIDS saying sex with others could become deadly. The boys became frightened.

Included in the statement, both claimed they were given wine and cognac before abuse.

Both boys, after becoming young men maintained contact with Dupre. The bishop informed them that their relationship was a logical expression of love and that God teaches love.

Before Dupre was to be named Bishop, he contacted the two men. He told them he would not accept the appointment unless they remained quiet. Both told him they would not speak of the abuse.

It was not long before a reporter from Springfield newspaper heard of the allegations.

2004

In February, the Springfield Republican asked Dupre to respond to the allegations brought forth by the two men who spoke to Scahill.

"The next morning, I woke up and heard the news that the bishop had resigned his position and had checked himself into a hospital the night before," said the reporter.

Shortly before Dupre's departure, Lavigne was defrocked.

The diocese maintained the public pressure had nothing to do with the defrocking. Sister McGeer disagreed, "I believe Richard Lavigne would still be a priest and Thomas Dupre would still be the bishop in Springfield had we not taken action."

Seven months later, Dupre was indicted for statutory rape, the first U.S. Roman Catholic bishop to be charged with sexual abuse. He pleaded not guilty and the charges were dropped because the statute of limitations had expired.

Dupre remains a Catholic bishop in good standing. His whereabouts unknown is both troubling and disgraceful.

Despite the laicization, Lavigne continued to receive a monthly stipend of $1,030 and $8,000 a year in health insurance. The payments would continue until May 2004. He continues to live in Chicopee, MA without restrictions. His probation period is over; however, he remains a registered level 3 sex offender.

If Lavigne seeks further financial assistance, a lay panel of financial and legal professionals would seek to determine if Lavigne is truly indigent.

If he were deemed indigent, money would be given to him from a newly created *Roman Catholic Holy Felon Fund* established by gifts from people who have expressed a desire to help priests removed from ministry for sexual abuse. Several victims of clergy abuse stepped forward to express their displeasure with the manner Dupre had been handling the allegations of abuse over the last decade.

Stephen Block, one of the plaintiffs stated, "Dupre is the person responsible for putting us through this long, tortuous legal exercise. I wonder if things will change with him gone."

John Stobierski, the attorney for up to 30 victims stated, "If he was a child molester, now we understand why this diocese was out of step with the rest of New England and the country in responding to victims."

Six bishops throughout the country had resigned in the past two years because of clergy sexual abuse.

As recent as February 2004 an Albany N.Y. bishop was accused by an Albany man of having sexual relations with his brother that drove his brother to suicide in 1978 at the age of 25.

About $100,000 in gifts were donated by a handful of lay people the last few months, according to diocesan officials.

Lavigne continues to maintain his innocence of all allegations, except the two to which he pled guilty. He blames many of his problems on the media. He continues to live in Chicopee.

The negotiations on behalf of Lavigne's victims were due to be reached. Settlements would range from $80,000 to $300,000 per victim, depending on the nature of the individual complaint.

When hearing of the laicization, Fr. Scahill accused the church of being hypocritical by allowing Lavigne to receive the holy Eucharist.

"Why is it this same church doesn't offer the same compassion to millions of good Catholic adults who have been married and divorced and who are no longer welcome at the Eucharist table?"

It was priests like Lavigne who turned the Roman Catholic collar into an object of fear, loathing and derision by the young victims of sexual abuse.

Failure on the part of the church to quickly and forthrightly cast out men who used the collar to abuse, cast a permanent stain on the institution.

Hampden County Superior Court judge ruled that the impounded documents of the murder of Danny Croteau, would be released to the public.

The release would make public autopsy and chemical reports of the victim, several investigators' reports, laboratory reports and summaries of statements. Some names would be redacted within the file, but all documents and evidence would be included for public access.

The victim's father, Carl Croteau Sr. wanted the records released hoping they would encourage additional witnesses to come forward with evidence that might finally bring a close to decades of grief for Danny's family.

"We asked D.A. Bennett to go the last mile, and he has been very good to us."

Acting on the advice of council, Carl Croteau submitted a sworn affidavit to the Superior Court of Hampden County.

The lengthy affidavit was precise and detailed. Attached was Carl Croteau's previous statement submitted after the conviction of Richard Lavigne, 1994.

Croteau described all events he remembered beginning the day Danny's body was discovered floating in the Chicopee River 31 years before.

His account included conversations, observations, encounters and direct quotes all in chronological order, in a language simple, and devoid of 'legalize'.

Throughout the document, Carl Croteau wove a story that substantiated his firm belief; Richard Lavigne was Danny's murderer.

Danny's father referenced State Police Lt. Fitzgibbon, the chief investigator at the time. He stated clearly Fitzgibbon's views of the case. Fitzgibbon indicated he was interested in prosecuting Lavigne for his crimes. He told Carl "his hands were tied."

Lt. Fitzgibbon died in 1985.

It was Croteau's belief the D.A. was not entirely frank with him. He believed the excuse was the District Attorney's office and the Diocese of Springfield were blocking any action on Danny's murder.

Within the affidavit, Croteau explained his relationship with Father Leo O'Neil who later became Bishop. He described his relationship as very good and states without a doubt O'Neil knew in the late 1960's that Lavigne molested boys and never did anything about it.

Carl was aware that Gregory Croteau had met with O'Neil shortly after he became a Bishop in the 1980's and told him that he was a victim of sexual abuse at the hands of Lavigne.

Bishop O'Neil died in 1997.

In his affidavit, Mr. Croteau requested a condition be put on the release. The condition that information of the specific act of the killing or any items of physical evidence only the killer would know be withheld to protect the possibility of a prosecution in the future.

Carl has been interviewed by the media and whenever the opportunity is afforded him, he speaks out on Danny's behalf.

"Lt. Fitzgibbon told me 'a lot of mistakes were made' in the early days of the murder probe."

The Lieutenant said they should have pushed harder to search St. Mary's rectory and to examine the clothes the priest wore the night of Danny's death.

"The police went there, but the priest who answered the door wouldn't let them in." Lt. Fitzgibbon told Croteau.

It is important to the Croteau family that the truth be told and not be kept secret any longer.

To date, thirty-five years have passed since Danny was murdered and even more than that since some of his brothers were molested. He was pleased when the court released the files.

Bennett believed he could get the indictment, but doubted he could get a conviction. He was not convinced the case could clear the 'reasonable doubt' hurdle.

Carl Croteau disagreed. "I think the evidence would sway a jury. If he's acquitted, we could live with that."

"Why not take a shot? I think we owe that much to Danny."

In addition, the others who traced the fracturing of their lives to Lavigne.

Peter Bessone and his cousin David Bessone were among those left in Lavigne's wake.

As the two grew up, Peter sank into a haze of drug and alcohol abuse. David left the state and went to college. Both carried the secret they vowed to keep.

Christmas, 1985 David called his cousin Peter and pleaded with him to get off drugs. When David hung up the phone, he lit a Hibachi grill in his apartment and let the fumes fill his lungs. He was 23.

In 2003, Peter was 40, and in the advanced stages of leukemia. He did not know how long he had to live, but he hoped it would be long enough to see Lavigne defrocked.

Peter watched as a priest knelt at David's grave to say a prayer. The ground was soaking wet, but Rev. Scahill knelt down anyway.

Peter dropped to his knees to pray over his cousin's grave, then collapsed into the priest's arms and wept.

Father Scahill agreed to an interview. Generally, he shunned the limelight in respect for the many victims he had counseled.

"I think Lavigne has gotten away with murder for more than 30 years. But the people who have enabled him are worse than him." Scahill has counseled many of Lavigne's victims. Some became suicides, but others began a downward spiral.

"Those are the ones that kill themselves by inches."

Several clergy were interviewed on the heels of the surprising news of the bishop's decision to resign before his 75th birthday, which is the mandatory retirement age.

"He has a personal sense of fairness; he was always trying to be fair to everyone." Responded Sniezyk, the vicar of clergy.

The Rev. Farland, co-vicar of clergy expressed shock and confusion when told about the allegations. He said, "Bishop Dupre is a sensitive man, a great listener and very pastoral." Farland continued, "He is as honest as you can get. That has been my experience with him."

Dupre was described as an extremely introverted person who struggled at the need to be more open with people while serving as bishop.

Monsignor Richard Sniezyk was appointed temporarily head of the diocese. The Monsignor stated,

"I can assure you if any individual brought forth a complaint against any member of the diocesan community, including the Bishop, it would be thoroughly investigated."

The Catholic Church was indeed in turmoil.

Cardinal Bernard Law resigned after accusations of failing to remove abusive priests from ministry.

Bishop Thomas Dupre resigned immediately after two allegations of child rape were brought forth.

Richard Lavigne, a convicted child molester was classified a level 3 sex offender, and defrocked.

Several sexual abuse cases had been settled and as many as 30 additional cases were pending settlement.

On March 10, 2004, the Vatican appointed the Most Reverend Timothy A. McDonnell to replace Thomas Dupre as Bishop of the Diocese of Springfield.

His assignment would be difficult. Unlike Dupre, Bishop McDonnell was described as jovial and charismatic with a sense of humor. However, his staff described him as authoritative with a hands-on style; a welcome change from his aloof predecessor.

All agreed Bishop McDonnell stepped into a difficult situation. The number of Catholics within the Springfield Diocese had dropped from 320,000 to 240,000, a considerable decline.

He was introduced to the diocese exactly four weeks after Dupre's resignation.

Bishop McDonnell was scheduled to take the helm on April 1, 2004.

On the eve of the installation for the new bishop, the diocese announced a fund for clergy abuse victims had been set up. "The Fund for Healing and Hope" in addition to the installation of the bishop marked the start of a refreshing, positive approach by the diocese.

Thomas Martin and Martin Bono, two of Lavigne's victims agreed the idea that the fund would be run by an advisory board made up of victims' family members was favorable. The advisory board would determine how the money was to be disbursed.

They suggested the allotment Lavigne was receiving should be shifted to the newly found fund.

Warren Mason, who had approached Fr. Scahill with the suggestion the parish hold back funds suggested the diocese take the $100,000 donated to "The Felon's Fund" and put it into the "Victims Fund" or returned to the donors.

Second to the healing of the victims, the allocation of 'funds' would be priority issues all hoped the new bishop would take seriously.

The Most Rev. Timothy A. McDonnell was installed on April 1, 2004. He was the eighth bishop of the Diocese of Springfield.

McDonnell addressed the diocese in attendance at St. Michael's Cathedral recognizing what he considered top priority; healing the pain and damage caused by clergy abuse. He apologized on behalf of the church.

Joseph Croteau noted the new bishop's apology was the first from a church official in the Springfield diocese.

"His apology was big for everyone."

Many victims of abuse had been personally invited to attend the installation ceremony.

Martin Bono who had a pending suit against the diocese said,

"As I listened to him, I felt as though the church was empty and that he was talking only to me and the other victims." Bono rarely attended church but added, "For me, it was so healing. I am so glad I went to church today. I am so glad. I feel he has started the beginning of my healing."

Bishop McDonnell had a long gnarly road to look down. Systematically he hoped to straighten the road and pave it with regained confidence of the crippled diocese.

One decision was to disassociate the diocese from the dubbed, "Felon Fund" that had been sanctioned by his predecessor, Thomas Dupre.

The clergy abuse scandal continued to plague the diocese.

Michael A. Graziano was the voice of the local Catholic Church. For years, Graziano appeared on weekly TV shows fielding questions about the clergy abuse scandal.

Graziano resigned less than a week after the new bishop was installed. McDonnell placed the 47-year-old highest-ranking lay member of the diocese on immediate leave. Graziano was accused of sexual misconduct. The allegations were said to have occurred in 1985.

The accused administrator submitted a letter of resignation citing personal and family reasons.

The news of the allegations against Graziano was sad, however, the bishop's immediate attention to the matter was a good sign.

Within weeks of Graziano's resignation, a complaint alleging that Deacon James Martone engaged in sexual misconduct with a minor was received. The deacon was immediately placed on leave by the newly appointed bishop.

Rev. James Scahill would feel the power of McDonnell. After a heated exchange over the "Felon

Fund," the bishop ousted Scahill from the Presbyteral Council.

Scahill objected to the bishop's decision to dissolve the fund and redirect the money to tuition aid and scholarships for children.

The bishop was asked about the circumstances of Scahill's removal. The bishop replied, "The council is meant to be an advisory group to the bishop. Scahill was an adversary member."

According to Scahill, McDonnell expressed criticism and said, "You attacked me personally. You basically called me a coward and said I was a lackey of the Vatican."

Scahill replied, "I didn't use the word lackey."

Scahill added, "The bishop told me I caused as much damage to the diocese as Lavigne."

A lengthy heated exchange ensued as Scahill left the room.

The actions toward Father Scahill were not received favorably among the parishioners.

Victims spoke in defense of their pastor. They expressed shock and disbelief when hearing the bishop compared Scahill with Lavigne.

For two years, Scahill, the pastor of St. Michael's Church of East Longmeadow held back weekly collections totaling more than $50,000, the percentage that was supposed to go to the bishop's office.

Again, the Roman Catholic Diocese of Springfield faced turmoil. Now, the battles were carried on in the infrastructure of the church.

Scahill defended his work with victims and their families.

"If the people of St. Michael's and the pastor who they asked to shepherd their concern had not done what we started two years ago with God's help, many victims would not have come forward to begin their healing and I suspect that Richard Lavigne would still be a priest and Thomas Dupre would still be our bishop."

After thirty-eight years, and 40 sexual abuse victims, the final tie between Lavigne and the church was severed.

In one sentence, a spokesperson for the diocese stated the financial support of Lavigne would end on May 31, 2004. The announcement was celebrated by St. Michael's parish. The monies that had been withheld in protest of the financial support of Lavigne would be handed over to the bishop. The parish suggested the money be used in future settlements with clergy sexual abuse victims.

Rev. Scahill estimated Lavigne had received $300,000 in benefits over the past 12 years. In addition, the diocese was forced to pay $1.4 million to victims of the defrocked priest. Presently, the diocese was nearing a settlement that would amount to $7 million to be paid to sexual abuse victims.

Rev. Scahill praised the bishop.

"During his first two months with us, Bishop McDonnell has taken several important steps to clean house."

During the first three months of being installed as bishop, McDonnell removed five clergymen.

Deacon James Martone accused of sexually abusing a minor beginning in 1991.

Rev. Ronald Wamsher accused of abusing several minors more than 10 years before.

Michael Grazziano, president of the Catholic Communications Corp accused of sexual misconduct occurring in 1985.

John Russell, former Catholic priest accused of abusing a minor more than 30 years before.

Rev. Andrew Dodo a visiting chaplain from Nigeria accused of abuse at Baystate Medical Facility.

It appeared the bishop ruled with a no nonsense iron fist.

Federal charges against Dupre and the diocese were also being considered. Legal experts stated the Springfield Diocese scandal may meet all the criteria of the Racketeer-Influenced and Corrupt Organization Act (RICO) charges.

Thomas Dupre remained at St. Luke's. Vicar Sniezyk said he has corresponded with Dupre who replied to Sniezyk concerning his condition.

"I'm starting to come out of the fog of what I've been through."

In the meanwhile, Dupre remained a retired bishop in good standing and received full retirement benefits. The retired bishop received a minimum of $1,500 a month, appropriate housing and board, complete health insurance benefits, an automobile, all expenses for trips to provincial, regional and national bishops meetings and workshops as well as possible occasional visits to the Vatican.

Dupre owns a home at 90 Beaver Road in Ware, MA.

2005

Most Rev. Bishop Timothy McDonnell faced another heart-wrenching ordeal. One of Lavigne's victims, Shawn Dobbert would not be laid to rest with Catholic funeral rites.

Dobbert's mother would say goodbye to her son, 37 at a funeral service in St. John's Episcopal Church in North Adams, MA.

Shawn's attorney, John Stobierski spoke for the grieving mother.

"Despite her lifelong pledge to Catholicism, she felt a burial in the Catholic Church would have been hypocritical in that it was the church where Shawn was molested and he had rejected organized religion as a result of his molestation."

Shawn Dobbert was found dead in his apartment. His death believed to be suicide.

Stobierski stated Dobbert was one of his most "tortured" clients. Dobbert had confided in his attorney two years ago and said that Lavigne conditioned him to believe that only he could love Dobbert because he was overweight and unappealing to others.

In closing, Stobierski said Dobbert died before knowing how much he would receive from the settlement, but noted that Dobbert knew it would be a minimum of $80,000.

Twists and turns would continue throughout the Springfield Diocese. Many believe it would be decades before the church would be stable. Abuse victims continued to come forward. The defendants would be on every level of the hierarchy.

Several priests would come forward and disclose their abuse at the hands of priests. As altar boys, they would describe the actions of their parish priests, yet they chose to enter the clergy. Each would be astonished when learning they were not alone.

The list of clergymen accused of abuse would continue to grow.

I n March, 2006 a bill was proposed to the legislature. If approved, the bill would abolish the statute of limitations in criminal and civil cases involving sexual abuse of children. Under the current law, sexual crimes against children that took place 15 or more years before cannot be prosecuted.

The bill would give people the opportunity to come forward and hold people accountable for the harm they caused and to start healing.

As a result of countless cases, lawmakers are on the brink of passing legislation to remove the legal barrier that prevents victims of sexual abuse from pursuing criminal charges and civil claims against their abusers.

Another bill to eliminate the $20,000 limit on liability for churches and other nonprofit organizations has the support of lawmakers.

Most of the abuses occurred more than 15 years prior because the victims did not disclose the incidents until they reached adulthood. Most victims were unable to come forward because in some cases, the abusers threatened or manipulated them.

With the passing of the new bill, the abused would be allowed to come forward without time restraints provided by a statute of limitations.

There would be no statute of limitations on child abuse cases in the Commonwealth of Massachusetts.

It should be noted; numerous clergymen faced allegations but are not included in this book.

From the Author

Failure to include all the victims and their allegations in no way implies they are not equally significant and as credible as those mentioned. To include every complainant would be near impossible. In addition, the incidents are very similar and would be repetitious to the reader. However, the similarities and repeated accusations serve to bolster the credibility of the victims, and were not considered any less serious.

At the time of this writing, Richard Lavigne was believed to be the only Catholic priest ever implicated and/or suspected of a murder...until the following was disclosed:

Reverend Gerald Robinson, a 66-year-old priest from Toledo, Ohio was arrested in April 2004. The priest was charged with the murder of a nun.

The body of 71-year-old Sister Margaret Ann Pahl was discovered in the chapel of the Ohio hospital where she and the Reverend worked. She was strangled and suffered as many as 30 stab wounds.

The murder occurred *26 years ago*, April, 1980 (on the Saturday before Easter Sunday)

At the time of the murder, Reverend Robinson was suspected, but not charged because of insufficient evidence.

On April 20, 2006, jury selection was completed and the trial for the murder of the 71-year-old nun began on *Friday, April 21, 2006*.

On Thursday, May 11, 2006, an Ohio jury returned a verdict. The 66-year-old priest was found guilty of murder and sentenced to life without parole.

EPILOGUE

The Springfield Republican covered the church crisis aggressively and is credited, in part, to the decision to release the Croteau investigative files.

A retired state trooper once attached to the Northwest District Attorney's office in Northampton MA was hired by the Springfield Republican to investigate the 1972 unsolved murder of Danny Croteau.

In August 2004, R.C. Stevens, a private detective, began an aggressive probe. Stevens suspects a ring of about 10 pedophiles, many of them priests, operated a sexual abuse ring that preyed upon children at the time of Danny's murder. He believes the 'ring of pedophiles' passed the boys from one predator to another. Stevens says,

"In the initial investigation, everything pointed to Richard Lavigne. Meanwhile, we have 10 arrows, seven of which point to Lavigne, but three that don't...this is not a witch hunt."

Carl and Bunny Croteau continue to wait for justice. As they wait, they enjoy nine grandchildren and five great grandchildren. Their faith has never diminished. They maintain,

"They can't take God away from us. That's the one thing they can't have."

The Reverend James Scahill continues his work as pastor of St. Michael's Church, East Longmeadow, MA He continues to counsel victims of abuse. When addressing the "Felon Fund" Rev. Scahill believes a "Victims Fund' would be more in keeping with Christ and Gospels that call for care for the least among us. As for violators of children, the pastor quotes,

"Jesus suggests a millstone be fastened around their neck and they be thrown in the sea."

Ronald and Mary Bernardo continue to live in their McKinley Terrace home, Pittsfield, MA. They preserve the memory of Jimmy and live their lives in private. Chief Gerald Lee retired in 1996; Anthony Aiello of the Pittsfield Police Department is presently Chief of Police in Pittsfield. District Attorney Gerard Downing died of a heart attack while shoveling snow in the winter of 2003. Clint Van Zandt has retired, but continues to consult in high profile cases.

George and Dee Ziegert relocated to nearby Feeding Hills, MA. Their oldest daughter Lynne married and purchased her parent's Agawam house. She has been with her present employer since 1989. Lisa's brother David lives in California with his wife and two sons. Sharon, the youngest of the Ziegert's children lives in Eastern Massachusetts with her husband and infant daughter. A white ribbon continues to be displayed in the midst of a floral arrangement in the front yard of the Ziegert's home. The Lisa M. Ziegert Memorial Fund continues today. Chief Stanley Chmielewski retired; Robert Campbell of the Agawam Police Department is presently Chief of Police in Agawam. Lisa's case remains unsolved.

In 1996, James Lusher married his friend and soul mate, Christine. He continues to live in his Ridgeview Terrace home in Westfield MA. Jamie's sister, Jennifer married and lives in Westfield with her infant daughter, Jamee named for her brother. Jennifer's husband is in the armed forces and has been deployed to the Middle East. He is expected to return in June 2006. Jamie's mother, Joanne Lavakis lives with her husband Bill in Blandford, at her mother's home. Jamie's grandmother passed away. Chief Benjamin Surprise retired; John Camerota of the Westfield Police Department is presently the Chief of Police in Westfield. Jamie's case remains unsolved; his body has never been found.

The Piirainen family have remained in Grafton, MA Ed Lemieux, Maureen's husband and Holly's grandfather passed away in 1997. Zachary, Holly's youngest brother lives with his father, Rick. Zach will graduate from high school, class of 2006. Andrew, now 21, is enlisted in the Air Force demolition unit. Presently he is stationed in Utah. Maureen Lemieux continues to work as a dental hygienist. Holly's case remains unsolved.

Robert and Frances Wood live in a small hamlet in upstate New York. Robert continues to be a spiritual leader in the community. Sara Anne Wood's body has never been found.

Stephen Dominicchi, now 27, lives in Florida. He works diligently in the banking/financial business and is a successful young man. His ordeal with his 'best friend' is slowly fading from his memory, but he does not perceive it will ever be completely forgotten. Stephen's mother, Linda died at the young age of 46. Stephen continues to feel the void she left with her passing. Stephen's sister Monica lives in Massachusetts with her young son.

Richard Lavigne lives in the private sector at his Haven St., home in Chicopee, MA. With his 10-year probation behind him, he lives unrestricted, but is required to register with the Chicopee Police department annually as a level 3 sex offender. He maintains his innocence and quietly states,
"My silence has been my salvation."

Thomas Dupre remains in parts unknown. He is still a bishop in good standing. All charges were dropped because they exceeded the statute of limitations. He was the first U.S. Bishop ever to face charges of sexual abuse. Assistant District Attorney David Angier retired from the prosecutor's office to pursue other interests.

Lewis Lent is confined at the Colonial Correctional Facility, Bridgewater, MA He is serving a life sentence, without parole for the first-degree murder of Jimmy

Bernardo. In addition, a 25 year to life sentence for the second-degree murder of Sara Anne Wood and 17 to 20 years for the attempted abduction of Rebecca Saverese. All sentences are to run consecutively. He has refused to disclose the gravesite of Sara Anne Wood, and has not confessed to any other abduction/murders.

'Yesterday is history...Tomorrow a mystery, but today is a gift, so we call it The Present.....'

SNAP (The **S**urvivors **N**etwork of those **A**bused by **P**riests) is a support group available to those wounded by religious authority figures. **SNAP** is a non-profit, independent and confidential organization with no connections to the church or church officials.

Printed in the United States
57772LVS00001B/15

9 781425 940553